The
English
Pilgrim

MARTIN BLAKE

The English Pilgrim

authorHOUSE®

AuthorHouse™ UK Ltd.
1663 Liberty Drive
Bloomington, IN 47403 USA
www.authorhouse.co.uk
Phone: 0800.197.4150

Published by AuthorHouse   07/16/2013

ISBN: 978-1-4817-6860-3 (sc)
ISBN: 978-1-4817-6861-0 (e)

Library of Congress Control Number: 2013911710

This book is printed on acid-free paper.

I

THE ALREADY DULL LIGHT OF late afternoon was fading to a steely blue-grey as I broke off from my reading, yawned, stretched and then tried to rub life back into my frozen fingers. My gaze drifted across to the south side of the cloister and the blackened stones of the warming room, aptly named since Brother Anselm set fire to it in his anger at being ordered to fast for three days as punishment for stealing food from the kitchen, as it happens incinerating himself in the process, whether by accident or design only God can say.

The work prescribed for me to read during that Lent, St Jerome's *Contra Jovinianum* was, I regret to say, stultifying to me, however worthy and uplifting others might have found its contents. I rose from my desk and whispered to the librarian, Brother Bartholomew, that I needed to visit the latrine. He did not even look up from his own work, let alone acknowledge the implied request for his permission. I turned and headed in the opposite direction out of the cloister, past the infirmary with its perpetual odour of pungent herbs and decaying flesh, and towards the farm buildings beyond. A fat nursing sow raised her head briefly as I approached, then allowed it to sink back into the mud. In among the lay workers who tended the animals was the hunched shape of Brother Stephen, who never took advantage even of the brief periods when we were allowed free conversation with one another, but who was now conducting an animated discussion with the chickens as he scattered grain for them. He was lightly dressed, seemingly immune to the cold March wind.

Beyond the perimeter of the Abbey, a looming mist hung over the fens and meres on which our island of Croyland seemed to float. A number of men cast nets from small flat-bottomed boats, exploiting the endless shoals which rendered it unnecessary for the Abbey to maintain its own fishponds. Others checked larger nets concealed in hides for trapped water fowl. The distant fields and

1

the high banks beyond which protected them from inundation were barely visible in the gloomy haze. I pulled my cloak more tightly around me to keep out the easterly breeze; some said that when the wind came in from that direction, there was nothing to impede it from blowing right around the earth, picking up cold damp air from the boreal regions as it did so. Whether the east wind originated on the other side of the world or the rough, unwelcoming sea a few miles away, it provided a telling reminder to the residents of Croyland that the warmer days of summer were to be cherished as a gift from God.

I pitied those who toiled in the open air all through the year, their bodies prematurely broken by excessive physical exertion and by our harsh climate. Old monks claimed that in their youth winters had been shorter and summers hotter; at first I dismissed these notions as no more than the dewy-eyed reminiscences of those who have reached the stage in life where they know each day will bring increasing discomfort. Nevertheless, I knew only too well that the last few years had brought harsh winters, late springs and poor harvests. Outside the blessed walls of our Abbey, many had starved despite our attempts to relieve the distress of those most afflicted. Some blamed these miseries on the sins of our King, Edward the Second, whom they accused of being an ungodly man. As a relatively junior brother, I could only leave such judgements to others.

When I had grown more agitated by the cold than by the prospect of continuing to read a tedious tome, I made my way back to the cloister. The other monks seated along the north wall seemed as unengaged as I had been, and watched my steps until I resumed my place at my desk. Brother Bartholomew looked up, seemingly either unaware of or unconcerned about the direction from which I had appeared, and immediately returned to his work. I tried to read on, but within a few minutes was yawning once more. At that moment the already gloomy light suddenly dimmed further. I looked up to see a large figure standing alongside, apparently trying to attract the librarian's attention but unable to form the words he had come to deliver. At length the sniggers of the other brothers caused Bartholomew to raise his eyes.

'What is it, Brother John?'

John was a young man of unusual size, clumsy gait and twisted features. He also had the misfortune to speak with a paralysing stammer. Most assumed him to be an imbecile, but on occasions when speaking to him alone I had discovered that he could with some effort express himself quite lucidly. From their behaviour towards him, not many of his fellow monks had bothered to delve beyond his unfortunate exterior. At times I even wondered if, for some obscure reason, it suited John to allow himself to be cast in the role of buffoon.

Bartholomew rolled his eyes impatiently. 'Come on boy, whatever it is you have to say, spit it out.'

John began to enunciate his message as best he could, in other words incoherently, to a background of ill-suppressed ridicule. The more he suffered mockery, the more he panicked and stammered and the redder his face grew. The most we could piece together was that our Abbot, Father Simon, wanted to speak to someone, but it seemed that we would wait until Vespers to find out the identity of the interviewee. At length Brother Peter, who occupied the desk next to mine, lost patience, gave a cruel imitation of John's stuttering speech and gestured by waving his arm that John should simply point to the person to whom his message was directed.

In that moment, my mind went back to the occasion when my heart first went out to Brother John. I had reached the age when young men feel the desire to assert their opinions, to right wrongs and put lesser mortals in their place. From the church at Croyland, the shortest route to the outer stairs to the latrines was along a narrow passage between two buildings, and one day, while crossing the end of this passageway, I looked along it and saw the tormented face of John. He was hopping from foot to foot, clearly in urgent need of the facilities which lay so tantalisingly close. In front of him, with his back to me, was one of our lay farm workers, a man named Edwin, who never made a secret of his contempt for the monks for whom he toiled. Once I had seen him relieving himself on the threshold of the chapter house, knowing that the next time we entered we would be stepping on his urine.

On this occasion, he was prodding Brother John in the belly with a pitchfork. As I walked towards them, seemingly unnoticed by either, I heard Edwin cursing John in the most vile terms, telling him that he was a monstrous perversion of nature although, needless to say, these were not the precise words he used. Within moments Edwin achieved his heart's desire, in other words John lost control of his bladder, the outpouring from which flooded the ground at his feet. John began to sob, while Edwin erupted into gales of laughter and another fit of cursing. He drew his pitchfork back to jab it into John with renewed vigour, but I grabbed the end of the handle, and when he felt the resistance he spun around. He cursed me with even less inhibition.

'Watch your tongue, Edwin,' I said. 'Life's hard for a vagabond thrown out onto the highway. You should reflect on how lucky you are to work on this demesne. God doesn't favour everyone as much.'

'Lucky? You lot wouldn't care if my children starved.'

'Are they starving, Edwin?'

'No. But you wouldn't care if they were.'

'Well, since they're not, that can only be your opinion. Can't it?'

He seemed to ponder for a moment, until his anger became even greater, as if enraged at being drawn into a battle of logic. He spat into the pool of urine at John's feet, then pushed past him and strode away. John's moist eyes were cast down in the manner of a dog which has just been punished for chasing its owner's sheep. He looked down at the wet ground beneath him, then turned and shuffled back down the passageway, shaking the drips from the bottom of his cloak.

As I walked away, I saw Brother Peter leaning against the wall behind me, smirking.

'Did you enjoy watching that?' I said.

He stared back, slowly shaking his head, not in denial, but in contempt of what he saw as my innocence. From that moment on, he and I never exchanged a word.

Back in the cloister, John raised his trembling hand and directed it towards me.

My fellow monks fell silent. Why would Abbot Simon, a man whose company more often consisted of bishops and nobles, want to speak to a humble brother such as myself? For a moment I stared blankly.

'Well, you'd better go,' Brother Bartholomew said to me. 'Don't keep Father Simon waiting.'

I rose unsteadily to my feet, all eyes fixed on me, then set off to walk around the cloister to where the Abbot's quarters lay in the south-west corner. Still sensing the glare of my fellows burrowing into my back, I turned instead and cut across the open garth, catching my foot in the drain as I mounted the kerbstones on the far side. The staircase which led up to Father Simon's quarters at least took me out of sight of the cloister. I stopped half-way up and listened to my heart pounding.

I had never before had occasion to visit this part of the Abbey, though I had often watched Father Simon leading his more privileged visitors to the guest quarters alongside. At the top of the stairs an impressive doorway, its stonework finely decorated with scroll-work carving, surrounded an oak door of formidable proportions. My hand rose to announce my presence by knocking, then seemed to freeze. Taking several deep breaths, I finally rapped as hard as I dared. A surprisingly welcoming voice instructed me to enter.

On the other side of the door was a long room which I can only compare to a miniature of the great hall of a castle, or what I have heard of them. In front of me was a large hearth from which warmth emanated in a most reassuring manner. To the left I glimpsed a dining table already set for what seemed to be a banquet. The walls were lined with tapestries. To my right, patiently waiting for me to give him my attention, was Father Simon. Only his round face, with its alert eyes and topped with thinning grey hair, was visible as he sat behind a wide desk piled high with documents, some in ordered collections, others strewn chaotically. A single huge candle, the size of those which burned in the church, cast a wavering light from alongside. He indicated by nodding that I should take the chair in front of the desk, then placed a heap of documents on the floor next to him so that we could see one another. He rubbed his eyes. His voice sounded weary.

'Do you know, Nicholas,' he said, 'that the lands owned by this Abbey are dotted haphazardly across six counties of this fair land. The most distant are several days' journey away. I could employ an army of clerks, and still'—he waved his hand across his cluttered desk—'it would still not be enough to keep on top of all this. I often think it would make more sense to rent out our lands and simply live off the income rather than to manage them directly.

Sometimes I find it hard not to lose sight of the fact that many years ago I entered the Benedictine Order because I felt a spiritual calling. Now, here I find myself in the thirteen hundred and twentieth year after the Incarnation of our Lord . . .'

His voice faded. He stared into the air, as if conjuring a vision of himself as an idealistic young novice. It seemed to me an unlikely image. Even I knew that Father Simon was from a wealthy and influential family, and that idealism was not generally a trait of those from such a background. My attention was jolted when I realised that he was speaking again.

'Lady de Mortagne of Spalding is with child. All being well, she will give birth in about three months.'

I waited several moments, but no explanation of the significance of this news was forthcoming.

'I imagine that Lord de Mortagne is delighted,' I said.

'On the contrary, Brother Nicholas, nothing could be further from the truth. Lord de Mortagne was taking part in a diplomatic mission to Flanders six months ago.'

'Ah. I see.'

After a further lengthy pause, I began to wonder which of us might be finding this exchange more tortuous.

'I don't see, Father, how this has significance for us here at Croyland Abbey.'

'It has significance, young Nicholas, because it appears that Lady de Mortagne has assured her husband that the child was fathered by an incubus.'

Still unsure where this conversation might be leading, I felt it wise to measure my response.

'Such things have been known, have they not?'

'Doubtless they have,' Father Simon replied. 'Whether the father of Lady de Mortagne's child be incubus or earthly gentleman, I have no way of knowing. All I do know is that, for some reason, she maintains that the incubus informed her that he had been summoned by a monk of this Abbey.'

Father Simon was confiding this information to me for a reason, although it seemed unlikely that he was asking for my help in tracking down the culprit.

'But Father, who in this Abbey would have the knowledge and the skill, let alone the motive, to summon an incubus?'

'In all probability, no-one.'

'Then, surely, the absurdity of this allegation will be seen to be self-evident.'

'Once again, nothing could be further from the truth. Lord de Mortagne believes what his wife has told him, as clearly it is in his interest to do. That is why it concerns us. He has demanded that the culprit be rooted out and punished.'

'With all due respect, Father, that seems absurd. Why would anyone here want to do such a thing?'

'His wife maintains that a young monk whose advances she resisted swore that he would take his revenge by fair means or foul. You can see the direction in which this is leading. And before you ask, I don't believe for one moment that this aspect of her story is true. All that matters is that Lord de Mortagne chooses, or finds it convenient, to believe it.'

'And what does our Bishop say?'

Father Simon lowered his head a little. 'The Bishop is a close friend of Lord de Mortagne.'

He fell silent. I found myself wishing that he would come straight to the point.

'Father, I'm honoured that you feel able to confide this disturbing news in me. But I still don't see what I can do to help.'

'The Bishop has supported Lord de Mortagne in demanding that a young monk of Croyland Abbey, preferably the one responsible, be punished. I suspect that in reality he cares little who the sacrificial victim may be. Action must be taken for the sake of appearances.'

My heart began to beat faster.

'Everyone knows,' I said, 'that the lords of Spalding have been antagonistic towards this Abbey for centuries. To sacrifice an innocent brother just because—'

'What you say is true, Nicholas, but it doesn't alter the reality. We are not immune from ecclesiastical authority whether it be implemented fairly or unfairly. We all accepted that when we took our vows of obedience.'

In an instant I saw with blinding clarity the destination to which this conversation had led.

'You mean, Father, that you've chosen me to be the scapegoat?'

He stared down at the small area of the surface of his desk which was visible.

'Yes, Nicholas, the scapegoat is to be you.'

For some moments, I felt sure that this whole conversation must be a dream, a nightmare, a bizarre fantasy or some ill-natured jest. Its absurdity tempted me to laugh rather than to roar in outrage. A further glimpse of the Abbot's face convinced me with chilling certainty that I was not the butt of an elaborate joke. Nevertheless, the feeling which welled up most powerfully was not anger, but confusion.

'But why, Father? Why me?'

'Who else then? Brother J-J-John? Brother Stephen, who prefers the company of farmyard animals to that of his fellow human beings? I appreciate, Nicholas, that you've been a reliable and conscientious member of our community. Doubtless you're considering at this moment that others surely deserve such a fate more than you do. But I'm afraid that there can be no debate. Your fate is already decided. Yes, life can sometimes ensnare us with the grossest of injustices. Pray to God for an explanation, for I can give you none.'

A few minutes earlier I had been reading in the cloisters, bored but untroubled, knowing, if I cared to give it a thought, that the rest of my life was set on a fixed and unchanging course. In the time it had taken to walk to the Abbot's quarters, my world had been turned upside-down.

'Then may I ask, Father, what's to be my punishment for the crime I didn't commit?'

'You'll leave us within the next few days.'

Father Simon spoke these words in such a matter-of-fact tone that he might have been telling me that I was to read the lesson at Compline. Testing my vows of obedience to the limit, I rose and walked across the room, stopping in front of the hearth to stare into the flames. When I looked back, Father Simon was watching me, his face unmoved. I spoke from where I stood.

'So I'm to be ejected onto the highway? Left to fend for myself, like a common vagabond?'

The Abbot did not raise his voice. 'Of course not. You'll move to another, sufficiently distant, Benedictine house.'

I lowered my head, walked slowly back and resumed my seat.

'Will I be allowed to choose?' I said in the meekest voice I could summon.

'As I said, your fate has already been decided.'

'Then, may I ask, where am I to go?'

'To the Abbey of Claremont, near Avignon.'

'But that's . . . that's not even . . .'

Father Simon leaned forward and rested his hands on the desk.

'If you had been put on trial, even a show trial, for summoning an incubus, you would be staring at the prospect of a much worse fate.' He paused for me to take in the import of his words. 'I'm told you speak Latin and French with reasonable fluency, so you'll soon pick up the local tongue. And they say the climate is most congenial in those regions.'

I clenched and unclenched my fists, trying to summon up all the derision I could muster into my voice.

'And how exactly will I find my way there?'

The Abbot's voice remained placid.

'A papal legate will be passing by in a few days on his way back from Lincoln to Avignon. His papers of authority from his Holiness will guarantee you safe passage throughout your journey. Doubtless they carry other advantages too.'

I decided that, hopeless as the situation appeared, more might be achieved by softening my tone.

'But, why so far away? Why not a monastery in another part of England?'

'Or perhaps somewhere in frozen Thule? Think how much worse your fate could have been, Nicholas. The orders of a superior are not for you to question.'

Croyland had been my home for as long as I could remember, since early childhood. In my heart, I had hoped never to be cast adrift onto the raging waters of the world beyond. I understood that Father Simon had been given no choice in the matter, and that indeed he had tried to soften the blow in whatever way he could, but this did not prevent me from feeling bitter and angry. I had always known that grave injustices occurred all the time, that men lost their lives simply because they fell foul of someone more powerful and unforgiving than they. I had never imagined myself as the victim of such a miscarriage.

'What books will you take with you?' the Abbot asked.

The question took me aback. My choice of reading material hardly seemed a pressing matter in the light of what he had just told me.

'I never travel without my sacramentary and my pocket Gospel book.'

'Ah yes, that antique work, in its barbarous old script.'

I was so surprised that he had registered such a detail that I omitted to take offence at his slighting reference to my treasured possession.

'Barbarous, perhaps, by the standards of our day,' I said, 'but I cherish it. The script is descended from one used by Saxon scribes. I've been told it was copied about two hundred years ago at Worcester.'

'Ah, Worcester,' he said, nodding. 'They always were conservative at Worcester. Still, worthy and indispensable as those two volumes are, you'll need more to keep your spirits up and your mind alert. Here, take this.'

From somewhere beneath the heaps on his desk he produced a small book bound in the finest black leather. Its gold clasps glinted even in the candlelight. I inhaled the fresh animal scent of its cover, then opened the title page. It proved to be a copy of the *Confessions* of St Augustine of Hippo. I looked up at Father Simon who, for the first time since our meeting began, was smiling.

'How much do you know of the blessed saint?' he asked.

'He was African, one of the most influential thinkers in the history of our Church. I'm afraid I haven't read many of his works, but I've been told that his strict teaching on predestination has had a profound influence on doctrine ever since.'

The Abbot nodded. 'Indeed, that's so. Whether for better or worse is not for me to say. In any case, he spoke of many other matters of spiritual importance. But all agree that Augustine was a man of infinite charity. And he lived through the most turbulent times imaginable, the collapse of the Roman Empire. On his deathbed he learned that the Vandals were at the gates of the city.' He gestured towards the book in my lap. 'I have always found his *Confessions* a source of comfort and inspiration. The story of the saint's journey from doubt to error and then to faith seemed strangely appropriate for this moment.'

It would be a long time before I realised the full significance of these words. I turned to the opening page of the text, and the sight took my breath away. It was not just that the letters had been carefully and beautifully copied by a most skilful scribe, but I saw the initial of the first word, *Magnus*, erupting in an intricate and dazzling design of blue and gold foliage cascading down the inside margin, punctuated in places by acanthus leaves which squirmed out of the page. The artistry was captivating. As the longest stem curled around into the bottom margin, it metamorphosed as if by magic into the head of a hart.

'It's a book of great beauty,' I said. 'I shall accept it in the spirit in which it's given, but I can't help wonder why you chose this volume.'

Father Simon sighed deeply, and I knew that it was not for effect.

'You've lived a sheltered life, Nicholas, even though you came to us as a result of a tragedy. No, don't worry, I don't intend to go back over all that. It's a fortunate man, or an uncaring one, who can escape the pain of his own memories. But despite your suffering as a child, how often has your faith been tested in the fires of despair?'

Had the Abbot chosen these words deliberately? I shivered, screwed up my eyes and saw a blazing cottage, inhaled the acrid scent of burning wood and thatch.

'I'm not sure I understand, Father.'

'Let me put it to you this way. From time to time we need to subject our faith to the crucible of action. To expose ourselves to all the evil and the temptation which the world can throw in our way, and to show courage and resolution in standing opposed to it. Only in this way can we be sure that our faith is as robust as we believe it to be. At least once in our life, we have to test ourselves to the limit.

'Consider Brother Peter. He's in his middle years and has spent his whole life here, never venturing more than a short distance from this Abbey. His emotions are constrained, his imagination shrivelled. His understanding of the everyday trials of the people who toil outside these walls is minimal. Consider Brother Peter as he is today, and see yourself in years to come.

'You're facing a profound test at this moment, Nicholas. You may be a victim of circumstance, indeed of a great injustice, but don't let that blind you to the opportunity which is being offered to you. One day, I pray, you'll look back and see that this was the day on which God changed your life for the better. Changed it because He had other plans for you.'

I had no doubt that Father Simon was speaking from the heart, but his tone was one of sadness. He pointed once more to the book.

'So you see, Nicholas, it's as well to have the panoply of God's armour available. Just in case.'

'I'll care for the book well, and try to return it one day in the same condition.'

He waved his hand dismissively. 'Return it or not, as you choose. And may God be with you.'

So saying, he clasped his fingers in front of his mouth and resumed his contemplation of the space above my head. I rose and turned to leave.

'Oh, Nicholas,' he said. 'I appreciate that you may now want some time for silent prayer. If you wish to use it, my oratory is through that door.'

II

Father Simon's private chapel was surprisingly austere compared to his living quarters. It consisted of a small, bare room with a table at one end which I supposed could serve as an altar, and a crucifix on the wall above it. I knelt before it for some time but, no matter how hard I tried, the anger which kept welling up inside me prevented me from focusing on prayer. I heard the bell ring for Vespers, and Father Simon did not disturb me. I remained there until I knew the rest of our community would be in the church, then left.

As I reached the bottom of the steps leading down to the cloister, I fell to the ground in a heap. Picking myself up while biting my tongue to repress the curse which had flown to my lips, I realised that I had stumbled over the sprawling form of Brother John.

'John, what are you doing here? You must be frozen.'

'W-Waiting for you.'

'But you should be at Vespers with the others. Look, we can't be seen talking like this. You know it's forbidden.' I looked around. By now, it was too gloomy to see clearly beyond the garth and into the cloisters on the far side. 'Come inside the sacristy.'

I helped John back to his feet and led him to the store room where we stood among tables piled high with altar cloths, sacramental vessels, candlesticks and enough candles to illuminate the Abbey for a year. The door should have been locked, but Brother Joseph our sub-prior was notoriously lax. Very little light crept through the two high windows, but I could tell from his breathing that John was shivering violently.

'Why were you waiting for me?' I asked.

'What did he s-say?'

'Who, Father Simon? I can't talk to you about that, John. It's a secret, I'm afraid.'

'D-don't w-want you to go.'

'Who said—who told you I was going?'

John simply lowered his head. Had he been listening outside all the time?

'Look, perhaps I won't have to go. Then again, I was always going to have to go at some time. We can none of us be sure . . .'

I was talking nonsense because I had no idea what to say. John sniffed hard. I reached out and put my hand on his shoulder. He inclined his head towards it.

'What are you afraid of, John?'

'Being alone.'

'How can you be alone with all the other brothers around you?'

'You're m-my friend. Only friend.'

I wanted to reassure him that this could not be the case, but the words died on my lips because, of course, it was true. He began to sob. My departure would be more devastating for John than for me, and I felt ashamed of my earlier selfish concern with my own future. Then he straightened his head and took a deep breath.

'I can c-come with you.'

'John, if only that were possible. I'd love to have you with me as a travelling companion. But this is something I have to do alone. I can't really explain any more. But I'll tell you what I'll do. I'll ask Father Simon if I'm allowed to write to you when I get there. He can arrange for one of the brothers to read my letters to you. How does that sound?'

John placed his hands over his face and released a wailing sound like a wounded animal caught in a trap. It hardly seemed possible for the human voice to express such misery. I clasped him by the shoulders, but had no words left to say.

There was no way of knowing how long remained to me at Croyland. Father Simon had been vague about the date of arrival of the papal nuncio with whom I was to travel, so there was no choice but to be prepared to leave at any moment. My fellow brothers, who clearly knew of my fate but, I hoped, not the reason for it, made a point of avoiding me. Little as I wished to bring forward my departure, it was difficult not to feel some sympathy for the condemned criminal who at length longs for the hour of his execution and his final release from mental torment.

In between the regular cycle of the monastic offices, I was not allowed to play any significant part in the life of the Abbey. Father Simon became busier than ever during those days, to the extent that he barely showed his face. It seemed that I was in the same relation to him as Brother John to me. Indeed, I could not deny that I had been trying to avoid John for the same reason.

It was a considerable surprise, therefore, when Father Simon got to his feet after our morning conclave in the chapter house and announced to the brotherhood, in the most direct and straightforward manner, that I would be leaving the next day. He then departed, leaving all eyes fixed on me. I prayed for a hole to appear in the floor through which I might drop out of sight. My prayer was not granted.

That night, when we rose for Matins, Brother John's bed was empty. Maintaining silence, we descended the night stairs and processed into the church. I had always found it an eerie place in the middle of the night as the flickering candlelight cast moving and ever-changing shadows, but on this occasion my circumstances seemed to have dulled my anxieties until, in the draught from the open door, I heard a creaking sound which seemed to emanate from above the nave. Others stopped and listened, a collective shiver passed through us and we rushed as one past the chancel screen and down the steps. There, visible only as a faint shadow in the minimal light, a squat body hung from the rope secured around its neck. Unnoticed, I slipped back out of the choir door, leaned against the cold stone of the archway and vomited.

To general consternation, it took some time to retrieve Brother John's body. Indeed, it must have been quite a feat for someone with as little agility as he to make his way along the roof beams above the nave and attach a rope. I doubt that I would have had the courage to do it, but then, I reasoned, John had nothing to lose. In the end we threw another rope over the beam and secured it, and Brother Stephen, armed with a knife, managed to climb up. We stood back as he began to slice through the knot. We had placed blankets beneath, but they had little effect in breaking the fall of John's body. His bones cracked as he struck the stone floor. Most distressing, we saw that the length of the drop when he hung himself had partially severed his head from his body. Had he been left hanging much longer, the separation might well have been completed.

We wrapped his body in the blankets and gave it a temporary place of rest in the Lady Chapel. I prayed with all my heart that the Virgin would intercede on John's behalf to mitigate the eternal punishment he would inevitably suffer for his crime. At first light, Father Simon called us all into the chapter house and addressed us in a tremulous voice, saying that Brother John's death was obviously a tragedy but that, given the bizarre circumstances, we should not assume that he had taken his own life without investigating the alternative. Strictly speaking he was correct, of course, but in all probability he was groping for a way to believe that John's soul could be saved, and perhaps to dampen the feelings of guilt which would inevitably flow from the conclusion that, within the supposedly safe confines of our community, his life had been made so intolerable that he decided to end it.

We remained there for some time in silent prayer. Over and over, I asked myself whether there was anything I could have said or done to ease the torment I now realised John had felt at my coming departure. Doubtless others asked themselves whether their own behaviour towards John had contributed to his misery. Our Abbot must have seen his death as forming the final link in a chain of consequences which he had not initiated, but in which he had played his part.

By the time we left the chapter house I was overcome by fatigue, but also knew for the first time what people meant when they described themselves as weary in soul.

III

AROUND MID-MORNING, I WAS SUMMONED to Father Simon's quarters. There I was introduced to the long-awaited papal nuncio, Vittorio di Collini, a balding man of about fifty years with sharp features and a hooked nose. When the Abbot told him that I was to be his travelling companion to Avignon, he looked at me with evident disdain. His dark, knowing eyes suggested a man of the world who had no wish to be saddled with the burden of an innocent such as myself. As a diplomat, he restricted himself to conveying his feelings through non-verbal gestures.

'Signor Collini has just been ferried upriver from Spalding,' Father Simon said. 'I gather he's unaccustomed to making such slow progress on his travels.'

Signor Collini's expression conveyed beyond any doubt that he was not in the highest of spirits. His attention was clearly focused on the journey which still lay ahead. Father Simon also seemed less than at ease; I formed a strong impression that he was equally keen to see both of us on our way.

We set off, ill-matched pairing that we were, in drizzling rain from the gatehouse. Every personal item I possessed was contained in a bag small enough to sling over my back. No-one appeared to bid me farewell, nor, indeed, did the scowl on Vittorio's face seem to augur well. Perhaps it was caused by the inclement weather, but I strongly suspected that he felt it beneath his dignity to be journeying in such lowly company.

After a short walk to the riverbank, we came to the boat on which Vittorio had arrived, its boatman in no better humour than the papal nuncio. We travelled as close as the course of the river would allow to the town of Peterborough, at which point we disembarked. Vittorio had somehow arranged for horses to be there waiting for us, I could not imagine how. Carrying papers signed by his Holiness clearly opened more doors than I could have imagined.

Given that we had a long journey in store, I decided that it would be helpful to know more about my travelling companion, so began to quiz him about his mission and the duties he carried out on behalf of his Holiness. He stubbornly refused to respond to my efforts to engage him in conversation, and took to riding far enough ahead to make any social intercourse impossible. The only time he responded was when I asked which port we were making for.

'Dover.'

My knowledge of the topography of our island was limited, but I felt sure that our arrival in France would have been hastened by taking a ship from one of the ports on the eastern coast, such as Sutton or Lynn. I reconciled myself to the thought that Vittorio, as a seasoned traveller, must know better than I, and indeed it crossed my mind that he might wish to minimise the length of our crossing out of concern for his fellow-traveller who, perhaps he knew, had never before undertaken a sea voyage. The journey across land to Dover would in any case allow me to see parts of England outside my own region, albeit at the expense of considerable discomfort to my nether parts.

It seemed logical that our itinerary would take us through the great city of London, which I had always wanted to see, but instead Vittorio seemed bent on a more circuitous route. To my greater consternation, it transpired that he had no intention of availing himself of ecclesiastical hospitality overnight. Rather, his preference was for inns of highly variable quality, at many of which he was greeted as a regular customer. After a few, for me, uncomfortable nights, I suggested that perhaps we should each follow our chosen path and meet up at Dover. Vittorio, it turned out, had a single letter of authority to cover both of us, which rendered me effectively at his mercy.

Our journey seemed never-ending, and certainly had not been planned to take us along major roads or through the most scenic parts of our wondrous land, but when at long last I saw the city of Canterbury spread out before us, I realised that we were nearing the end, at least of the first stage. Surely Odysseus could not have been more relieved to see the shores of Ithaca. To my surprise, we made our way directly to the Archbishop's Palace, where Vittorio disappeared inside without indicating how long he would be. I was desperate to see the famous cathedral and pay homage at the tomb of the blessed St Thomas, but it seemed I had been left to take care of the horses. When Vittorio re-appeared some considerable time later, smelling strongly of wine, he was grinning broadly. Whatever the business he had been conducting on behalf of his Holiness, it had clearly been completed satisfactorily. I was cross, and very cold.

To my even greater surprise, we spent that night in the guest quarters of the Abbey of St Augustine. For once, Vittorio seemed content to spend the evening in my company, and the Abbey's hospitality wanted for nothing in epicurean terms. After we had eaten, the prior, a rotund, jovial fellow, joined us to help consume several bottles of wine. His fund of humorous, and often bawdy, stories from the monastery's long history kept me so amused that I must confess I drank more than I was accustomed to, indeed more than was wise. Vittorio and the prior were still enjoying themselves riotously when I was forced to excuse myself and retire to bed.

The next morning, I nursed my head from its pillowy grave and saw that Vittorio's bed, while rumpled, had already been vacated. I made a lengthy diversion to the latrine, where my bowels repaid me for the previous night's over-indulgence, giving me time to recall an episode from what already seemed my past life at Croyland.

A few years before, there was an elderly monk at the Abbey named Luke. He had reached the stage in life when Saturn begins to exert its influence and phlegm becomes the dominant bodily attribute. In other words, his faculties were failing, and although he still enjoyed reasonable physical health he had become increasingly forgetful and confused.

One day, Luke went missing. A search of his usual haunts proved fruitless, and his fellow monks began to fear that he had wandered out into the town and either become disoriented or fallen into the river. A novice, however, had the idea of looking in the one place no-one had considered, the latrine. Sure enough he found Luke there, although not using the facilities for their intended purpose. From his belt hung the keys to the Abbey's treasury. Luke held a box from which he was taking silver coins and dropping them one by one into the foul conduit running beneath, laughing maniacally as each landed with a dull splash. The novice watched in astonishment for some time, unsure whether his eyes were deceiving him. At length he took Luke by the arm, gently persuaded him to release his hold upon the box of coins, and led him to the infirmary, still shrieking like a demon.

From that time on, the old monk was kept under a degree of constraint and not allowed to walk about unaccompanied. All shook their heads sadly as they watched him pass, led by the arm by one of the younger monks, often giggling to himself. It was agreed that Luke had lost his wits, but I struggled with the thought that what he had done was the sanest act that any man could commit. On one occasion, I dared to ask him what had prompted him to do it. His eyes returned the most piercing stare, then a smile crept over his lips and he gave a slight nod of the head. To this day, I have no idea what this gesture meant. And to the best of my knowledge, no-one ever thought it worthwhile to retrieve the coins from their noxious repository.

When at last able to do so, I made my way outside and saw my travelling companion already saddled up and about to depart. Whether he would in fact have set off without me, I will never know. I told him that I would like to visit the shrine of St Thomas before we left, but he sneered and said that if we left immediately we could make Dover before the end of the day. Something in his manner conveyed the message that the matter was not open for further discussion.

We rode through the day with greater urgency than at any stage of our journey. Perhaps the prospect of finally leaving England was enticing to Vittorio, but as one unaccustomed to riding I found it hard to keep up with him. To enhance my discomfort, during the afternoon it started to rain heavily and remorselessly. The inclemency of the weather did not seem to bother Vittorio, but by the time we finally arrived at Dover, my mood was as sullen as the sky. Even the sea had a sickly green hue.

He walked brusquely up and down the quay in the failing light, demanding to know who would be setting sail for Boulogne the next morning. Most of the mariners responded to him with a surly sneer until he came to one who, from his speech, was a fellow Italian. They spoke quickly and abruptly, but at the end of their conversation they shook hands, presumably to confirm that Vittorio had succeeded in arranging a passage for us. The ship on which they negotiated had a shallow draught and was little bigger than a barge. Vittorio did not deign to explain to me the nature of the transaction, and simply remounted his horse and departed.

I followed him, expecting after the previous night that he would head for the substantial and, I had heard, well-appointed abbey overlooking the town, but instead he led the way to an inn on the waterfront. Its external appearance did not fill me with confidence, and my opinion was only reinforced by what greeted us within. The interior was dark and smoky, and as we entered a silence descended over the customers, primarily seafarers, which only after some moments was overtaken by the returning murmur of conversation. Vittorio gestured towards an empty table, and I placed my bag down and gratefully took a seat.

'We stay here tonight,' he said, the first words he had spoken to me spontaneously since our departure. Even so, I groaned at the import of his message, even whilst understanding the reasoning behind his decision, the tavern being only a short walk from the quayside to which we were bound to report in the morning.

To my surprise, he then walked away and disappeared through a back door. A buxom girl came over, a woman of easy virtue when not serving at table, I guessed, and I ordered wine and a light supper of pork and bread, assuming that Vittorio would be covering the cost, even if he was making his own arrangements. The food was welcome even if not entirely wholesome, but by the time I had finished my meal I had still seen no further sign of my companion. By now weariness had overtaken me and I decided to retire to the dormitory. As I stood up I noticed Vittorio at a table in a dark corner, talking with some animation to a fair-haired young woman.

I slept poorly that night. At regular intervals, some drunken mariner would barge into the room accompanied by a whore, or in one case two whores, and stumble around with much shouting and laughing until he found a spare bed. Needless to say, that would not be the end of the noisy interruptions to my rest. At length, once drink had taken its toll on them all, I did drift off into a tortured sleep. I recall dreaming at one point that I was in a sinking ship, the water rising rapidly towards my head. All I needed to do to save myself, at least temporarily, was to walk to the stern of the ship and climb onto the rear deck, but my legs were paralysed and the seawater as dense as honey. As the water closed over my head I must have cried out in my sleep, since I woke with a start to hear foul curses directed my way from the other sleepers in the dormitory. I turned over and saw next to me the bed which presumably had been reserved for Vittorio. It had not been occupied.

IV

THE NEXT MORNING, I RETURNED downstairs to find that the rain had ceased, but there was a strong wind blowing, and the prospect of the sea crossing filled me with foreboding. To comfort myself, I read the Gospel passage in which St Mark relates how Christ calmed a storm on the Lake of Galilee and so assuaged the disciples' terror. Having thus calmed my own fears, I ordered a light breakfast and searched for Vittorio, but could find no sign of him. It occurred to me that he had not even deigned to share the intended hour of our departure. I rushed to the stables at the back and found no sign of our horses. I found a lad cleaning out the stalls and demanded to know where the beasts were.

'We've taken them up to the abbey. Signor di Collini's orders.'

I hurried down to the quayside in case Vittorio were prepared, or even intended, to leave on his own. The boat on which he secured our passage was still docked and in the process of being loaded, its cargo consisting mostly of bales of wool which the captain was anxious to raise from the deck to prevent them from being damaged. It occurred to me that the only damage they could suffer on the voyage was from the ingress of water. I was aware that baling was a normal activity on board ship, even in relatively clement weather, but even so found a great anxiety welling up inside me which no fervency of prayer could disperse. I took some relief from the ship's name, the *Santa Maria*, which at least seemed a favourable omen.

I asked one of the seafarers if there had been any sign of Vittorio, and he shrugged his shoulders, whether to say that he did not know, or that he did not understand me, I had no way of ascertaining. At length, the boat seemed to be fully loaded and the captain ready to depart, but my companion remained conspicuous by his absence. The captain became increasingly impatient, and finally dispatched one of his men to a large house on the quayside. A short while later he emerged with a clearly disgruntled Vittorio a few paces behind, still adjusting his clothing. The seafarers exchanged jocular comments which I could not understand. One of them made the sign of the cross, which induced a general outburst of laughter.

No sooner had we cast off than it began to rain once more, and the crew looked up and emitted comments which, by their tone, I took to be curses. Vittorio, seated alongside me in the stern, seemed to share in their assessment of our native English weather. Since his arrival on board he had not acknowledged me in any way, and it now seemed clear that he could not wait to leave my home land far behind. It crossed my mind to wonder how a man of such narrow temperament could have found himself in a post which required him to travel constantly to other lands on papal business. Perhaps I still had a great deal to learn about the ways of those in the higher ranks of the Church's hierarchy.

We had barely left harbour before the ship began to pitch and roll in a most alarming way, and water to make its way over the upper strakes and onto the deck. The crew took to baling, the expressions on their faces making it clear that they were relishing this day no more than I. It was not long before I realised with a shudder that my breakfast was about to enjoy its release from the prison of my stomach. Vittorio, seeing the unmistakable signs of the apocalypse to come, grabbed me and held my head over the side of the boat, where I fed the fishes and seabirds with food which, in my generosity, I had already partly digested for them. Looking back, this was the first physical contact of any kind, however brusque, that there had been between us since we set out from Croyland. He dragged me back, chuckling to himself and clearly finding my condition a source of entertainment. I felt no better than before evacuating my stomach, but Vittorio seemed to find a vein of sympathy whose existence I would not previously have suspected.

'Not enough wine,' he said enigmatically. I shrugged. 'Wine protects the stomach, especially Italian wine. Apulian is best. Dark and rich, like a good woman.'

He doubled up with laughter at his own joke. I was more concerned to know what happens when an already empty stomach attempts to void itself.

'Turn over,' he said. 'Lie with your face on the deck.'

I did as he suggested, and found to my surprise that it had a beneficial effect. He patted me paternally on the shoulder.

Once I had come to terms with the possibility of arriving at Boulogne alive, I contemplated the paradox of Vittorio's behaviour. Only in my time of distress had he shown any human feeling towards me at all. Did he find me so amusing in my current state that I had taken his mind off more sombre matters? Or had I indeed unearthed another side of his character, a more generous one hidden until now? After a while he tapped me on the shoulder again; when I looked up he was offering me a leather bottle. I frowned, wishing to know what it might contain before committing myself to sample its contents.

'Apulian wine,' he said, and winked at me.

Somewhat against my better judgement I drank some, then waited for what seemed the inevitable consequence, but to my surprise found the sensation most reviving. He beckoned me to drink more, and I decided that his remedy was indeed a pleasant and effective one. The wine was robust and, if a wine can taste dark, it certainly did. My spirits began to lift and, even though the improvement in my health served to make me aware once more of the piercing cold, I also realised that someone like Vittorio, a well-travelled man of worldly experience, could be a most useful companion.

Towards midday the sky began to clear, and I saw for the first time the coast of Normandy as a thin line on the horizon. The captain looked round at me, pulled his cloak closely to him, pointed up towards the sky and made an expansive gesture with his arms whilst smiling broadly. I took him to be indicating that the north-east wind, though cold, was enabling us to make good time on the crossing. Hoping that I had interpreted his gestures correctly, I smiled back and nodded, pointing at the coastline up ahead. He in turn nodded vigorously, confirming my surmise, and I allowed myself the thought that people can communicate a surprising amount without the use of words. Indeed, it sometimes appears that words themselves can be a source of confusion, given their ability to be misinterpreted or misheard. At that moment, as the only Englishman on a ship full of Italian speakers, I felt no sense of alienation, and indeed began for the first time to feel that it was possible to look upon my forthcoming life as an adventure rather than an onerous and undeserved duty.

We hugged the coast until, as the light was beginning to fade, we drew into the harbour at Boulogne. When I felt dry land under my feet again I at first felt a little unsteady, but remembered to give thanks to God for His safe deliverance of the *Santa Maria* from the perils of the sea. Listening to the cries of the sailors, merchants and peddlers who crowded the quay, I was reminded that my knowledge of the French tongue had not often been honed in conversation, so that I could make out little of their speech.

The captain judged it too dangerous to unload the cargo in the failing light, and ordered three of his men to spend the night on board to watch over it. This, needless to say, met with an angry response which the captain ignored. The rest of us repaired to a tavern where he and his more favoured crewmen proceeded to pour down their throats prodigious quantities of a strong local drink, distilled from apples to judge from its smell. Vittorio sat with us, and although I expected to be excluded from the conversation as the only non-Italian speaker, he diligently translated for me the most interesting parts, at least those he judged suitable for my ears. The captain and crew soon became very drunk, and took to fighting with a group at a neighbouring table. Vittorio leaned across to me and explained.

'Our men are Genoese, the others Venetians.'

He raised his eyebrows and shook his head, as if the significance of this distinction should have been obvious. I nodded as though it were. He took me by the elbow and led me out of the tavern and along the quay, then through the door of a very different kind of establishment.

At first sight we appeared to be in another tavern, but of a much more civilised and sedate kind. Vittorio ordered food and drink for us and, once enjoying the comforting feeling of a full stomach and the warming effect of the wine, I began to feel very much at home. The lilting, ethereal tones of a dulcimer drifted from a side room. As soon as we had finished our meal, two slim, dark-haired young women came and sat at our table, bringing with them another bottle of wine. Vittorio was soon in animated conversation with them, and one began trying to converse with me, but she spoke very quickly and in a strange accent, so that I had to indicate by gestures that I could not understand her. She shrugged her shoulders as if to suggest that whether I spoke or not was a matter of little concern. Vittorio leaned across.

'Which of them do you prefer, Nicholas?'

'They're both very attractive,' I replied, 'and, I'm sure, very lively company.'

He roared with laughter, then translated my words to the young women, who roared with laughter too. Why my words had provoked such amusement, I had no idea. I decided that I must try for the moment to see every new experience as an opportunity to increase my understanding. At length Vittorio said to me:

'I think it is time to retire upstairs.'

In truth I was extremely weary after such a long and demanding day, and felt more than ready to take to my bed. One of the young women took me by the arm and led me upstairs, showing me a well-appointed room which, to my surprise, contained only one bed. After my night in the dormitory at Dover, this was luxury indeed. I lay down and my strength left me immediately. The young woman kindly helped me off with my boots, and I honestly believe that by the time she had succeeded in removing the second, I was fast asleep.

V

THE NEXT MORNING I WOKE bright and early and feeling refreshed, not to mention joyful that the Lord had finally blessed us with bright sunshine. I said my morning prayers and went downstairs, only to find the establishment deserted. After some time people, male and female, started to appear one by one, and I sat down to try to control my hunger until breakfast appeared. It seemed that I was the only person there lively and awake. Had something intervened to deprive all the other occupants of a good night's sleep? I saw the young woman who had helped me upstairs the previous night and smiled to thank her for her assistance, but to my surprise she snorted and turned away.

At length Vittorio appeared, looking as unwell as I must have done on the voyage from Dover. I asked him the nature of his malaise, but he simply gave me a puzzled look. It has to be said that, whilst all men and women may be creatures of God, their ways and customs offer a bewildering variety. At length our host served us a perfunctory breakfast of bread, cheese and honey. Vittorio picked at his for a few moments then pushed it aside, saying that he was going out to procure horses. Gazing around at this scene of red-eyed torpor I was led to conclude that, whilst the inhabitants of France might have a robust and energetic approach to life, this outlook did seem to take its inevitable toll. It was a blessing that my own background had led me to adopt a much healthier regime.

Vittorio returned in due course and indicated with a sweep of his head that it was time for us to depart. Once outside he suggested that, whilst we were on the road, I should remain silent whenever we were in the company of local inhabitants, since it was possible that the presence of an Englishman would not meet with general approval. England and France had not been at war for some years, but in this matter I could only accept his greater wisdom, without fully appreciating why an Italian should be more welcome to them.

We journeyed over the next few days to Rouen, a fine city with quite one of the most splendid cathedrals I have seen. It proved to be a busy inland port, with heavy traffic on its broad and surprisingly deep river heading for Paris in one direction and the sea in the other. This has made it a prosperous city but, I was told, had also been its downfall, since many centuries earlier savage and pagan Norsemen used the river to raid deep inland. The name of Normandy itself was said to preserve the memory of their no doubt unwelcome settlement in this region.

From Rouen we made our way on towards Paris, following broadly the route of the great river until, from the top of a rise, in the far distance we could make out the outline of the city. I had never had the chance to explore a city as majestic as Paris, and hoped that Vittorio would allow us time at least to visit the famous cathedral of Nôtre Dame and the renowned abbey of France's national saint, Denis. However, as we passed the fields outside the city walls we saw that a great multitude had assembled there and, needless to say, felt a compulsion to investigate further. It soon became clear that they were listening intently to a man speaking on the far side of the crowd. Vittorio and I exchanged a glance and spurred our horses to reach a position from which we could hear the speaker's words.

We dismounted on the edge of the crowd, a short distance from the cart from which a young man in a rough woollen cloak was addressing his seated audience. Our arrival naturally aroused some interest. One pox-scarred man dressed in rags looked up at our distinctive clothing and spat on the ground at our feet. Vittorio fixed him with an angry stare, and he slowly turned away. But the speaker also seemed to have observed our arrival and began to address his remarks in our direction. Even to my untutored ear it was clear that, for all his fluency as an orator, he spoke in a coarse dialect and was not a man of great learning. Nevertheless, his words were having a powerful effect on the crowd, a gathering of men, largely young, with a sprinkling of women and children. Vittorio was listening intently, a fact which had not gone unnoticed to the speaker. I sensed a rising hostility to our presence, and before long the young man on the cart began pointing in our direction.

'We've heard enough,' Vittorio muttered, and we remounted our horses. He led us away at pace as insults and worse were hurled after us.

We did not stop until it was necessary to allow the horses a period of rest. It was clear that Vittorio intended to avoid the city and, indeed, make rapid progress to get past it. As we sat on the ground and watched the horses grazing, I took the first opportunity to ask him about the events we had so recently witnessed.

'You've arrived in this land in disturbed times,' he said.

'What was going on? Who were the people gathered in the field?'

'They call themselves the Pastoureaux,' he said. 'The "Shepherd Boys". Which doubtless some of them are, but by no means all. The young man who was addressing them may have had the tongue of a simple rustic, but he learned the art of rhetoric somewhere. They claim to have been inspired by a vision from God to go and liberate the Holy Land from the infidel. How such a contemptible rabble could believe that they can carry out what kings and armies have failed to do, I cannot begin to imagine.'

'What did he say which inflamed them so much?'

Vittorio looked at me sternly. 'I will tell you the most devilish things he told them. "Those in authority over us may be placed there by God, but in this land they carry out the work of the devil. The King in his palace taxes us until we starve to pay for future crusades to liberate Jerusalem which he has no intention of carrying out. When we, his subjects, try to meet with him to discuss our discontent, he sends us away at the end of his soldiers' swords and threatens to cut us down.'

'Is that true? About the King?'

'Of course it is. King Philip has no more intention of undertaking a crusade to the Holy Land than the King of England does. But the young man went on to say some outrageous things about Christ's holy Church. "Our priests grow fat while we waste away, our bishops and archbishops consort with moneylenders and whores instead of providing the Church with the leadership it so obviously lacks."'

'He said all these things?'

'Oh, and plenty more. "There is only one place left to take our grievances, and to demand that the King fulfil his pledge to go on crusade to free the Holy Land. We'll march all the way to Avignon to see his Holiness Pope John and tell him to get off his lazy arse, and woe betide him if he treats us dismissively. Indeed, woe betide anyone who gets in our way or incurs our displeasure."'

'No wonder King Philip was keen to get rid of them.'

'Indeed. But his gesture has caused us a major problem.'

'Us?' I said. 'You and me?'

'We have simply found ourselves in the wrong place at the wrong time. Or the right place at the right time, depending on your point of view. Anyway, destiny may weigh heavily on our shoulders.'

Vittorio was becoming increasingly excitable, his Italian accent more and more pronounced. I was, I confess, becoming more and more alarmed.

'Then what must we do?' I asked.

He looked at me in astonishment. 'Why, it is obvious. We must ride like the wind to warn his Holiness.'

We embarked upon a headlong race from Paris to Avignon, travelling at such a speed across the country that the journey seemed to pass in a blur. In each major town and city we passed, from Auxerre to Autun to Lyon, Vittorio demanded audience with the secular and religious authorities to find out if they had any news of these so-called Pastoureaux. I could not see how such a rabble on foot could possibly have overtaken us, but perhaps Vittorio believed that there was another detachment of this peasant army further advanced on its journey. That his enquiries were met with blank stares and incomprehension brought him no peace of mind; he insisted on continuing our careering progress towards Avignon, reciting each day a litany of disasters which would of necessity result from any reduction in our pace, from the downfall of the Holy Roman Empire to the return of the Antichrist. I just had time to notice that, once we began to follow the course of the River Rhône, the local population no longer spoke in French but in a tongue Vittorio said was known as Occitan. To me it was incomprehensible, sounding if anything more like Vittorio's Italian speech than the tongue of the areas of northern France we had just passed through. However, I had little time to dwell on such matters. Such was his anxiety that, wherever we stopped overnight,

Vittorio would retire to his bed at an early hour in order to be sure of a prompt departure at dawn the following morning.

By the time we saw Avignon in the distance, I was concerned that he was intent on riding our horses to a premature grave. I had no idea what to expect from my first sight of the city and was surprised to find that, despite being the ecclesiastical centre of western Christendom, it was completely circumscribed by massive walls. The Papal Palace itself from the outside, and to some extent the inside, resembled a defensive fortress far more than it did the episcopal and archiepiscopal palaces of England. Indeed, work was clearly continuing in many areas to strengthen the fortifications still further. There was no time to dwell on this observation as Vittorio had raised the alarm immediately on our arrival, and had thereby unleashed chaos. The captain of the papal guard dispatched reinforcements onto the battlements and sent heavily-armed patrols out into the surrounding countryside. It seemed that it was only some time later that he troubled to enquire of Vittorio exactly where we had seen the huge mob which was on its way to destroy the very heart of the Papacy. On discovering that they had been camped outside Paris, he fell into a stormy silence. Indeed, he appeared to have quite lost the power of speech. With blazing eyes he turned to stare at me inquiringly; I could do no more than shrug my shoulders.

The Papal Palace did, nevertheless, remain in a heightened state of alert. For myself, as a complete stranger, this proved to be a considerable inconvenience as I was constantly required to prove my identity to all level of officials. Matters were made even more difficult by my linguistic ignorance. In the end I retired to the room which had been assigned to me, located in a small turret at the top of a tower, but one which at least afforded me a wide view of the Rhône. There for the first time I opened the copy of St Augustine's *Confessions* which Father Simon presented to me. I read with great joy the opening chapter, containing the blessed saint's paean to the Unknowable God, feeling by the end the shallowness of my own appreciation of the nature of our Creator. Was Father Simon more perceptive than perhaps I had given him credit for when he observed that my faith was incomplete in not having been tested in action?

One passage had such a profound effect on me that I decided to commit it to memory; perhaps in the future it would be meaningful to look back on it and to see whether my response had changed over time:

What are You, my God? What, I ask, if not the Lord God? For who can be the Lord God except our God? You are the highest, the best, mighty and all-powerful. You are most merciful and just, hidden yet omnipresent, most beautiful and strong. You never change and yet we cannot comprehend You. You who are unchangeable change all things, never new and never old, renewing everything. You bring down the proud. You are always active yet always at rest. You bear up and fill and protect, create and nourish and bring to perfection.

Whether those who lived and worked in the Papal Palace had remained aloof from the temptations which power and wealth always bring in their wake, and were indeed worthy torch-bearers for all those seeking leadership along the path of true Christian living, as yet I had no way of knowing.

VI

The following morning, both Vittorio and our horses seemed to have disappeared. A helpful guard who, it turned out, had spent time in the north, informed me in French as broken as my own that the Abbey of Claremont was a short way to the south-east, and advised that if I followed the old Roman road, which he said was named the Via Domitia, I could not fail to spot it nestling majestically on a hilltop. This seemed in line with the name of the Abbey, clearly from the Latin *claram montem*, 'bright mountain'. He even arranged for me to be provided with food and drink for the journey. Seeing his hospitable attitude as a favourable omen, I set off in that direction in good heart.

I located the road which the guard had described, and found it reassuringly easy to follow. Indeed, the Via Domitia turned out to be in a surprising state of preservation. I later discovered that it had once stretched all the way from Italy to Iberia, a feat of engineering and organisation which it would be hard to match even in the present day. It soon became clear, however, that the definition of 'a short way' needed to be re-interpreted in this land where settlements tend to be more widely separated than in England. When I finally saw the outline of what I took to be a monastery on the skyline, darkness was falling and I had long since used up my rations. There had once been an adequate path leading up the hillside, but it was now crumbling into disrepair and full of potholes. By the time I reached the top, I was exhausted.

The sight which awaited me did nothing to raise my spirits. The gatehouse was unoccupied, not surprisingly given that it was in a ruinous state. I walked past the seemingly-derelict church, across an open courtyard and into the Abbey's cloisters, once roofed but now quite open to the elements. There were niches around the ambulatory, a few still containing weather-worn statuettes, presumably of saints, but most now empty.

With a heavy heart I retreated back into the courtyard, contemplating the real possibility that, in the period since Father Simon made the arrangements for me to move here, the Abbey had been abandoned. As the darkness increased, however, I noticed the light of a candle burning within a structure standing isolated from the main complex of monastic buildings. I walked over and knocked on the door. For a long time there was no response, then, as I was about to give up, it slowly creaked open. Around it peered the angular, wrinkled features of a very old man. He looked me up and down, then beckoned me inside with a slow curl of his hand.

The room was so gloomy that at first I could make out little detail. It reeked of many years of damp, decay and neglect. The air within was barely warmer than the evening air outside. The old man gestured towards two fragile-looking chairs in front of the unlit fire and said something to me in what I now knew to be the local tongue, so I asked him if we could converse in Latin. He looked at me with some puzzlement, then nodded, although it seemed to require a considerable effort for him to speak the universal language of the Western Church.

'Is this the Abbey of Claremont?'

'It is.'

'I'm looking for the Abbot.'

'I am he.'

'In that case you'll be expecting me. I am Brother Nicholas.'

He stared at me, frowning and tilting his head from side to side. My name clearly meant nothing to him. Or was he deaf? I raised my voice.

'I've been sent from the Abbey of Croyland, in England. By Father Simon, the Abbot there. I'm sure he must have written to you.'

He rested his chin in his hand and fell into a pensive silence. I waited, and waited. At length he looked up.

'Why are you here?'

'I was hoping that would already have been explained to you. But I see that my arrival here was not expected.'

The old Abbot's face crumpled. He seemed not only surprised, but perplexed. The arrival of a stranger was clearly not an everyday event at Claremont. He picked up a walking stick, rose groaning to his feet, took the candle which provided the room's sole illumination, then walked out the door.

I followed him through the darkness to a nearby building, windowless as far as I could see, at least on the side from which we approached. He placed his meagre weight against the warped door, with no effect. He tried again, with the same result. His efforts were finally rewarded when it was opened from the inside. He showed me into what turned out to be the kitchen. It had an enormous brick oven on the far side, which at one time must have served a large community, but there was precious little sign that much food preparation still took place. Cleaning the surface of a table was a short, rosy-cheeked woman of ample proportions. I heard the door slam behind me.

The woman was clearly as nonplussed as I by the situation. I gave what I hope she interpreted as a friendly smile. She stared as if trying to make out who or what I was, then said a few incomprehensible words to me. I tried my inadequate French on her, but she just shrugged. Then she said something which took me aback.

'Do you speak the English tongue?'

'Yes. Yes I do. I'm from Lincolnshire. How do you know our tongue?'

'I grew up in Bordeaux. My parents served in the house of a noble English family. We all had to learn how to speak like them.'

I felt such an overwhelming sense of relief that I leaned back and laughed in a freer way than I had done for a very long time.

'In that case,' I said, 'I am very pleased to meet you. My name is Nicholas.'

'I am called Eleanor. You must be hungry. I'm afraid we can't afford much food here, but you're welcome to what we have. Please, sit down.'

I did as she requested. She busied herself on the other side of the kitchen with her back to me.

'How many is "we"?' I asked.

'Just Abbot Julian and me now,' she said. 'Oh, and Brother Guillem, but he won't be with us much longer, God willing. He's been confined to his bed in the infirmary since the beginning of the year. He longs for eternal rest. Things have been difficult. It wasn't always like this, but times change.'

Eleanor placed in front of me a platter containing some bread, clearly not baked that day, a slice of dry cheese, an apple and some salted meat. From which animal it originated, God alone knew, but I began to devour it greedily. She produced a bottle of wine and poured some into two cups, placing one in front of me and then sitting herself opposite. I tasted the wine and tried not to grimace; it would probably have been at its best at least a couple of years earlier. Still, I was thirsty and grateful for any gesture of hospitality.

'What crime did you commit to be sent here?' she asked.

'Is that the only reason why anyone would come?'

'These days, yes.'

It may have been hunger or fatigue or simply the opportunity to talk freely in English to another human being which liberated my tongue.

'I was accused of impregnating the wife of a local nobleman.'

Eleanor drank deeply before replying. 'So, did you fuck her?'

As I choked, I thumped my chest to suggest that a particle of food had gone down the wrong way, but her grin indicated that my subterfuge was in vain. It was some moments before I could clear my throat to reply.

'I'm an ordained monk of the Benedictine Order.'

She frowned and narrowed her eyes, apparently unable to see how this constituted an answer to her question.

'I've never had carnal relations with a woman, let alone another man's wife.'

She shrugged her shoulders and smiled. 'You should let me have your clothes.'

'Excuse me?'

'They are filthy. You stink. I am sorry to be so, what's the word, blunt. Anyway, I will wash your clothes for you. When you go to bed.'

She gazed distractedly around the kitchen as I finished my meal. It had been in no sense a visit to a gustatory Empyrean, but I had eaten every last crumb. I even sucked the last droplets of meat fat from my fingers. Eleanor watched me, running her tongue over her lips. She refilled our cups.

'It's a lonely life here,' she said.

'I can understand that it would be. Do you have a husband?'

'I did. My husband was a merchant. He left on a trading voyage to north Africa, and never returned.'

'That's terrible. It must be agonising not knowing what happened to him.'

'Huh. I don't need anyone to tell me what happened. Knowing him, he died of the sailors' pox in a brothel in Tangier. To be honest, I'm better off without him. Most of the time. But what about you? Why did you become a monk? Apart from the obvious reason.'

'I don't remember ever making a decision,' I said. 'I was orphaned when I was quite young. I was brought up in the monastery, and never really knew any other life.'

'How did your parents die?'

I took a deep breath and looked up at the crumbling roof timbers.

'I don't remember. Still, there's something reassuring about the monastic life. Events occur in cycles, daily, weekly or yearly. I suppose we always know where we are.'

I looked down to see that my cup had been refilled, as if by an invisible hand.

'The opposite of life for the rest of us, in a way,' she said. 'We have no certainty that the harvest won't fail, or that we'll be able to pay our taxes and avoid being thrown into prison. Still, I don't think I envy you.'

I was feeling very weary, and my eyes began to swim. In my fatigue, the wine had gone to my head. Nevertheless, I drained my cup and wiped my mouth with the back of my hand.

'I'll show you to the guest quarters,' she said, then laughed. 'Well, somewhere to sleep anyway.'

She led me to the side of the kitchen and up an ancient flight of stairs, and opened a door. I looked inside and saw a bed which quite clearly had already been slept in. I must have frowned.

'It's all right, it's mine, but tonight your need is greater. It's comfortable, I assure you. And warm.'

'But where will you sleep?'

'Oh, don't you worry about me. Now get undressed and let me have your clothes.'

I waited for her to leave, but she gave no sign of doing so.

'Don't worry. I've seen a lot of naked men.'

'That may be so, but . . .'

She sighed. 'All right, I'll turn my back.'

I hurriedly removed my clothes and jumped into bed. She picked them up from the floor, sniffed them with distaste and bade me goodnight. I wondered for a moment what I would do in the morning if she had not returned them in time. The thought was soon overtaken by welcome sleep.

Some time later, I awoke, imagining that I had heard the door open. After a few moments I reassured myself that, the whole Abbey being in a state of dilapidation, nocturnal creaking sounds must be a constant fact of life. When I awoke in the morning, the sun was already up. I recalled a dream, its context elusive, but the memory remained vivid that a human form had curled up alongside me in the bed.

I looked around and found my clothes neatly folded on the floor, exuding a gentle aroma of wood-smoke.

VII

I DESCENDED TO THE KITCHEN and found that two cats had devoured the majority of a plate of bread and cheese which, presumably, Eleanor had left out for me. A third had knocked over a cup of water and was lapping it from the surface of the table. They had ignored an apple which sat alongside, presumably put off by the numerous maggot-holes in its skin.

Since my arrival, no bell had rung to mark the hours of the monastic offices. Indeed, with Brother Guillem incapacitated, what would be the point of Abbot Julian ringing it for his own benefit? It was possible of course that, like much of the rest of my surroundings, the bell had already deteriorated beyond any useful purpose. I made my way to the chapel and found the main door sealed by rusting chains. Managing to force an entry through a small door in the south transept, I discovered every surface inside thick with dust. A long-dead pigeon lay on top of the altar like a bizarre sacrificial victim. Its live counterparts entered and departed at will through a hole in the roof, and the floor was covered with their droppings.

I stood outside, holding my cloak tightly against me to keep out the cold. My spirits were at their lowest ebb. The long journey from England had, it seemed, been to no purpose, and I had no idea where to go or what to do now. Was it even possible that Father Simon had decided to compound my punishment, knowing full well that nothing but desolation awaited me here?

I went to Father Julian's quarters and found him with his back to me on his knees, seemingly at prayer. Eleanor was in the process of lighting a fire, making use of the meagre stock of wood which lay scattered around the fireplace. As I entered she half-turned her head, and a smile broke out across her lips. Once the wood was smouldering, and it seemed capable of doing little more, she left, and as she passed her eyes for a moment flickered towards me.

At length the Abbot drew himself painfully to his feet and turned to face me. His expression was no more welcoming than it had been the night before. I decided to come straight to the point.

'There seems little point in my remaining, Father. Some kind of mistake has clearly been made in sending me here.'

He silently repeated my words, then nodded, and did not take his eyes from me.

'Unfortunately,' I continued, 'due to the circumstances of my departure, I cannot return to England. But I don't know where to go from here.'

He lowered himself slowly into his chair and stared into the fire, or rather the billowing smoke. I waited for some time. Was he thinking, or simply hoping that I would leave? At last he broke the silence.

'Can you write Latin as well as you speak it?'

'I would like to think so.'

'Then you should go to Avignon. They are always looking for bright young men like you. Go to the Palace and ask to see Paul Dalbon. He's an old friend of mine. Tell him I sent you.'

Having said this, he closed his eyes and soon began to snore. I let myself out, and headed back towards the gatehouse. As I was about to leave the monastery, I saw Eleanor step out of the kitchen. When she saw me she stopped and, without a smile, raised her hand in a gesture of farewell.

In the course of the return journey to Avignon, my feelings of apprehension grew more and more strong. Suppose Father Julian had invented the name of Paul Dalbon simply to get rid of me? Suppose Avignon proved to be full of ambitious young men searching for employment? In any case, I had spent my life as a monk, and could not be sure my talents would be at all suited to the huge engine of administration which the Papal Palace represented.

It was evening by the time I presented myself to a uniformed guard at the main entrance. His face formed itself into a sneer even before I opened my mouth.

'I am here to see Paul Dalbon,' I said in Latin.

The guard stared. Apparently he did not speak Latin. I tried again in my school-room French. This brought a more positive response although, since neither of us spoke the language well, conversing took some time.

'Never heard of Paul Dalbon,' the guard said. 'What does he do?'

I had, of course, no idea, but felt obliged to convey a self-confidence which I certainly did not feel.

'He holds a senior post in his Holiness's administration. I'm surprised you're not aware of that.'

'What do you want with him?'

'I have a matter to discuss with him.'

'If you're looking for a job, you're wasting your time. People are always turning up here wanting a job, and they all get sent away.'

'That's as may be.' I heard my voice begin to quiver, whether through anger or fear I could no longer tell. 'But I assure you that, when you tell Paul Dalbon that I have been sent by Father Julian of Claremont, he will want to see me.'

I expected him to burst out laughing at the mention of Claremont, but the name seemed to mean nothing to him. Perhaps those who worked within these walls heard little of the world outside.

'What do they call you?' the guard said.

'My name is Nicholas,' I replied with as much dignity as I could summon. He rolled the name around in his head, clearly bemused. I repeated it in its French form.

'Wait here,' he said, and walked away. Soon, the darkness was punctuated only by the light of the blazing torches on either side of the gateway. I was cold, hungry and by now despairing that Father Julian's introduction would be of any avail. I sank down onto my haunches to ease my tired legs, until roused by the grating of boots on gravel.

'Come with me.'

I struggled to follow him across the tenebrous courtyard, guided only by the sound of his feet. When I heard a door open, I walked through into a gloomy corridor which quickly turned at right-angles. The guard hammered on a door, then spun on his heel and disappeared.

A voice from within, seemingly that of a reticent but educated man of about forty years, invited me to enter. I found him in a large chair surrounded by candles, reading.

'I'm looking for Paul Dalbon.'

'Then accept my congratulations. What do you want from me?'

'I asked the guard to inform you that I've been sent by Father Julian of Claremont.'

'Typical. He forgot to mention that part. What in the devil's name were you doing at Claremont?'

'It's a long story. May I sit down?'

'Of course. Please pardon my lack of hospitality.'

He dragged a considerably more humble chair across the room until it was within the ambit of the candlelight.

'So what did Julian send you to say?'

I took a deep breath. 'He expressed his hope that you would be able to find employment for me.'

His expression did not change. 'Did he now? In that case, perhaps you'd better tell me this long story. The salient facts, anyway.'

Even had I the inclination to lie, it was a skill which I had never acquired, so I held nothing back. My listener's face gave nothing away. By the end of the tale, it was a struggle not to hang my head.

'Well, well. Fate has dealt you an unfortunate hand. Still, who are we to query the mysterious ways of God?'

'But, technically, I don't have the permission of my Order to be here. I was sent to Claremont, not to Avignon.'

He frowned. 'And how could you possibly serve God better at Claremont than here, working directly for his Holiness, God's representative on earth? I dare say there are people in this place with considerably more guilty secrets than yours. Anyway, at least the Benedictines will have given you a sound education. So, what can you do? We're too busy to carry passengers, unless of course they happen to be the bastard sons of bishops and cardinals.' He chuckled to himself.

'I can read and write in Latin.'

'So can everyone else here.'

'And I have some knowledge of the French tongue.'

'Most are fluent in it, apart from the Italians, of course. You'll have to do better than that.'

He seemed to be trying to find an excuse to employ me, but I was doing little to help my own cause. As I struggled for any other skill or talent to offer Paul Dalbon as inducement, it seemed that all I had ever really learned was the detail of monastic ritual. I had one last chance.

'My native tongue is, of course, English.'

He sat up in his chair and stroked his chin. 'Hmm. Relations with your homeland have been, how shall I say, interesting at times. Do you have a family there?'

'No. Not any more.'

'Good. Not for you, of course, or them for that matter. But it simplifies matters if there are no family ties.' He clasped his hands and twirled one thumb around the other, then leaned forward and lowered his voice. 'Life's not always easy or straightforward here, you should understand that. In some respects, the Palace functions like a royal castle, treasury and chancery all rolled into one. Things are not always what they seem on the surface. Do you see what I'm saying?'

'Yes, I think so.' I had no idea what he was talking about.

'Sometimes it pays to just keep your head down and let others manage their own affairs. If you can work within those constraints, I think I can find a place for you here.'

What choice did I have? I thanked Paul Dalbon profusely for his generosity. As I prepared to leave, I pointed out to him that I had nowhere to stay.

'That's not a problem. I'll find you a room here while you get yourself settled.' He looked me up and down. 'And you'll need some new clothes. In fact I know just the person to help you find your way around, a very promising young man who'll make quite a name for himself one day. I'll arrange for him to come and see you tomorrow. Come back and see me the day after.'

A liveried servant showed me to a room at the top of a very high tower. I was exhausted by the time I reached the top. The room was small, cold and a very odd shape, being constrained by the tower's curved outer walls. Nevertheless, it contained the one essential item at that moment, a bed with some blankets. I gave thanks to God for His grace in delivering me into what seemed like the haven of the Papal Palace, little knowing that the future He had in store for me would be anything but settled and peaceful. In my blissful ignorance, I soon fell into a profound sleep.

VIII

THE NEXT MORNING, THE SUN was streaming in through the slit which constituted the room's only window. It bathed the room in an unearthly glow, gilding the grey stone walls. Indeed, it seemed like the dawn of a new phase of my life, one which filled me with anticipation and excitement. Not very long before, the idea that I could have left the monastic cloister for the vibrant world of Avignon, travelled across new lands to start a new life, and could relish the experience, would have been unthinkable. I lay on my bed and realised that I was smiling to myself.

I was stirred from these thoughts by a loud rapping on the door. When I opened it, standing outside was what I can only describe as a human peacock, a young man dressed in the most flamboyant style. He wore a tight red jacket over a white lace shirt, equally tight black leather trousers and long pointed shoes. The crowning feature was a broad black hat adorned with brightly-coloured feathers from an assortment of birds, including crane and pheasant. Below it was a pale but vibrant face with sparkling eyes. He removed the hat, swept it before him and performed an extravagant bow. He introduced himself in the Latin tongue.

'Francesco Petrarca, at your service, my friend. May I call you Nicholas?'

Without pausing for a reply, he strode into the room, threw his hat on the bed and stood at the tiny window, breathing deeply. As he took in the view, he began to speak rapidly in what I recognised as the Italian tongue. My face must have conveyed my confusion.

'A thousand apologies,' he said, reverting to Latin. 'In my excitement I naturally spoke in my own tongue. From now on, I will try to speak good Latin.'

'I travelled from England with an Italian. A papal nuncio. Unfortunately, he wasn't talkative enough for me pick up any of his native tongue.'

'Ah, a nuncio. They're trained to say no more than what they have to say. Except in private, to whores, of course.'

He laughed and threw himself onto the bed next to his hat.

'They reserve these lofty rooms, Nicholas, for young guests such as yourself, you know, since the fat old ones, who are the majority, would never survive the climb. Even so, the air is fresh up here, unlike in the streets below. I have never encountered such a stench, even in my student quarters in Montpellier.'

'You're a student at the University?'

'I was a student of law. Sadly my days of leisurely learning are over. I must soon return to Italy, to Bologna, to undertake some, how shall I say, more intensive study.'

'Paul Dalbon seems to think highly of you. I'm sure he could arrange employment for you here.'

He turned around slowly, narrowed his eyes and lowered his voice.

'This place stinks of death and corruption.'

For some moments we stared at one another, until his face softened and he began to smile.

'Do you have any wine?' he asked.

'I'm afraid that the generosity of my hosts doesn't seem to extend that far.'

'That's because the greedy bastards are keeping it all for themselves. Come, let's leave here. I'll show you the delights, the attractions and the despicable dereliction of Avignon.'

Without another word he picked up his hat and strode from the room. By the time I had gathered myself and put on my cloak he was half-way down the staircase.

'Wait for me, Francesco,' I called after him, and heard laughter drifting upwards in response.

Once we were outside the bounds of the Palace, he led me towards the river and into the premises of a tailor. After he had conducted a rapid exchange with the proprietor, presumably in the local Occitan tongue, of which as yet I understood not a word, the latter began to measure the length of my arms, legs and torso. While he did so, Francesco said to me, in Latin:

'The fool wanted until next week to make you some clothes. I told him we need them by the end of the day or we'll take ourselves elsewhere and make sure that he gets no further custom from the Palace. That seemed to concentrate his mind.'

I was more than a little alarmed. 'Francesco, I appreciate what you're doing, but I've no money to pay for this.'

'Don't worry, I told him to send his bill up there.' He nodded in the direction from which we had come. The people in the papal accounts office are too lazy to ever check anything.'

He led me away from the river and down streets of decreasing breadth, until it seemed that we were walking through a dark tunnel. Above us, the eaves of the houses on either side almost met, effectively blocking out both light and air. The stench was every bit as overwhelming as Francesco had suggested, and we stepped carefully in a vain attempt to avoid the refuse and waste, probably both animal and human, which littered the streets.

Without warning, he veered down an alleyway. I followed him with some trepidation, but discovered that it opened out into a sheltered and fragrant courtyard, mercifully free of the malevolent odours which assailed our nostrils on the way. Lemon and olive trees grew around its perimeter, and we sat at a table just beyond their shade. We seemed to be in the courtyard of a large private house, but Francesco vouchsafed no explanation. Within moments a fresh-faced girl emerged with a tray holding a flagon and two rough pewter cups. As she placed it on the table, she leaned forward until her breasts seemed on the point of escaping from her dress of their own volition. I turned away hurriedly, but not before noticing that she and Francesco exchanged the broadest of smiles. As she turned to leave, he slapped her on the buttocks and, to my surprise, she giggled.

'The lovely Marie,' he said as he poured the wine. 'I can introduce you to her if you wish.'

I frowned. 'I'm still subject to the vows I took when I entered the Benedictine Order.'

'Ah, you're a monk? Tell me how you came to end up here.'

I recounted once again, as briefly as I could, the story of my recent life. He listened with what seemed like genuine interest.

'I see you're already partially detached from your monastic calling,' he said, glancing at the top of my head. 'When was your tonsure last shaved?'

'Yes, you're right. I suppose there hasn't seemed much point. Still, unless and until I'm released from my vows . . .' I shrugged.

'In that case,' he said, 'shouldn't you have permission from your Order to be here?'

'I've been thinking about that. Paul Dalbon wasn't bothered. I suppose I could argue that Father Julian gave me temporary licence when he recommended I come here. But if I don't go back to the monastic life at some stage, I'll have to find a way of resolving the issue.'

'Well, if any arms need twisting, at least now you're working in the right place.'

On the journey from England, Vittorio had invariably insisted on being served the finest wine available, and I found it difficult to conceal my dislike of the unpalatable liquid served in this establishment, whatever it might be. At one point I caught Francesco looking up and grinning, and saw a plump woman about thirty years of age waving to him from an upstairs window.

'Avignon is a city of no culture,' he said. 'A man must find some way of passing the time without causing harm to his fellows.'

I decided not to question him on this enigmatic statement. He, at least, appeared to be drinking the wine with relish.

'How do you know Paul Dalbon?' I asked him.

'My father was a civic official in Arezzo. He decided to try his luck here, hoping to be absorbed into the already vast papal administration. To my good fortune, he sent me to Montpellier rather than leaving me to rot here, but on my visits to Avignon I seemed to catch Paul's eye. I don't know why.'

Recalling the startled reaction of the city's inhabitants to his attire as we made our way through the streets, I felt tempted to give Francesco the explanation he sought, but decided to hold my tongue. I found myself, nevertheless, becoming a little envious of his lack of inhibition in expressing himself through his appearance. I felt a twinge of apprehension wondering what style of clothing he had ordered for me.

We talked for some time about Avignon and his uncomplimentary view of his Holiness and all the paraphernalia which surrounded him. Now away from the Palace, he felt no need to disguise his thoughts or even to lower his voice. Indeed, the more wine he drank, the more it became clear that he held a similarly derogatory opinion of virtually every figure of authority in this or any other land. He was in fact a remarkably, and perhaps dangerously, free-thinking young man. Could Paul Dalbon have had some deeper reason for wanting our paths to cross?

We conversed for some hours, and by the time we finished a second flagon of wine the fragile warmth of this early spring day had begun to diminish. Francesco slammed his cup on the table and rose, wavering, to his feet, then regained his balance and began to make his way back to the street. I followed more closely this time, noting that no payment seemed to have been expected for the wine, at least on this occasion. Perhaps my companion was a sufficiently regular customer to be trusted by the host to settle his dues at a fixed time.

We made our way in silence past the wharves and quays which lined the east bank of the river, listening to the incomprehensible cries of the lightermen and warehousemen, some no doubt remarking in suitably ribald manner on the appearance of my companion. We strolled towards the remains of what had once been a substantial stone bridge. Passing through an impressive archway to gain access, we walked as far as we could, in other words to the point where the bridge had seemingly collapsed into the river, and sat with our legs hanging over the edge. The Rhône sparkled below us in the late afternoon sun, drifting languidly towards the sea many leagues to the south. The river traffic was substantial, and barges processed past us like so many pieces of giant driftwood. The scene was strangely calming.

'Why do you despise those in authority over us?' I asked. 'Surely they hold their position, for better or worse, because God has placed them there.'

Francesco stared down at the oily waters below, and said nothing. Just as I concluded that he intended to ignore my question, he replied without looking up.

'Do you know why Avignon only has half a bridge?'

'Bridges always seem to have a tendency to collapse. I suppose like church towers they're sometimes too heavy to support themselves.'

He smiled. 'Across the river is the territory of the King of France. Avignon belongs to the King of Naples, did you know that? Many years ago, King Louis the Eighth decided to punish the people of Avignon for supporting the Cathars, so after wreaking destruction on the city he decided to demolish the half of the bridge which lay on his side of the river, leaving the townspeople with the useless remnant which remains. I suppose that, rather than demolish it, they've always felt it's better to leave it here as an act of defiance.'

I pondered whether this had provided any meaningful answer to my question, but decided not to press the matter.

'What do you believe in, Francesco? I mean, really believe in?'

'I believe in learning and knowledge and books and ideas. I want to know everything there is to know about everything. I've been collecting books since I was first able to read. Not the contemptible sort which are written here, about canon law and the need for orthodoxy in all matters. I'm talking about books containing the words of the great thinkers of the past, those who flourished under the Greek and Roman civilisations. Do you know the Greek language?'

'No, I'm afraid not.'

'A pity, neither do I and I've just acquired a Byzantine copy of Plato's *Timaeus*. I don't trust the Latin translations.'

'To put it another way,' I said, 'the only writers you admire are those who lived during a bygone era and were pagans.'

He turned to me, and a flicker of a smile played on his lips.

'Ah. There you overstate the case, my friend. The book I have read more often than any other is by one of the most revered Christian theologians. Can you guess what it is? No, don't bother, I'll tell you. The *Confessions* of St Augustine. Have you ever read it?'

'I have a copy in my room, but I must admit I've barely started it.'

'Then read avidly, Nicholas. Learn to know this book as your closest friend, the friend you turn to for help and support and advice. It will never let you down.'

Francesco's eyes took on a distant look and his lips flickered, as if he were reciting the text in his mind from memory.

'I had a tutor at one time who'd studied at the University of Oxford,' I said.

At first my words drew no reaction from him, but at length he seemed to become aware of my presence once again. His eyes sparkled more than they had done at any time since our first encounter.

'I knew that there would be a deeper bond between us,' he said. 'As scholars we have suckled at the same breasts, those of the nine Muses. Come, Nicholas, don't look like that, it was a mere poetic flight of fancy. Do you like writing letters? I write them obsessively. I shall write to you while you're here in order to keep your spirits up. I suspect that, living and working in this place, from time to time you'll need something to lift you from the jaws of despair.'

'Why do you say that?'

Francesco's face set itself into a stony expression with such abruptness that I was taken aback. When he spoke, however, his voice conveyed tones of melancholy rather than anger.

'What was it that Jesus advised his disciples when he sent them out into the towns and villages to preach the Gospel of the Kingdom of Heaven? "Be as wise as serpents." If your future lies here in Avignon, then you, Nicholas, will need to be as wise as a serpent.' He clapped his hands. 'Now, it's time to eat. Do you like music? I know a place where the most exquisite harpist performs, although sadly a dolt who can play a few notes on the flute sometimes joins in, but at least the food is on the acceptable side of execrable. I shall pay, or at least add the cost to the credit facility which the owner has graciously afforded me. I'm sure my father will pay it off soon. Anyway, Nicholas, we shall think of it as our Last Supper, until we meet again on the other side of—well, come, let's go and dine.'

Francesco showed the way to a quarter of the city filled with taverns and places of private entertainment, to express the matter delicately. Indeed, there seemed a free interchange of both customers and employees between the two classes of establishment. We entered a large, smoky room which offered a quiet respite from the cries and laughter without. In one corner played the harpist Francesco had mentioned. His playing was indeed of a rare beauty, thankfully unaccompanied by the less accomplished flautist. We ate chicken and vegetables and drank more wine. Francesco and I conversed only occasionally, but I felt very much at ease in his company. I realised now why Paul Dalbon was convinced that he had a bright future before him.

When we returned to the Palace, he bade me farewell, saying that he would be spending the night elsewhere.

'When do you leave for Bologna?' I asked.

'Tomorrow. And I wouldn't have chosen to spend my last day here in any other way. Remember what I said, Nicholas. And I shall write to you, you have my word. Now, if you'll forgive me, I must say some farewells.'

He turned on his heel and walked away, then stopped and looked back.

'We forgot to pick up your clothes. Make sure that scoundrel has them ready first thing in the morning. Tell him you'll have him excommunicated if he hasn't.'

Later that night, when the meagre supply of candles in my room had exhausted itself, I lay on my bed thinking about Francesco Petrarca. At times I had been taken aback by his anti-authoritarian attitudes and his undoubted weakness for the offspring of Eve. Nevertheless, something about this effervescent and engaging young man reached into my heart in a way that left me anxious and confused. It was as if, having spent mere hours with him, I had experienced the equivalent of years in the company of the more mundane individuals who had populated my life up to that point. I doubted that I would ever meet him again face to face, but hoped that he would be true to his word and communicate with me by letter from time to time. I guessed that he of all people would be capable of finding a way of keeping his promise.

Groping in the dark, I found the copy of St Augustine's *Confessions* which Father Simon had given me, and held it against my chest as I drifted into sleep.

IX

Paul Dalbon set me to work, not surprisingly, amongst a group of young men dealing with correspondence from England, Wales, Scotland and Ireland. The documents we dealt with were mostly legal in nature, asking for advice on aspects of canon law, or related to political and diplomatic matters, visits by papal legates and such like. Occasionally we saw a letter of a more sensitive nature, such as those asking for a certificate of exemption from the rule imposing prohibited degrees of marriage between relatives. We were, of course, sworn to secrecy.

At first, my tasks were limited to ensuring that every item was safely and securely recorded and placed in the archives, but in time I was trusted to reply to the more straightforward types of query, following standard forms of wording, needless to say. I soon found that the Palace had its own customs and practices. Some of my colleagues scoffed at the script which I had learned in England, declaring it old-fashioned, a historical relic. It transpired that in these regions new forms had been adopted, styles not yet known in my homeland. I tried to adapt, but habits ingrained since childhood are almost impossible to eradicate.

I cannot in all honesty say that I found the work stimulating, although most of my colleagues seemed to find it even more tiresome than I, and applied themselves only when subjected to direct pressure from our master. They made no secret of the fact that they considered anywhere north or east of Paris to be backward and barbaric, even though I saw no evidence that any of them had ventured that far afield. Presumably, they had only taken up employment there in the hope of subsequent advancement to more responsible and lucrative positions, or because they were considered unfit for more demanding work. Nevertheless, I settled into my role and, indeed, found its routine comforting after all the uncertainties I had endured since my expulsion (as I saw it) from England.

I became quite friendly with one of my colleagues, the only one in fact who made any real effort to acknowledge my presence, an attractive and ebullient local youth named Bartolomeo, dark-haired and olive-skinned. His education had been limited, but he had a lively mind, and never needed to be taught twice. In our spare time, he undertook to teach me his native Occitan tongue, and we turned my room into an impromptu classroom. I expected Occitan to be a variant of the French widely used in England, but was disconcerted to find that it was nothing of the sort, having remained much closer in crucial respects to its Latin ancestor. In time, however, I found that most of the historic developments which it had undergone as it separated from its parent tongue over the centuries were regular and, within limits, predictable, and Bartolomeo proved to be a most able teacher. I became, in fact, an enthusiastic student, and eventually developed the confidence to engage others in conversation in the shops and taverns I visited. At first they found my efforts risible, but later began to show grudging respect for the pace at which I became fluent.

One warm evening, Bartolomeo and I rested on the broken bridge where I had previously conversed with Francesco Petrarca. Despite his assurances, I had not heard from him since his departure to Italy. Doubtless his law studies kept him very busy.

'You don't seem to be like the rest of us,' Bartolomeo said.

'I'm not sure what you mean, my friend.'

'Well, young men generally have a reason for wanting to work in a large, impersonal place like the Palace. Most are there through nepotism, because a well-connected relative put in a word for them, and they think it's their birthright to enjoy a lucrative career without doing much work. There are a few, like me I suppose, who come from more humble backgrounds, and still feel vaguely privileged to be working for such important and powerful people.'

'I assume,' I said, 'that you mean powerful in a political sense, rather than spiritually.'

'Even I'm not that stupid. If I want to benefit from spiritual wisdom, I'll ask a hermit, not a cardinal. But what about you? I can't seem to put you into any category. Were your parents high-born? If you don't mind me asking, that is.'

'I grew up in a small labourer's cottage.'

'Then . . .'

'Strictly speaking, I'm a monk of the Benedictine Order.'

Bartolomeo's eyes widened. 'Strictly speaking?'

'I was transferred to Claremont Abbey. Which, as you probably know, barely exists any longer. The Abbot, to my good fortune, knows Paul Dalbon. What else can I say?'

He fell silent, perhaps inwardly debating whether it would be impolite to press me further on these revelations.

'Shall we go to Petro's taverna?' he said. 'He has a new serving-girl, and I think she's been looking at me with interest.'

In so far as I could judge through the sepulchral gloom of the tavern, the serving-girl possessed undoubted physical attractions, but she was no more attentive to Bartolomeo than to any other of her numerous admirers. As she leaned forward to serve us wine, I was forced to avert my gaze for fear that my eyes would be sucked into the chasm between her breasts. As she walked away Bartolomeo gazed after her wistfully, but she did not look back.

The following weeks passed uneventfully, and I began to feel that a life in the service of the Papacy could be an appealing prospect, particularly for one fortunate enough to achieve advancement within this vast and dizzying edifice. I well knew, however, that such matters were often resolved on the basis of criteria other than innate ability.

The weather in Avignon proved a good deal more variable than I had expected. A fair amount of rain fell in late April, although as spring progressed it grew steadily warmer week by week. In any case, the thick stone walls of the Palace kept the internal rooms at a more or less even temperature. Outside in the streets, the stench of which Francesco had complained grew more unpleasant, even in the relative cool of the evening. The river appeared to be making its contribution to the infernal aroma. Any rotting carcase which washed up onto the banks would be pushed back into the stream by men with long poles to the accompaniment of a volley of curses, most of which Bartolomeo felt it would be indiscreet to translate for me.

This comfortable if unchallenging routine was disrupted one day without warning. I was drafting a letter on an arcane point of canon law when Paul Dalbon walked into the room. This was an unusual event in itself; I had seen him perhaps a handful of times since my first meeting with him. To my greater surprise, he walked straight to my desk. His expression did not suggest that he had come to pass the time of day.

'Cardinal de Savigny wants to see you tomorrow,' he said.

The room fell silent. I did not dare to look around, but knew that every pair of eyes was fixed upon me.

'May I enquire why?'

'You can enquire, but it won't do any good.'

I tried to prevent the rising sense of alarm from creeping into my voice.

'May I ask, where do I find the Cardinal?'

'You don't find de Savigny. He finds you.'

Having said this, he turned abruptly and left. No-one moved or spoke, as if the moment had somehow been frozen in time. I returned to the document on which I had been working, but my words had been reduced to a series of meaningless lines and curves which swam before my eyes.

The next morning, about an hour after dawn, a liveried servant knocked on my door. He did not bother to state his business, and showed considerable impatience, as if I should have known that he would arrive at precisely that moment. We descended the spiral stone staircase to reach the bottom of the tower, then set out across the main courtyard. The servant walked in silence, keeping just ahead of me and maintaining a brisk pace. By the time we arrived at our destination, a set of apartments on the other side of the Palace, my breathing was so heavy that I was grateful when he instructed me to take a seat in the hallway. From merely inspecting the wall-hangings I realised that my new surroundings were considerably more luxurious than any part of the complex to which I had so far been allowed access.

After a short time, another servant appeared and beckoned me with a nod of the head towards a door across the way. I found that I was entering a grand ceremonial hall rather than the intimate private apartment I had expected. Long tables and benches were stacked out of use along the sides, but I could imagine that on ceremonial occasions, with scurrying, brightly-uniformed servants in attendance, this would be a most impressive space. My eyes were drawn upwards to the lofty, vaulted ceiling, decorated with sweeping and extravagant celestial scenes dominated by unclad, and very clearly female, angels

At the far end, behind a large table, sat a man about thirty-five years of age, writing very quickly. He had thick black hair, and his features were as sharp and alert as those of a hunting dog. His robes were trimmed with sable. From both his clothing and his bearing, I knew that this was the man I had been fearing to meet.

I stood in his presence for some time before he finally acknowledged me. I felt his dark eyes probing, as if attempting to read my thoughts and intentions without taking the trouble to interrogate me. When he finally spoke, his sonorous voice, though not loud, was effortlessly commanding. He would have been as much at home at the helm of a large banking house in Florence, or leading a diplomatic mission for the Emperor himself.

'You must be Nicholas the Englishman,' he said, in Occitan rather than Latin. I thought I detected an accent somewhat different from Bartolomeo's. I tried to formulate a response to his opening words, but none came. He made me feel even more uncomfortable by smiling.

'Do you know who I am?'

'I can only assume that you are Cardinal de Savigny.' Had my reply sounded abrupt or impertinent? His face betrayed no reaction. His eyes, however, continued to ask their own questions.

'I am Cardinal Bertrand de Savigny,' he replied. 'I had hoped to make your acquaintance earlier, but these have been, how shall I say, interesting times. There are disturbances in this land, some of which I believe you experienced on your way here in the company of Signor di Collini.'

'Ah, yes,' I replied. 'The Pastoureaux. Vittorio—Signor di Collini seemed to think they were a major threat to his Holiness.'

'Quite so,' the Cardinal said. 'I don't entirely blame him. As papal nuncio, it's his job to be the eyes and ears of his Holiness wherever his duties take him. In that sense he was only fulfilling his mission. Indeed, his Holiness takes Signor di Collini's warning very seriously. Our reports suggest that these Pastoureaux are committing acts of violence and murder wherever they go, even robbing and desecrating churches in their blind hatred. I fear we'll be hearing more of them.'

He paused. Once again my tongue was frozen. He allowed the tension to hang in the air before continuing.

'I can assure you that everything I say to you has the blessing of his Holiness. I must also stress that you and I are about to discuss matters of great importance and equal delicacy. I have been informed that you are a man who can be trusted to show loyalty and discretion.'

He waited, presumably for me to confirm that this was in fact the case. In truth, I was not yet sure if what he had said was correct.

'Perhaps I should apologise,' he continued, 'for the fact that you have been given no explanation for your summons here. You'll soon find that, in matters which touch upon his Holiness, information and knowledge are far too valuable as weapons to be given out lightly. Nevertheless, I intend to tell you as much as I can without compromising his work or that of the members of the Papal Curia. It goes without saying that this information is not to be shared with anyone else without my express permission. Do you understand that?'

Despite the exalted position of the Cardinal and the ease with which he exercised power, I found myself becoming irritated by his determination to patronise me at every opportunity. I had no idea what secrets he was about to reveal to me which could be of such importance. Indeed, I had not asked to be told any secrets. I was out of my depth in such surroundings. In which case, why was I in the presence of Cardinal de Savigny?

'Your Eminence will understand,' I said, 'that I have very limited experience of the world in which I now find myself. I'm flattered that someone has seen fit to pass on to you a report praising my integrity. But perhaps I'm not the most appropriate person in whom to confide secrets of the kind you spoke about, whatever they may be.'

For the first time, the Cardinal looked uncertain. To my surprise he stood up, walked briskly around the table, took me firmly by the arm and led me towards a pair of large and sumptuous chairs positioned to one side of the hall with a small table between them. As he sat down, he gestured to me to do likewise, then raised his arm towards the back of the hall where, I noticed, the servant who had shown me in was still waiting. He disappeared, and returned moments later carrying a silver tray bearing a wine jug and two tall-stemmed glasses, finer than any I had ever seen.

He poured the wine, stood momentarily to attention, then turned and resumed his place at the back of the hall.

'Nicholas,' the Cardinal continued, 'I already know a lot about you. I know of course that you have only spent a limited time in this region, but have taken the trouble to learn our language, with some fluency. Equally importantly, I know that you have a reputation for—how shall I say?—a certain independence of mind. Unlike some, you're not swayed by fine robes or fine rhetoric. You prefer to weigh the evidence and draw your own conclusions. Am I correct?'

A voice somewhere in my mind advised me to be cautious of this naked flattery.

'I think,' I replied, 'that I try to make the best use of the powers of reason which God has given me. Sometimes, however, we all have to accept the judgement of those wiser or better-informed than us.'

Bertrand de Savigny smiled, picked up his glass and drained it. He indicated to me to do likewise, then refilled both. I felt the wine glide across my tongue like honey, then caress my dry, nervous throat as it passed down. It was the best I had ever tasted. Even Vittorio would have been envious.

'I'm beginning to feel,' the cardinal said, 'that you're not as far out of your depth here as you make out. You have what I might call a diplomat's way with words. But there is something I must ask you directly. What experience do you have of matters touching on heresy and the Inquisition?'

A clamorous warning bell rang.

'In all honesty, very little,' I replied. 'England has, on the whole, remained largely free of the influence of heretics, thanks to God's mercy. In my homeland we have found little need for Inquisitors, so far at any rate.'

'Then God's mercy has indeed been great to you. In this land we have struggled for many years to eradicate heresy, yet still we can't rid ourselves of it. You'll have heard of the Cathars?'

I nodded.

'We've been waging a war to eradicate their accursed heresy for a century now, and still there are rumours that in the mountain fastnesses they continue to spread their poison.'

He leaned forward as if about to confide one of his promised secrets. Goodness knows from whom he intended to conceal it, since the servant presumably knew that he would pay for any indiscretion with his tongue, or worse.

'And do you know, Nicholas, what I believe to be the heretics' most formidable ally?'

He waited, apparently expecting me to furnish an answer to this problematic question. I thought for some moments, then said:

'I am afraid that, as I've indicated, I have very little knowledge of such matters.'

'Nicholas, I'm speaking of the failure of our priests to adequately teach the people the true way of Christ and his holy Church. When the heretics use false arguments to ridicule our sacraments and our Scriptures, too often there is no-one to help the people understand why their arguments are false, since too many of our Catholic priests are themselves ignorant. And heresy breeds where ignorance abounds, Nicholas.'

I took a deep breath. 'Presumably, then, this has something to do with the reason why I'm here.'

Cardinal de Savigny eased himself back in his chair. His face suddenly looked lined and tense.

'I need you to be my eyes and ears, Nicholas. I fear—that is, his Holiness fears—that dark days are on the horizon for God's Church. Already we see around us the signs of God's displeasure towards His people. For several years now, summers have been cool and sunless and harvests have failed as a result. Peasants have died in their thousands. We hear of outbreaks of plague. We hear of endless conspiracies as those who hate God's Church band together to hatch plots against her. Kings and princes threaten, imprison and kill God's servants. Everywhere there is unrest, with lawless bands roaming at will through the countryside, having abandoned their homes, their families, their fields and their lords. And I need hardly remind you that the Holy Land remains in the hands of Saracen infidels. When all these things come together, Nicholas, we can only conclude that God is warning us of the wrath to come.'

He brought the tips of his fingers together in front of his mouth and closed his eyes. When he opened them again, it was as if his apocalyptic address of moments before had never been delivered.

'So you see, I need you to be my eyes and ears. Can you perform that role for me, Nicholas? I need you to report truthfully what you see, so that I can pass it on to his Holiness. I need you to travel across this land, making a report of what you find. I need to know more than what I read in the bland reports I receive from abbots and bishops. And there is something I must share with you, a matter of the deepest sensitivity. I'm particularly concerned about reports I have been receiving from the city of Narbonne, and I would like you to spend some time there. Observe how the Church is fulfilling its mission in that city. Keep your eyes and ears open, find out how far churchmen are failing in their duty and what heresies fester there. This is a matter of great concern to all of us. I need a detailed eye-witness report of all the failings of the Church's servants in Narbonne. I hope that I can trust you to do that for me.'

I swallowed hard. 'I'm honoured that you feel I'm capable of carrying out such a task. But wouldn't it be better to entrust it to someone who knows this land as a native, who can blend into his surroundings?'

'No, that's the whole point. It's precisely because you arrive here with fresh eyes, Nicholas, with no preconceptions, that I've decided that you're the one to take on this responsibility.'

His wording seemed to have left no scope for me to refuse. I saw my secure and comfortable life of the last couple of months slipping away.

'If his Holiness wishes me to carry out this task, I have no option but to agree. But it's still my opinion that I'm not well-equipped to fulfil it.'

Cardinal de Savigny relaxed in his chair. 'I'd have been concerned if you'd said otherwise.'

I sighed, more audibly than I had intended. 'In that case, I'll do my best. How long will this task take?'

'I can't say. Reliable people will meet up with you at pre-agreed destinations to bring back your reports. It goes without saying that, if you are to succeed, you must use discretion in revealing who has sent you and the nature of your mission. My representatives will ensure that you're adequately funded for your needs. I have arranged for you to stay on the first night of your journey with the Countess Maria at the Castel de Caneto. If you set off early tomorrow, you'll arrive before darkness falls.

'Tomorrow? So soon?'

'Time is pressing, Nicholas. God's enemies are closing in on us. You'll find the Countess's hospitality first rate. You may as well enjoy one last night of comfort before—well, before whatever God in His eternal wisdom has in store for you. I will hold you in my prayers, Nicholas.'

The Cardinal rose to indicate that our audience was at an end, and I did likewise, bowed, then turned and headed for the door. I looked over my shoulder before leaving. He was already back at his desk, writing furiously.

X

FOR THE REST OF THE day, I tried to keep away from Bartolomeo, partly from a desire to avoid an awkward farewell, but also from cowardice. I could not face having to explain to him that, whilst I did not distrust him, I was sworn to say nothing of where I was going and why. I knew that eventually he would come to look for me in my room, so early in the evening I went out to walk by the river. My spirits could hardly have been lower if I had just been placed under sentence of death. I tried to tell myself that God must have some purpose for me, that it was not His will to allow me to remain comfortably and anonymously in Avignon, but the thought did nothing to reassure me.

I decided to head for the establishment where Francesco and I had enjoyed the music of the harpist, hoping that its celestial beauty would soothe my anxieties. I found a table in a dark corner and ordered a meal and some wine. After a few minutes the evening's entertainers appeared, two musicians neither of whom, sadly, played the harp. One plucked a lute so battered that its strings rattled and reverberated in a most unharmonious way. The other turned out to be the execrable flautist of whom Francesco warned me. Just when it seemed that the evening could not drag me any lower, Bartolomeo walked through the door. He walked over to the proprietor who, after some animated discussion, pointed towards my table.

I managed to force a smile as he approached.

'Nicholas, you certainly know how to disappear. I went to your room, I've visited every establishment in Avignon looking for you. This was the last place I could think of to try. You certainly know how to be elusive.'

'I wasn't trying to be elusive. I just, you know . . .'

'Wanted some time to yourself? I understand. I hear you're leaving us tomorrow.'

So, Bertrand de Savigny's rules of secrecy had not been as watertight as he tried to make out.

'For a while. Anyway, sit down, help me get through this wine.'

Bartolomeo sat on the bench opposite. In the gloom, I could not see his face properly.

'Where's de Savigny sending you, then?'

I shrugged, although I had no way of knowing if he could see the gesture.

'It's all a bit vague. I'll know when I get there, apparently.'

'Come on, he must have said something.'

'Not really. I don't think he wants me to know too much at this stage. Sometimes it's better not to ask questions.'

I had not intended this as a pointed remark to my friend, but his reaction suggested that he took it as such. I saw his face turn until it was in profile.

'Make sure they keep my room free,' I said. 'I'll need it again when I get back.'

Bartolomeo turned to look at me again, but his eyes were in shadow, and I could not judge his expression. The darkness was beginning to unnerve me.

'Are you sure about that?' he said.

'Of course. I'll be back as soon as I've finished whatever it is I'm supposed to be doing.'

He took a long draught of wine, then rested his elbows on the table, brought his hands together and placed them in front of his face. His eyes were moist.

'I hope so,' he said. 'I really hope so.'

There was a sick feeling in my stomach as I thought of poor Brother John, and I remembered all too clearly why I had hoped to avoid Bartolomeo on that night. The music was, if possible, becoming worse with each successive tune. I finished my wine.

'Come on, my friend, this place is dreary tonight. Let's find somewhere to cheer us up. I know, we'll go back and see your friend Petro.'

The tavern was as I remembered it. Customers in search of food and drink mingled with those seeking less nourishing, but equally corporeal, fulfilment in the establishment next door. The serving-girl who had attracted Bartolomeo's attention had been replaced by one of, to my eyes, suspicious youth. I suspected that she had not long since arrived, probably from the countryside. I hoped for her sake that she knew the kind of life she was taking on.

We ordered more wine, and as she served us she gave a thin and clearly forced smile. I felt an outpouring of sympathy for her.

'You don't have to pretend you're so pleased to see us,' I said. 'A simple greeting's enough for the likes of us.'

'The master says I have to smile all the time. That way we'll get more trade.'

She walked away with her fixed smile still attached.

'She's pretty,' Bartolomeo said, 'but very young. I hate to think what a few years of this kind of life will do to her.'

'Don't you ever feel that you'd like to settle down and let a good woman make you happy?'

'I've not really given it much thought. What about you? Sorry, stupid question. Forgive me.'

'Don't worry. I doubt that many in monastic orders go through their whole life without wondering what a different kind of existence might have been like. Anyway, you're a caring sort of person. I think you'd make a good husband and father.'

He averted his eyes. 'In some ways, perhaps.'

We finished our wine and then ordered some more. I would not feel in the best of health the following morning for the start of my journey, but was rapidly ceasing to care, like the soldier who drinks as much as possible in order to forget that the next day he will go off to war. As the evening wore on, that seemed an increasingly fitting analogy. The atmosphere around us was becoming raucous. What worldly pains were all these carousers trying to nullify?

Bartolomeo's eyes were becoming glazed and his speech slurred, until at last it seemed doubtful that he would be able to make his way home unaided. Feeling somewhat less than steady on my own feet, I helped him to his, and steered him towards the door. The serving-girl was being molested by some foreign merchants who grasped her buttocks and breasts as if she were an inanimate object. As we passed, she looked up at me with tears in her eyes, pleading for rescue.

On the way home, Bartolomeo draped his arm around one of my shoulders and rested his head on the other. This seemed an unnatural position for one whose body was almost uncontrollably relaxed. When we reached the Palace, I propped him against a door jamb while I recovered my breath and cleared my head. He toppled forward, threw his arms around me and began to kiss my neck. With considerable difficulty, I cajoled him to his room and, when I released him, he collapsed onto his bed.

Bartolomeo lay there, breathing heavily, murmuring to himself. I put my ear close to his mouth, and heard the words 'I love you.' To whom he was addressing them, I could not imagine. I waited until he began to snore, then took my leave of him, as it turned out for the last time.

XI

By the time I set out from Avignon, I was relieved that the period of waiting, short as it had been, was over and that my journey was finally beginning. I found my way back to the Via Domitia and set off westwards in good spirits, whistling to myself a tune I had heard in the tavern the previous night. Other travellers passed by at frequent intervals, but most were on horseback or driving ox-carts and hurried past with a perfunctory wave of the head. I felt tempted to leave the road and strike out across country, but all I knew of the location of the Castel de Caneto was that it was a prominent landmark to those who made their way along the Roman road. The prospect of becoming lost on my first day was too much to contemplate, so I resolved to take no risks.

Once again, I marvelled at the handiwork of our Roman forebears beneath my feet. Of other material remains of that civilisation there was little sign, although from their appearance I suspected that several churches along the route were at least partly constructed from re-used Roman materials. No wonder, then, that the remains of so few buildings of that period were to be seen above foundation level.

By mid-afternoon I had consumed my food and most of my water, and was beginning to hope that the castle was now close at hand. Still I walked on, and it was not until the sun was low in the sky that I finally observed the outline of a large fortified complex on a hill to the north. I turned and trudged up a path for some distance until I came upon the castle's main gateway, where I was admitted after no more than a token request to state my name and my business. So indifferent were the guards that it was quite impossible to tell whether they had been told to expect me or not.

Inside a high and well-appointed, even luxurious, reception room, the Countess herself greeted me with the easy familiarity which seems to be natural among those of her social status. She was a fair-skinned, statuesque woman I guessed about five years older than myself, with a well-preserved beauty. Seeing my obvious fatigue, not to mention the dust which covered my outer clothing, she instructed a servant to show me directly to my room in order that I might wash and rest before the evening meal. It turned out to be above the kitchens, clearly not a room reserved for her most distinguished guests, but with a soft sheepskin on the bed, comfortable and more than adequate for my needs. I looked out of the one narrow window as the sun set the western horizon ablaze, then lay on my bed and soon drifted into a peaceful sleep.

When I awoke it was growing dark, and surely the evening's festivities had already started; on the first day into my journey, it seemed, I had distinguished myself as an impolite guest. I tidied myself, washed my face, brushed off as much of the dust as I could and rushed down to the dining hall, where I found to my relief that the first guests were just arriving. As far as I could tell, they consisted of members of the local minor nobility, and appeared on the whole to have an easy relationship with the Countess. To my surprise, she invited me to sit next to her at the head of the table, although making no attempt to introduce me formally to the other guests, nor indeed did she show any curiosity about me or my mission during the whole of the evening.

The food presented was generous in the extreme; the centrepiece of the table was a swan beautifully decorated with flowers, vegetables and colourful ribbons, its wings gracefully half-extended as if drying its feathers. By the end of the meal my appetite was more than sated, and I reminded myself to ask for God's forgiveness for committing the sin of gluttony.

After we had eaten, entertainment ensued in the form of a performance by a troubadour whose name I did not catch, but it was certainly not Blondel. The heyday of Occitan troubadours was said to be long past, and sadly the efforts of this particular example did nothing to suggest otherwise. Most of the pieces he performed were third-rate songs of courtly love, tedious and repetitive although, to be fair, the rest of the assembled company appeared to enjoy them more than I. Perhaps, I thought, it was a style of music one needed to learn to enjoy.

One piece, however, caught my interest; at its core was the great hymn to our Lady, *Ave maris stella*, 'Hail, Star of the Sea', but interwoven with this was a lengthy poem about the crusade against the Cathars some hundred years earlier. The composer, whether this troubadour or not, whilst having little sympathy for the Cathars, saw the crusade as nothing less than a war of occupation against the Occitan people, and its outcome as the beginning of the end of the region's culture, language and independence, rather than the triumph of right-thinking Catholic orthodoxy over heresy. The reaction of the troubadour's audience indicated that they shared these perverse sentiments. I made a note in the back of my mind to investigate further the source of these feelings as and when the opportunity might present itself.

The day had by this stage taken its toll on me, and I was grateful to be able to bid my hostess goodnight. As I did so, the Countess called over a pretty young serving-girl whom she introduced to me as Esclarmonde, inviting me to summon her specifically if I found myself in need of any assistance. The girl looked at me with curiosity, as if weighing up in her mind the sight before her. She gave a half-smile, then turned and resumed her duties clearing up the dining table. With some relief I retired to the sanctuary of my room, knelt to pray at the side of my bed and then collapsed into it. I went to blow out the candle I had brought up with me to illuminate the staircase, then, watching the flickering shadows on the walls of my strange surroundings, decided to leave it burning. My last waking thought was of puzzlement that I had seen no sign of the Count, or indeed heard any reference to him.

I had only been asleep for a short time when a creaking from the door-hinges roused me, and I became aware to my horror that someone was entering the room. I froze, not daring to look, heard an extended rustling sound, then felt someone get into my bed beside me. Breathing heavily, I turned to see the face of Esclarmonde lying on the pillow next to me. She pulled back the sheepskin to reveal that she was naked. For some moments I gaped open-mouthed, which for some reason caused her to giggle. Silently reciting the *Te deum* to keep my loins in check, I slowly reached down and covered her up once more, trying hard not to touch her in the process. To my surprise she seemed to become upset at this.

'What's wrong?' she asked. 'Don't I please you?'

'Esclarmonde,' I replied, edging away as far as the width of the bed would permit, 'there has clearly been some confusion, and it's not your fault. The Countess must have failed to make clear that I'm a man of the Church, a member of the Benedictine Order.'

Her brow furrowed. 'I still don't understand. Haven't you been sent by Cardinal de Savigny?'

'Yes but—I'm sorry, Esclarmonde, you cannot remain in my bed. Please go.'

She shrugged her shoulders. 'I understand. I'll send up one of the kitchen boys in my place. Or perhaps you would prefer Leonardo, the stable-lad? He's very popular with many of the Cardinal's men.'

I looked at her face for any sign that she was mocking my lack of sexual avarice, but it was clear that she was not. My mind was in a state of utter confusion. I noticed that she wore an amulet around her neck on a cord. She saw me staring at it, and held it out.

'Does it bother you? The Countess gave it to me. It would be inconvenient for me to bear a child now, wouldn't it?'

'You mean it prevents . . . by some kind of magic?'

She looked at me with an expression bordering on pity.

'Why are you monks and priests obsessed with magic? Here, smell it.'

I leaned forward, closing my eyes to avoid gazing on her flesh. The amulet smelled of a concoction of herbs which I could not identify.

'Does it work?' I said.

She gave me the pitying look once more. I shook my head to clear it, then held it in my hands.

'Esclarmonde,' I said, 'I wish to understand exactly what's happening here. Are you saying that the Countess expects you to—to do this for any visitor who comes here from Avignon?'

'Of course not,' she replied indignantly. 'Only for those sent by Cardinal de Savigny.'

'But that's little better than—'

'Whoredom? Tell me—no, I don't want to know your name. Where have you come from? Before Avignon, I mean.'

'From the Abbey of Croyland, in England.'

'I see,' she said. 'Have you travelled much?'

'Not until I arrived on these shores, no.'

'That doesn't surprise me. Let us say that you still have a great deal to learn about the world beyond your monastery walls.

You dare to call me a whore. But compare me for a moment to a high-born woman who marries a man whom she despises simply because he is wealthy. She shares his bed even though she loathes him, and all for love of his money. That woman is more of a whore than I.'

In truth, this did seem a novel way of presenting the issue.

'I'm sorry,' I said, 'I realise that you have to carry out the tasks allotted to you by your mistress. But the kitchen boys? The stable lad?'

'As I said, you have a great deal to learn.'

'Then teach me something else. What does your mistress gain from this arrangement? Does the Cardinal pay her to provide this service on his behalf?'

Esclarmonde stared, then burst out laughing. Her expression suggested that my pathetic innocence had plumbed new depths. To my consternation, she sat up in bed, making no effort to cover herself. Rather than remain looking up at her naked body, I sat up beside her, staring straight ahead.

'Have you seriously not realised?' she said. 'The Countess is Cardinal de Savigny's—'

'Stop!' Esclarmonde put her finger to my lips to remind me of what should have been obvious. I continued in a whisper. 'I cannot, will not believe that a senior member of the Papal Curia could possibly—it simply can't be true.'

'The choice is yours, believe it or not as you please.' She sighed deeply. 'Look, you seem to be a kind and gentle man. If you don't quickly learn the ways of this world, there will be many less scrupulous people only too eager to take advantage of your innocence. I can say no more. But for now, I ask only one thing. Don't send me away. If my mistress thinks that I've failed to please one of the Cardinal's men, she'll punish me. I promise to be as discreet as you wish, and I'll be gone before dawn.'

I looked at Esclarmonde and saw that her eyes were moist. Her tears seemed to me as genuine as any I had ever seen.

'You may remain,' I replied, 'but you must keep your distance. I don't wish to be subjected to even greater temptation.'

She wiped the back of her hand across her eyes, then turned and smiled.

'I'll agree to whatever you demand,' she said.

71

Esclarmonde was as good as her word. She lay down and turned away from me and did not attempt to approach me. Indeed, I cannot deny that, as one who does not always welcome the onset of night, solitude, silence and darkness, I found it strangely comforting simply to know that another human being was in such close proximity. Esclarmonde's world was far removed from mine; she was perhaps fourteen years of age, but had already had to learn so many vital lessons. In terms of experience, I was by comparison a babe in arms. And despite her loose sexual morals, I wrestled with the paradox that she seemed to me an essentially good person.

At one point I became aware that I had turned over in my sleep and placed my arm across her and my hand upon her breast. Waking abruptly, I snatched it away. She took hold of my hand and gently replaced it. As I drifted back into sleep, I felt her nipple harden under my fingers.

I awoke at dawn and, true to her word, Esclarmonde was gone. On her pillow I smelled the scent of jasmine. I did not see her again, and left the castle two hours later. As I departed, one of the Countess's servants handed me a note informing me that I was to head for the house of Father Robert, a man apparently well-versed in the Cathar heresy, in the village of Servian.

Continuing westwards, I forced myself to relive the events of the previous night as a way of reinforcing my shame at not having been more decisive in distancing myself from temptation. Needless to say, the devil took the opportunity to try to convince me that what I remembered most of all was the proximity of illicit pleasures, and I was forced to kneel at the roadside to pray to the Lord for strength to resist these thoughts. I was also deeply disturbed by what Esclarmonde had told me about the Cardinal and the Countess. I am only too aware that we all share in the essential sinfulness of human nature, but surely what she told me could not be true? The idea that the Countess is the Cardinal's concubine is unthinkable enough, but that she also procures sexual favours for his chosen friends and associates . . .

As if I were St Paul on the Damascus road, I received a dazzling illumination. In fact, I despised myself for not having seen the truth earlier. The whole affair had clearly been a huge jest at my expense. The Countess had decided to take advantage of a young, innocent

English monk, and had enlisted Esclarmonde in the execution of her unworthy scheme. I felt immensely foolish at having believed the web of falsehoods which Esclarmonde had spun for me but, more than this, overwhelmingly relieved that I no longer had to concern myself with the ominous import of her story. Now I knew that not only was the Cardinal's reputation intact, but that Esclarmonde had not intended her behaviour towards me, brazen as it was, to be taken seriously, I stepped out with a much lighter heart. As I passed a hedgerow, however, I felt sure that I detected the scent of jasmine.

XII

A COUPLE OF DAYS LATER I entered the village of Servian, only to discover that my arrival had coincided with a local festival, and one of a distinctly secular kind. On every street were boisterous crowds, and I was pushed and jostled all the way, albeit in a good-humoured manner. The house of my contact, Father Robert, turned out to be set within a walled courtyard next to the church, from within which the noise of the carousing outside was at least muffled.

On my arrival, the priest eyed me suspiciously, although he had clearly been expecting me. We sat down at his kitchen table and he produced two large cups of wine. The wine was of good quality and the refreshment more than welcome. I had no way of knowing if he was aware of the reason for my visit, so decided to come straight to the point.

'I understand it must seem strange that you've been given no explanation for my arrival here.'

Father Robert avoided my gaze. 'If you're on business from Avignon, that's enough. I'm not sure I want to know any more. People from Avignon always say that their mission is of vital importance but highly confidential. But if it's not a stupid question, why did they send an Englishman like you out on papal business? Please don't be offended.'

'I'm not. In fact I've asked myself the same question. Apparently it's because I'm an Englishman who happens to have learned to speak Occitan. Cardinal de Savigny positively wanted an outsider. Whether there were other, unspoken reasons remains to be seen.'

I thought that Father Robert raised his eyebrows at the mention of the Cardinal's name, but could not be sure.

'So what have you been told to find out? No, on second thoughts don't answer that, the less I know the better. If the Inquisitors come calling, I want to be able to plead ignorance with a clear conscience.'

At first I took this to be a jest, but my host's face remained serious. Perhaps it was time to change the subject.

'Father Robert, the Cardinal appears to hold suspicions that the Cathar heresy has somehow lingered on in these parts. Can you tell me anything about that?'

He sat back. 'The Cathars? What would I know about them? If they were around, they obviously wouldn't come near me.'

'But you'd know if their beliefs live on?'

'No, I don't know whether they do or not. Presumably that's what you're here to find out. In which case, good luck.'

'To be honest with you, Father, I'm not sure what I'm looking for.'

He raised his eyes to the ceiling. 'Then what in God's name was the point of sending you on this mission?'

I stared down at my hands. 'I have no idea.'

He watched me for a long time, and I could not bear to meet his gaze. He was treating me as an object of ridicule, and at that moment it seemed precisely what I deserved. At last he relented.

'Look, I'll do what I can to help you. In some respects, the practices of the Cathars are—or were—a parody of our own. They have their own version of our sacraments, they use a bastardised version of our liturgy. But some say that their beliefs go back to the early centuries of Christianity. And they're certainly widespread; I've heard that Cathars have turned up in Italy, Flanders, Germany and elsewhere. But do you know why people listen to them?'

'You speak of them as if you know they're still around.'

'Their priests, if you can call them that, they call themselves perfecti, live simple lives. They're not wealthy. They don't preach in great stone churches and cathedrals. Often they hold meetings in the homes of sympathisers, including members of the nobility, who protect them. Do you wonder that they're so hard to eradicate?'

'Now I'm confused,' I said. 'I thought that the heyday of the Cathar heresy was a century ago. Even I know that the last Cathar stronghold in the Pyrenean Mountains was taken over seventy years ago, but you talk as if they're a living presence.'

He looked askance. 'I can't say if they are or otherwise. I'm just telling you what I've heard.'

'If that's all there is to the Cathars, I don't understand why the Church was prepared to go to such lengths, at the cost of such loss of life, to eradicate them.'

'There were many reasons why the crusade against them took place, not all of them to do with faith and beliefs. Even you must have picked up the resentment people here still feel about being ruled by northerners.'

My mind went back to the song which the troubadour performed at the Countess's banquet, and the reaction it stirred up among the audience.

'You said, Father Robert, that their beliefs seem to go back a very long way.'

'They have things in common with some of the heretics the early Church had to battle, the Gnostics and the Manichaeans who seduced St Augustine for a few years. They see this world as a battleground between good and evil.'

'I'm sure that's the way it appears to many good Catholics.'

'It's a question of definition. In their view everything material, including the human body, is inherently evil. Good only resides in the non-material, the spiritual. The purpose of this life is to shake off the evil effect of the body and to be re-born as a spiritual being.'

'But if you believe that,' I said, 'doesn't it logically follow that Christ's sacrifice of his physical body on the cross could never enable us to achieve redemption and salvation?'

'Precisely. They don't accept that Christ died for our sins on the cross. And because the Catholic Church preaches that he did, they consider us to be as damnably heretical as we consider them. They teach that God's Church is wicked and hopelessly corrupt, which of course is why they were so ruthlessly suppressed.'

I noted that, despite his earlier ignorance of the Cathars' current standing, Father Robert had continued to use the present tense.

'Some of their other beliefs,' he continued, 'are simply bizarre. Do you know what they think happens to the human soul after we die? It's reborn in another body. If it's the soul of someone who's lived a good life, it enters the womb of a newly-pregnant woman and takes over the embryo. If it's the soul of a wicked person, it's condemned to be reborn in an animal: the greater their sins, the more lowly the animal.'

'I've heard that many in India and the Orient hold similar beliefs.'

'Indeed, but it's obviously incompatible with our teaching on Judgement and the Resurrection. The Inquisitors had great fun asking them in which of their succession of bodies they'd be resurrected on the last day. But I've heard that many unrepentant Cathars still went to the stake singing and praising God.'

At times, Simon appeared nearly as hostile to the Inquisition as to the heretics. He leaned forward, as if to confide a dangerous secret.

'You know I said the Cathars don't believe that Christ died for us on the cross? Some teach that he actually married Mary Magdalene, and that they had children.'

I made the sign of the cross. He grinned, but his face quickly turned serious once more.

'And yet still many people have always been drawn to their teaching. Nicholas, you need to understand that a small, out-of-the-way village in this region has nothing in common with the world you're used to in England.' His earnest tone made these words sound like a warning. 'Take my advice, go back out into the streets and see for yourself what's going on at this moment. It'll convey what I'm trying to tell you ten times more eloquently than I can.'

He rose to his feet and took my empty cup. 'But one thing I must warn you. Don't let on to anyone that you're a man of the Church.'

'Because you think I'll learn more by blending in with the crowds?'

'No. Because these people hate the Church and everyone who represents it.'

These words still rang in my ears as I made my way towards the main square of the village, seemingly the focus of festive activities. At one end, on an impromptu throne perched on an equally impromptu dais, was a man in elaborate costume, apparently either sitting in judgement on the proceedings, or perhaps in the role of master of the revels. Approaching more closely, I was shocked to discover that his costume represented a crude parody of the robes and accoutrements of his Holiness himself. The crozier he held was nothing less than a tree branch carved into the shape of a phallus.

On his head, secured by a scarlet sash, was a pair of breeches, the legs hanging down in front of his shoulders. His throne turned out to be a milking stool. Remembering Father Robert's advice, I made my way quietly away in search of more innocent entertainments.

In the next street, I found groups of young men and women rushing this way and that, as if in some maniacal game of chase-the-rascal. On closer inspection, some of them proved to be in a state of partial undress. One young man had quite lost his breeches, which were being carried away by a group of young women who threw them to one another as he approached each in turn. In the frantic pursuit, the breasts of one of the girls had fallen free, but she was quite heedless and made no effort to secure her modesty.

A little further on, I saw a game taking place in which young men were set a riddle by a young woman. If they answered the riddle correctly, their reward was to throw a bucket of water over a naked woman of distinctly ample proportions who sat patiently nearby, seemingly enjoying the game as much as anyone. If the young men failed, a group of four women would, with some force, divest them and hold them secure while the bucket of water was tipped over them, invariably amidst shrieking and ribald remarks about the young man's supposedly inadequate genitalia. In more familiar surroundings, such goings-on would have been offensive to me, but I confess that in that place, at that moment, I was touched by the innocent simplicity of their behaviour. I had been told many times at Avignon that the people of the region had a tendency to be carefree and uninhibited, albeit sometimes to the extent of risking their own perdition. Indeed, when I thought of England I had often envied them the congenial climate which, it seemed to me, contributed so strongly to their open-hearted enjoyment of life.

The high-spirited and good-humoured mood was about to change. As if in response to some unseen signal, four figures in white cloaks, Cistercians as I took them to be, appeared from different quarters, and began to berate and, in some cases, to scourge the revellers. When one of them passed close to me, I saw a fury in his eyes which, in someone of a different calling, I would not hesitate to describe as demonic. At that moment, the devil himself put the thought into my mind that perhaps this was why feelings against the Church ran so strongly here, but I hurriedly pushed it to one side.

Without warning, I felt a paralysing pain as the scourge of one of the Cistercians cracked against my back. His words burned themselves into my memory: 'Cherish the pain, be scourged for your own salvation.' I fell to the ground and for a few moments could neither move nor even breathe. In a state of shock I gasped for air, and finally struggled to my feet in time to see the erstwhile revellers fleeing in all directions. The four Cistercians stood in a group in the middle of the square as one of their number led them in prayer.

Some time later, I sat with Father Robert as I revived my spirits with another cup of his wine. My hands were shaking. Pressing my spine against the back of my chair, I still felt a searing pain. At length I felt able to describe to him all that had happened, and he listened in attentive silence. Afterwards, he stroked his chin.

'Tell me truthfully,' he said, 'what was your reaction to our village revels?'

'My reaction was mixed. As a man of God, I could hardly endorse such licentious revelry, such brazen flaunting of—well, you must know better than I the kind of things which take place. And yet . . .'

I struggled to put into words my feelings about what I had seen. How frank could I be with a fellow man of God, one I had only known for a matter of hours?

'Let me dare to put words into your mouth,' Robert said. 'You secretly envied the people of the village for their ability to express joy in such an uninhibited way.'

He refilled my cup and I took another mouthful before replying. Was the wine beginning to loosen my tongue? And his?

'In all honesty,' I replied, 'I'm not sure. We don't have festivities of that nature in Croyland. It was something of a shock to me.'

'All right then,' he continued. 'How did you feel when the Cistercians intervened so aggressively?'

'That's easier to answer,' I said. 'I was disappointed, I would even say a little shocked.'

'Shocked?'

'Their reaction seemed—disproportionate. To use such violence against helpless people . . . I think I even felt a little shame.'

'Shame that the Church encourages the Cistercians to act in this way as its assault troops?'

I thought for a moment. 'In England, the Cistercians are seen as a contemplative order who tend to separate themselves, physically at any rate, from the rest of humanity. Their monasteries are often in remote locations. True, they've acquired wealth and influence in spite of this, but I'd be most surprised to see them acting in such a way in England.'

Father Robert sat back and gazed into the air, sipping his wine thoughtfully, then leaned forward and spoke quietly.

'Brother Nicholas, may I speak freely to you?'

'I'm sure that it'll be to my benefit if you do.'

'And can I be sure that our conversation will go no further? No, please don't be offended, I will explain.'

'On my word,' I replied, 'even the Inquisition couldn't drag it from my mouth.'

I meant this comment in jest, but he gave no indication that he interpreted it in that way. He took a deep breath.

'Even though you demonstrate what in some ways is a refreshing innocence, you still work in a more sophisticated milieu than I, Nicholas, and your grasp of our tongue is, I will accept, impressive. Nevertheless, I have concerns for your welfare. Grave concerns.'

'Then please express them.'

'To be frank,' he continued, 'I'm more puzzled than ever about the use to which the Church authorities at Avignon intend to put you. You have a good heart, but you're not a worldly man, and at this moment that makes you very vulnerable. Do you see what I'm saying?'

'No. I'm afraid I don't. You speak as if his Holiness and his advisers were our enemies, not our spiritual leaders.'

'To the people of this village, they are enemies. You've seen that today for yourself. And you've also seen why.'

I felt myself sinking in confusion.

'So what advice are you giving me?'

'Go back home as quickly as you can, by any means you can. I can find you a mule, make your way to Bordeaux, pretend you're a pilgrim or something, you'll be able to find a ship heading to England. Or go south to the coast, take any ship sailing westwards, just get away from here. You have no idea what you're getting yourself into, and I've no wish to see you destroy yourself.'

My head began to spin. I looked at Father Robert to see if he was being affected by the wine, but his eyes were clear and his face serious. It was becoming clear that my forebodings about this journey had been well-founded after all.

After we had eaten, he took me for a walk around the perimeter of the village so that we could clear our heads. It was a warm night. He explained that the village's substantial walls were a thousand years old, having kept guard over Servian since the days when it formed a tiny part of the Roman province of Gallia Narbonensis. We paused when we reached a passage-way through the walls which amply demonstrated their great thickness, but appeared to be of more recent origin.

'You see this?' Father Robert said. 'Simon de Montfort besieged the village a century ago in the course of his crusade against the Cathars, but it held out for some time. One night they managed to tunnel through the walls, I can't imagine how, they must have had help from inside. De Montfort's troops poured through under cover of darkness and went from house to house, slaughtering the people in their beds, burning them alive in their own homes. He'd decided to make an example of any community which resisted in order to intimidate all those he'd encounter in the future. The Pope and the bishops agreed this was the best way.'

When we returned home, he gave me a book which he said would help to illustrate the things he had been talking about. I thanked him for his kindness, put the book in my bag and gave it no further thought. That night I slept little, turning over and over in my head the things which he had said to me, the blunt warning he gave. What he told me suggested that, despite his protestations of ignorance, he knew of continuing Cathar activity. He had also offered up further evidence that the people of this region still felt themselves to be a conquered race, rather than an integral part of the wider French nation.

I had always suspected that I would be out of my depth, initially in any case. If that were true, of what value could my reports be to the Cardinal, let alone his Holiness? What was truly behind this ill-begotten mission on which I had embarked? And yet to return home as Father Robert had suggested was not an option for me given the circumstances in which I had left. I lay in the dark and listened to the nocturnal sounds of the natural world. An owl called from a branch outside my window, mice scuttled through the thatch above, a vixen called to her cubs in the distance. How less anxious were their lives than mine. I contemplated the words of our Saviour:

'How blest you are, when you suffer insults and persecution and every kind of calumny for my sake. Accept it with gladness and exultation, for you have a rich reward in heaven; in the same way they persecuted the prophets before you.'

What was I thinking? Jesus had been referring to the persecution he expected the disciples to face at the hands of the Pharisees and unbelievers. The oppression which faced me, according to my host, came from the very leaders of the Church of God. Could what he said possibly be true?

XIII

THE NEXT MORNING, FATHER ROBERT told me that I was to meet with the Cardinal's representative in Béziers in a couple of days to pass on the first instalment of my report. He invited me to stay longer as the city was only a short distance from Servian, but I sensed that he had made the offer more out of duty than for the pleasure of my company. I therefore replied that I would travel on without delay and use the time to familiarise myself with Béziers.

The sun was warm on my back as I headed into the countryside. I passed flourishing vineyards and groves of fruit trees and olives, enjoyed cordial conversations with those I encountered, and in no time the anxieties which had oppressed me seemed a distant memory. I began, in contrast to the previous day, to feel that I was fortunate to have been chosen by the Cardinal for this mission, and that my life had become considerably more rewarding than my former existence as a humble administrator in Avignon. Little did I suspect how short-lived this euphoria would prove to be.

I had not travelled far before, rising from a hill on the skyline, I spied the towers of Béziers' imposing cathedral. I stopped to rest in order to take in the majesty of the view, then after a few minutes set off with renewed vigour. By late afternoon I stood at the foot of the hill, looking up towards the walls of the city and, beyond, the soaring mass of the cathedral.

Béziers proved to be a city of substantial size. The true extent of its population was unknown, as I later discovered, but I hazarded a guess that its walls must have encompassed not less than twenty thousand souls. As a few hours of daylight remained, I started my tour at the great church of St Mary Magdalene, even at close quarters a most impressive structure though clearly not of any great antiquity, and in places still not complete, but nonetheless a worthy symbol of God's majesty, and of the triumph of his Catholic Church over the forces of heresy and darkness. Indeed, the very dedication of the church reminded me of the scale of the errors of the Cathars, given what Father Robert told me of their absurd belief that our Lord had married Mary Magdalene. That any rational being could believe such nonsense was extraordinary enough. That such gross heresy should have spread so widely and penetrated this society so deeply—well, doubtless the Lord had shown great forbearance in giving them as long to come to their senses as He had.

My journey from Servian had left me hot and dusty, and the interior of the church was by contrast airy, spacious and pleasantly cool. The soaring vault of its nave reminded me of the cathedral at Lincoln which I had occasion to visit several times, yet I had to admit that in some respects it was an even more impressive tribute to the skills of the draughtsman and the mason. The sleek, gracious columns seemed too slender to bear the colossal weight above, yet bear it they did. As I moved towards the chancel, I was surprised to find that the cathedral appeared to be lifeless, with no sign of human activity whatsoever. Genuflecting as I passed before the high altar, I continued into a side chapel, windowless and lit only by candles, where I knelt to enjoy a short period of silence and contemplation. Yet on this occasion the feelings of peace and tranquillity which such moments usually provide eluded me. I found myself in fact becoming restless and agitated. I began to hear distant muffled voices and turned to look behind me, but could see no-one. Concluding that the devil was, not for the first time, using his wiles to try to prevent me from communing with my God, I forced myself to turn back and closed my eyes once more. As on previous occasions when trying to shut the devil out of my mind, I began to recite the *Pater noster* slowly and rhythmically.

What occurred next defied my feeble understanding, and does so to this very day. I heard voices again, difficult to comprehend yet clearly in distress. My ears told me that they came from the other side of the wall in front of me, despite the massive thickness of its stones, yet another sense, I know not which, felt the sound emerging from the very stones themselves. I placed the tips of my fingers against the wall and felt a curious vibration emanating from it. As I listened the voices became louder and more insistent, the shrieks of tormented people pleading for salvation from God knows what horror. I could make out cries of 'For God's sake help us', 'Have pity, spare my children' and, most chillingly, an elderly and authoritative voice spitting out the words, 'May God's curse be on you for defiling His sanctuary with innocent blood.'

I leapt to my feet in terror and rushed out of the chapel, but the voices would not leave my head. Now I heard them from behind a solid oak door to my right. Despite the coolness of the air within the cathedral, sweat coursed down my face and my body and began to soak into my clothes. I was frozen with terror, yet still was drawn towards the closed door. Shaking as I placed my ear against it, I could make out the most terrible sounds from beyond. This time few words were audible; rather, I heard the screams of the suffering and dying, the desperate cries of children, and above all the merciless crackle of fire and flames. My hands were trembling and slippery with sweat, so that I could barely grip the handle of the door, but slowly it began to move. The voices became louder and louder, the noise of conflagration so insistent that I fancied that I could smell acrid smoke and burning flesh. When able to bear this no longer, I threw the door wide open. On the other side was a small, dark empty room, apparently nothing more sinister than a store room. The sound had come to an abrupt end. Once more, I was alone in the silent cathedral.

I ran back down the nave as fast as I could and burst back out into the fading light. The people of Béziers were going about their business as before, and the world could not have seemed more normal. I looked behind me, and the cathedral appeared exactly as when I had entered it. I moved out into the square, sat down against a wall and closed my eyes, praying to God for some kind of guidance, any clue which would help me to understand what I had just experienced.

Perhaps through divine inspiration, perhaps because my mind was desperate to find a diversion from my recent experience, I recalled the volume which Father Robert had given me and to which I had thus far paid scant attention. I took it out and turned to the first page; above the Latin text a hand had written in Occitan a title which I translated as *A Song of the Albigensian Crusade, by William of Tudela*. I had never heard of the author, but it proved to be a work recounting the history of the crusade led by the same Simon de Montfort whose handiwork Father Robert had shown me in Servian. It soon became clear that William of Tudela considered the crusade an opportunistic and cynical campaign to deprive the Occitan nobility of their power and their land in favour of the northern lords who followed de Montfort in search of rich pickings.

I began to search frantically for any reference to Béziers, and before long discovered a passage which described a siege of the city by the crusading army in the year of our Lord twelve hundred and nine. It related how the city's Viscount, on hearing of the approach of this mighty force, had left for Carcassonne, advising the people to look after their own defence. The Bishop of Béziers, a man of wisdom, advised the townspeople that they could not withstand the might of the crusaders, and should surrender in order to save their lives and possessions. It was well known, it seems, that the crusaders had adopted a policy of slaughtering the entire population of any town which resisted, in the hope of softening the resolve of those they would encounter in the future. The people of the city, however, arrogantly believed that their walls were impregnable, even to the forces of God, and determined to resist the coming attack.

In due course, on the very feast of St Mary Magdalene, the army arrived led by Arnauld Amaury, the Abbot of Cîteaux and papal legate, and encircled the city. However, despite the force arrayed against them, the people of Béziers remained obstinate, and even taunted the crusaders from the walls. Eventually, according to William, the head of the army's servant boys decided to take matters into his own hands, and led his ragged band of shrieking lads in a full-scale assault on the walls. For some reason this so terrified the people that they abandoned the defence of the city and fled to the sanctuary of their cathedral, the priests putting on vestments for a mass of the dead and ringing the bells as if for a funeral, while the servant boys pillaged the city at will.

Up to this point the narrative seemed reminiscent of other accounts I had read of the storming of cities during times of war. But I read on, and what came next caused a chill to run up my spine. The servant boys proceeded to ransack the city, rejoicing in the unexpected riches which had come their way. The northern lords, however, seeing that they were being deprived of the booty they considered rightfully theirs, drove the boys away. In their fury, the lads put Béziers to the torch. As the flames engulfed the whole city the cathedral was completely destroyed, the heat cracking it down the middle before it finally collapsed in ruins, engulfing all those who had sought sanctuary within.

I confess that there were tears in my eyes as I looked up from the page. Could this be true? Could this somehow be the explanation for my terrifying experience? I recalled that Jesus said on one occasion that if the people of Jerusalem had not cried out in praise, then the very stones of the holy city would have done so. But surely he was using a figure of speech?

By chance a priest was heading towards me, making his way to the cathedral. I hurried to my feet and intercepted him.

'Excuse me Father, may I ask you something? Is this present church of St Mary Magdalene on the same site as the old one? The one which was burned down by the crusaders against the Cathars?'

The priest narrowed his eyes, clearly trying to weigh up the kind of person he was dealing with.

'Yes it is,' he replied.

'And were the stones from the destroyed cathedral re-used in the new?'

'I'm sure they would have been,' he said, 'those which weren't too damaged. Building stone is far too valuable to waste. Why do you ask?'

I looked the priest in the eye. 'Father, I realise that you're very busy, but there is something else I must ask you, something of great importance. Is it true that the whole population of Béziers took refuge in the church, and was massacred there?'

The priest now gave me a hard stare. 'Friend, I've no idea why you're asking me these questions. The events of that dreadful day are a matter of record. All the accounts agree that there was a terrible slaughter. Surely you've heard the tale recounted by Master Caesarius of Heisterbach in his *Dialogus miraculorum* about Arnauld Amaury, the Cistercian Abbot of Cîteaux, who led the crusader army on that day? He recounts that some in the army were concerned that the population contained many good Catholics alongside the Cathar heretics, and that in practice it was impossible to tell them apart, so they asked the Abbot what they should do. He was more concerned that the guilty shouldn't escape than that the innocent should be spared and, it's said, gave a reply which is now part of history: *Caedite eos. Novit enim Dominus qui sunt eius.*'

So saying, the priest turned on his heel and continued walking towards the cathedral. I sat back down, his words, or rather those of Arnauld Amaury, ringing in my ears: 'Kill them all. For the Lord knows which are His.' I felt like a hammer-blow the full extent of my ignorance about the land in which I was travelling, and realised how insulated I had been from the real history of this region while living a cosseted life at Avignon. I was just beginning to understand why resentments here ran so deep.

XIV

THE NEXT DAY, I WENT to the administrative office in the episcopal palace and wrote a short report of what I had seen so far, which from Cardinal de Savigny's point of view was not very much. To date I had encountered no ignorant and indolent priests, and no Cathars. I mentioned the intervention of the Cistercians at Servian, but without commenting on the rights and wrongs of their behaviour. I decided to make no reference to anything Father Robert told me, or to my strange experience in the cathedral, more for fear of ridicule than anything else.

I had just completed the final sentence when I heard a rider outside. A few moments later a young man in a fresh white tunic and expensive riding boots entered and presented me with a letter of authority from Cardinal de Savigny to pass him my report. I handed it over, he perused it in a cursory fashion, looked up at me with what appeared to be disdain, then placed a bag of coins on the table and turned to leave without speaking a word. I asked his departing back where the next stage of my report would be collected. He replied without breaking stride.

'When you get to Narbonne, go to the house of Father Pierre. You'll be given further instructions in due course. Don't leave the city until you've been contacted.'

Although Béziers had much to commend it, I felt a strong urge to leave as soon as possible. The most direct route to Narbonne would be straight along the course of the Via Domitia, but a little to the north the scenic delights of the uplands beckoned. I considered the importance the Cardinal had attached to the state of affairs in Narbonne, whatever that might prove to be, and felt a sinking feeling in my stomach. Deciding that the quickest route there might not be the most efficacious, I headed away from the road.

Before long, an ascent faced me which turned out to be steeper than I had envisaged. I trusted that my young limbs would be a match for the task, especially as I was not in any particular hurry, but found myself envying the goats and sheep which were perfectly at home in this terrain, and their bleating seemed to mock me as they leapt effortlessly from crag to crag.

On reaching the summit I put down my bag and looked around. The air was cooler, and felt clean and crisp as it entered my lungs. The sky was an iridescent blue, shading down to turquoise above the sea towards the horizon. The soil beneath my feet was barren and dusty, but the summit was still carpeted by heather, lavender and saxifrage. On the yet higher slopes to the north rose a magnificent stand of pine trees. As on so many occasions since my arrival in this region I praised God for the beauty of His creation.

Moving on reinvigorated, I made my way across a broad plateau, unsure what lay ahead but calculating from the position of the sun that I was broadly heading in a westerly direction. After some time without encountering any human presence, a ramshackle structure appeared in the distance. In fact as I drew closer it became clear that it was constructed largely of mud and old fragments of timber. I knocked at the door to solicit a drink of water, and was met by a man and woman of extreme years, frail and crippled but with eyes bright and alert. The man brought a tin cup and accompanied me to their well at the back of the house, inviting me to draw from it as much as I wished. The water was chilled and clear, and at that moment tasted sweeter even than the Cardinal's expensive wine.

'Where are you heading, traveller?' he asked.

'My plan is to reach the next village by nightfall,' I replied. 'I should be able to find somewhere to stay there.'

The man's face was already so furrowed that it would be hard say whether he frowned or not, but his eyes betrayed anxiety.

'I advise you not to attempt that, sir. There's a severe storm coming.'

I looked up at the cloudless sky and smiled at the old man. 'Are you sure? I see no sign of it.'

'With respect sir, that's because you don't live up here. We learn to read every sign in the sky, every change in the wind.' He gestured with his head. 'Look up at the mountains to the north.'

There were a few wisps of cloud appearing above the highest peaks, but they were thin and at a great distance.

'I think there'll be plenty of time to reach the village before those clouds have the chance to cause any trouble.'

'No sir, I beg you, you must trust my judgement on these matters. You're passing through, but I've lived here all my life. I assure you there will be a storm. Look again.'

In the short time this exchange had taken, the distant clouds had swelled and darkened. I watched with the old man as they started to roll down towards us, seemingly gathering speed as they did so. On this occasion, the old man's knowledge of local conditions had proved more valuable than my educated arrogance. The tempest developed with frightening speed, and looked as if it could be with us in no more than a few minutes.

'Do you think the storm will be severe?' I asked with some trepidation.

'We can provide you with shelter for the night, sir,' the old man said. 'I don't think that conditions will be favourable for travelling until tomorrow. Please, come inside.'

My vision struggled to adjust to the gloom within. In the centre the old woman stood stirring a pot over a very smoky fire, her back bent, clearly in considerable pain. I asked if I could help her, but she smiled and waved me away.

'If I need help,' she replied, 'my husband Jean will provide it. He may look like a rascal, but he's a good man.'

They smiled at one another with obvious affection. I was already feeling very fortunate that they had deigned to take me in, a complete stranger foolish enough to try to cross the uplands without any knowledge of local conditions.

'My name is Nicholas, by the way,' I said, looking at the old woman.

'I'm Anna. From your appearance you remind me of a pilgrim. Are you heading for Compostela?'

'No. Not yet anyway. Although come to think of it, back at home I met people who had been on pilgrimage to the shrine of our Lady at Rocamadour. Perhaps I'll visit it too before I return.'

'My parents met on pilgrimage at Rocamadour,' she said. 'That's why they named me Anna, in honour of the mother of our Lady. They had very fond memories of Rocamadour. Apparently I was born exactly nine months later. I suspect that the Holy Virgin wouldn't have approved of everything they got up to there.'

Anna chuckled, and her husband pretended to give her a reproving look.

'Still, I'm glad they did,' Jean said. 'When a man and a woman love each other and they produce a daughter as wonderful as my Anna here, how can that be wrong?'

I was startled to hear the old couple come out with such views, but at that moment nothing could have been further from my mind than to rebuke them. Anna was clearly unashamed that she had been conceived out of wedlock, and I guessed that she had felt nothing but love and respect for her parents. Outside, thunder sounded in the distance, and the sky was growing more ominous by the minute.

My eyes had begun to adjust to the semi-darkness, and I now saw that the cottage, if that was not too grand a word for it, could not have been more sparsely furnished, confirming my impression that Anna and Jean were desperately poor. The only items of any value that I could see were a large crucifix, formed from what metal it was impossible to tell, and a statue of our Lady holding the Christ child. At that point, Anna carefully carried a pot of steaming soup to the table, then brought some bread from a porcelain container and placed it next to the pot. Jean set out three bowls and spoons. Poor as they were, they were about to share with a stranger what little food they had. This was the most unselfish act of human charity I had experienced in a long time. It inevitably reminded me of Jesus witnessing a poor widow donating a coin of minimal value at the Temple, and pointing out to the disciples that she had given more generously than the rich with all their gold. Anna and Jean asked me to say a blessing over the food, which I happily did. The soup was thin and the bread dry, but I can honestly say that it tasted better to me than the roasted swan I had consumed with the Countess on the first night of my journey.

After we had eaten, I got out my books and laid them side by side on the table. I could hear rain beating down on the roof, and from time to time glanced upwards with some anxiety. Jean and Anna were particularly taken with the copy of the *Confessions*, and gasped in delight when I showed them its illumination.

'Praise God for the skill which He gives to His servants,' Jean said. 'Will you read to us from this book, Nicholas?'

I thought for a moment. 'The book is in Latin, and not easy to read. It's a work both profound and in places beyond my feeble ability to translate. If you will allow me, I'll read something more familiar, but in its way even more profound.'

I opened my Gospel book to the well-thumbed pages containing the fifth chapter of the Gospel according to St Matthew, and read the words which had never meant more to me than at that moment, translating as I went along from Latin to Occitan:

Blessed are the poor in spirit, for theirs is the kingdom of Heaven. Blessed are the meek, for they shall inherit the earth. Blessed are those who sorrow, for they shall be consoled. Blessed are those who hunger and thirst after justice, for they shall be satisfied. Blessed are the merciful, for they shall receive mercy. Blessed are the pure in heart, for they shall see God. Blessed are the peaceful, for they shall be called sons of God. Blessed are those who suffer persecution in pursuit of justice, for theirs shall be the kingdom of Heaven.

I closed my eyes and allowed Christ's teaching to stir my heart as it had done on so many occasions before.

'What beautiful words,' Anna said. 'Where do they come from?'

For a moment I was too stunned to speak. They looked at me expectantly.

'You mean, you're not familiar with them?'

They looked at one another and shook their heads.

'But how can that be? Surely your priest reads to you from Holy Scripture?'

'Our priest?' Anna replied. There was a hint of disdain in her voice. 'We have no priest. We've had no priest for years.'

Jean waved his hand and shushed her, but she was undaunted.

'Our friend Nicholas is a man of learning, Jean, he must know these things go on. Sir, we have no priest because the Archbishop of Narbonne, a friend of counts and princes but no man of God, can't find anyone prepared to pay the price at which he wants to sell the benefice. It should be obvious to anyone that poor people can't pay generous tithes, yet our Archbishop seems determined to hold out. I fear that we shan't see another priest in our lifetimes.'

'You're telling me,' I replied, weighing each word as it passed my lips, 'that the Archbishop practises simony, to the detriment of the spiritual well-being, the very salvation, of the people of his archdiocese?'

'I told you that you should have said nothing of this,' Jean said to his wife. 'What can anyone do against these people? It will cause more trouble than it's worth.'

Anna glared back at him. 'Then are we to die without the benefit of the Church's sacraments? Without making our confession or receiving the last rites?'

'Please,' I said, 'I'm horrified by what you've told me. But I know someone who can do something about it. I'll plead your case at the highest level.'

Anna remained silent. Jean shook his head, then spoke sadly.

'Sir, I believe that you mean well. But those at the highest level, as you put it, are already well aware of our plight and have done nothing. Our Archbishop is too powerful. No-one can move against him, even—no-one, sir.'

'Mind you,' Anna said, 'we did receive great comfort from a preacher we heard in the house of Pierre the shepherd last year.'

'Oh? Please tell me more,' I said.

'He was a simple man, dressed poorly like us, and no great orator. But he spoke with such conviction that we hung on his every word. His preaching was like honey dripping into our ears.'

'Then perhaps all is not lost. Can you remember anything of what he said?'

'Oh yes,' she said. 'I'll never forget. He explained that this world is a constant battleground between darkness and light, between good and evil. And let's face it, no-one could doubt that. But he taught that individual men and women can rescue themselves from this world by living pure lives, that they can shed the burden of sin which we all carry.'

I nodded in agreement, since such teaching seemed incontrovertible. But Anna had more to say.

'All material things belong to the darkness, and spiritual things to the light. Hence our physical bodies are evil, and we must purge them in order to free our spiritual souls to return to the Heaven from whence they came. The preacher said that he never eats meat, and has remained unmarried. He also had some derogatory things to say about the Catholic Church and—'

'I think our friend has heard enough,' Jean interrupted. He glanced at me, and seemed to read in my face that I was becoming disturbed by Anna's account.

'Do you remember the preacher's name?' I asked.

'No,' Jean said.

'Yes, I think so,' Anna said, ignoring her husband. 'I'm almost certain he was called Guillaume.'

Later, I wrapped a blanket around me and tried in vain to find a comfortable position on the earth floor. I thought of the plight of poor Anna and Jean, devout Christian people deprived of the comforts of Christ's Church and her sacraments. Surely this was the very abuse of ecclesiastical power which Cardinal de Savigny spoke to me about before I set off? Surely this Archbishop of Narbonne was at the root of the evils which he had wanted me to investigate in that city. And surely the Cardinal would wish to put right this appalling wrong?

I also recalled Anna's account of the itinerant preacher who had visited the area only last year. Could it be that he was one of the Cathars whose influence Cardinal de Savigny told me to watch out for, and about whose activities Father Robert was so guarded? As yet I could not be sure, and decided to say nothing to my hosts, but to include what Anna had said in my next report to the Cardinal. I am sure that he will know what action to take.

For the first time, the reasons for my mission began to seem a little clearer in my mind. Outside the hovel which was my temporary home, the storm still raged. A pool of rainwater on the floor was slowly expanding in my direction.

XV

Soon after dawn the following day, I left Anna and Jean before they had a chance to offer me breakfast, feeling that I could not accept more of the hospitality which they could ill afford. Taking only water from their well for the journey, I set off along a route which Jean assured me would offer some of the greatest visual delights the region had to offer. His promise was to be fulfilled in ways I could hardly have expected.

Before too long I reached the edge of the plateau, and began to descend via a path more gentle than that by which I had ascended. In addition, this westward-facing slope was considerably more fertile than its eastern counterpart. I passed through stands of oak, ash and pine among whose branches flew brightly-coloured birds I had never seen in England. Their rippling song mingled with the screeching of cicadas to create the illusion that I had been transported not to France, but to an exotic destination in the distant Orient. From somewhere in the valley beneath me, I heard the melodious sound of running water.

As the path continued down the hillside, in the distance I could make out the sun's sparkling reflection on the river as it wound its way down the valley. The air became warmer as I descended through olive groves and vineyards on the lower slopes, then at the bottom came orchards of apples, pears and plums, all still heavy with blossom in this sheltered spot.

I sat by the river and watched as a young deer came down to drink on the opposite bank, splaying its front legs in order to lower its head to the water. After a while it caught sight of me, but did not react with alarm; when its thirst was quenched, it turned and trotted back into the woodlands beyond. If the Garden of Eden had been the original paradise on earth, I could not imagine how it exceeded the delights of the place in which I found myself, and smiled with sheer unbridled joy.

A rustling from behind attracted my attention. Imagining that it was another deer, I made my way silently back through the trees until I came to a path running parallel with the river bank. There, I was astonished to see a tall, slim, dark-haired young man walking away from me, clearly unaware of my presence. To my greater astonishment, he was completely naked, his pale skin glowing yellow as it reflected the dappled sunlight. He seemed in no great haste, nor did his movements suggest any sense of embarrassment at his condition. As he passed a large willow tree, a golden-haired young woman stepped out in front of him, also quite naked. Like the man, she was a vision of human perfection, unblemished and unashamed. She smiled at the young man, and then they embraced. Had a second Adam and Eve been sent to adorn this new Eden?

My question was answered when the young woman slid to her knees and, to my shock, began to perform an act of unspeakable depravity on the young man. As I watched in horror, she turned onto all fours like an animal on heat, then the young man knelt behind and began to fornicate with her in a suitably bestial fashion. For some moments I was paralysed, then I could think only of turning and fleeing with all haste. As I twisted, my tunic caught on a thorn-bush. While I struggled to free myself, the noise alerted the young couple to my presence. They separated, stood and looked around and, for one horrific moment, my eyes met theirs. I tore my tunic free and ran blindly back in the direction I had come, tripping over tree roots and frightening flocks of birds which scattered in alarm at my approach. I did not stop running until my strength completely failed.

When I had recovered myself I pressed on upstream, flinching at every unexpected sound, every snapping twig or rustle of leaves. Finally I arrived at a point where the stream looked readily fordable, and began to wade across. The water turned out to be deceptively deep and I soon found myself up to my chest, holding my bag above my head and struggling to keep my feet against the current. Several times I feared that I would be swept away, and had to pray to God for the strength and courage to press on.

By the time I emerged on the other side, exhaustion had taken its toll. I lay on the bank for several minutes to regain my strength, and was just rising to my feet when a sharp blow across my shoulders knocked me back to the ground, face down. Before I could turn over to see who had attacked me, a foot pressed down hard on my neck pinning my head to the ground. I felt one pair of hands searching my clothing, whilst another ripped at my bag to try to take it off me. Even though I knew that it contained nothing that would be of interest to the thieves apart from a little money, the great value to me of its contents made me determined not to let it go without a fight. But the thieves were strong and were just about to succeed in their nefarious endeavour when I heard the sound of hooves arriving in great haste, from which direction I could not tell.

The thieves released their grip on me, and I looked up in time to see them struck down by four uniformed men on horseback whilst another, presumably their sergeant, looked on, cowing the captives by encouraging his horse to rear up at them. For the first time, I had the chance to observe the men who had attacked me. One was of middle age, short and muscular but with a slight paunch, ugly and wearing ragged clothing. The other was equally bedraggled but thinner and only about twenty years of age. They might have been father and son.

The thieves were swiftly bound and dragged before the sergeant.

'No point taking these two back to town,' he said to his men. 'String them up over there.'

He nodded towards a large tree which stood nearby. Although there was precious little reason to show any sympathy towards the felons, I felt obliged to intervene.

'But sergeant, surely these men are entitled to have their case heard in a court of law before they're sentenced.'

'Why's that?' he replied. 'Do you think they're innocent?'

His men laughed. One of them spat on the ground.

'Of course not. But . . .' My intervention faded away into foolishness.

'Why should the townspeople pay to feed and water them in prison when they're going to be hanged anyway? Better to get it over with. Besides, this ford's notorious for thieves and cut-throats, they prey on ignorant travellers like you who struggle to get across. We make an example of these, and we discourage the rest.'

'But they should at least have the chance to make their peace with their Maker, and pray to Him to have mercy on their souls.'

At this, all the uniformed men began to laugh hysterically. To my astonishment, the older thief joined in.

'Don't you worry about us, Master Piety,' he said, 'we've already booked our place at the devil's table. Can't you hear him stoking the fires for us right now?'

I stood rooted to the spot, open-mouthed. The younger thief clearly did not share the elder's bravado. In his eyes, there was only terror.

'Go on, just get it over with,' the sergeant yelled to his men.

They dragged their captives across to the tree, tied ropes around their necks, then threw the other end of the ropes over two sturdy boughs. Keeping the ropes taut, they backed away and then hauled until the men were a little way off the ground. They tied the ropes to an adjacent tree-stump, then walked back to laugh and jeer as the thieves kicked and struggled, their tongues lolling, their eyes bulging.

At that point, the rope suspending the younger man slackened, and he fell to the ground in a heap. One of the sergeant's men cursed another for not having tied the end securely. The young thief barely had time to register his reprieve before he was hauled back off the ground and resumed his hopeless struggle for life. Both the hanged men soiled themselves as they lost control of their bodily functions.

I had never seen a man executed before, and was frozen in horror. I sank to my knees, closed my eyes and frantically recited the words of Extreme Unction, hoping to get as far through them as possible before the men gave up their souls. When I opened my eyes once more, their struggles were over. Whether my last desperate intervention had any merit in saving their souls from damnation, only God knows.

'Where will you bury them?' I asked the sergeant.

'Don't be stupid,' he said. 'I already told you, they'll be a warning to others. We'll leave them where they are.'

With that, the five rode into the woods and disappeared. I walked over and, standing on tiptoe, closed the dead men's unseeing eyes, then returned to the bank of the river, sat down and placed my head in my hands. It seemed that I had just lived through a waking nightmare. Two men had died, slowly and agonisingly, and one at least had laughed at the prospect. They may have been the lowest of God's creatures, but God's creatures nevertheless they were. Should I not have felt relieved at my salvation from violence and robbery, if not worse? Perhaps the thieves would have killed me if the timely intervention of the sergeant and his men had not prevented them. It seemed certain that they would have gone on to commit further crimes if not apprehended, to the detriment of other innocent travellers such as myself.

St Paul wrote that those placed in authority over us are placed there by God, yet Christ instructed us not to judge if we wish to avoid being judged ourselves. I found myself giving silent thanks for being a humble monk, rather than a doctor of theology.

XVI

THE WAY FORWARD ENTAILED A further ascent, although not to the heights I had reached the previous day. I hoped to reach Narbonne by nightfall, but among the hills I had been unable to catch even the smallest glimpse of the city, the way ahead always being barred by further summits. Hunger was beginning to take its toll when, surely by God's providence, I met a shepherd who offered to share his ration of bread and cheese with me. Although it was meagre fare, I ate it greedily. Fortunately the shepherd took no offence at my ill manners, and indeed laughed at my lack of judgement in travelling so unprepared. For the second time in as many days, I found myself considering the paradox that those who have very little tend to be more generous in sharing what they have than those who could much better afford to do so.

Evening was drawing near by the time I crested the summit of a hill to see laid out before me a distant prospect of the city of Narbonne. Its buildings glowed red in the radiance of the setting sun, the stones of its cathedral warmest of all. In the background, the sea had darkened to the colour of opal. I will not go so far as to say that it reminded me of a vision of the New Jerusalem, but the knowledge that my next goal was within sight raised my spirits. I found a sheltered spot to rest for the night, and gave thanks to God.

It was in good humour that I descended the hill the next morning, rejoined the Via Domitia and made my way towards the main gate of the city. The amount of traffic heading away from Narbonne was astonishing. Assuming that a market or festival had been taking place, I tried to engage several of the travellers in conversation, but to my surprise was met in each case with a terse response.

Enquiring among the guards at the city gate, I was told that Father Pierre's house was a little south of the cathedral, toward the quayside, and made my way in that direction. The streets were surprisingly empty at a time when it would have been normal to see crowds thronging them, in contrast to the large groups I had seen on the road outside. It seemed, in fact, that a large part of the population had simply melted away. A strange tension hung in the air.

Following the main street heading towards the river, I arrived at the house of Father Pierre, a simple wooden dwelling with a thatched roof. As I walked up to the door, a large black rat caused me to jump back as it scuttled from an alleyway out into the street. Something about its behaviour caught my attention, however, then I realised that, on closer inspection, it was staggering from side to side. At length it toppled over onto its side, seemingly panting for breath, and I saw blood begin to trickle from its mouth. Much as I find rats among the least endearing of God's creations, it was hard not to feel some sympathy for the creature in its extreme suffering.

I knocked at the door, and a gaunt elderly man opened it. He was short in stature, and his thin grey hair covered a dome-like skull. His lips were thin, and his hooked nose gave him the appearance of a gargoyle. He seemed anxious, and hurried me inside.

'You've arrived at a most inauspicious time,' he said. 'In fact I advise you to leave immediately, before it's too late.'

'But I'm under instructions—'

'Never mind about that. Just go. There's no time to lose.'

'Is the city about to come under attack?' I asked.

Pierre clenched his fists. 'I'd say that it's about to come under siege. Stories are circulating that the plague has arrived on a ship which has just returned from the Levant. I suppose it may be just a rumour, but people are taking no chances. Those who can do so are preparing to flee the city before it's too late.'

'But I've been sent here by—'

'What in the devil's name does that matter now?'

'And what will you do, Father Pierre?'

'Me? I have no choice, obviously I must stay. It's my duty before God.'

'Then I'll stay with you. If the story's true, your services will be in great demand. I can help you.'

He looked at me as if I had spoken in a foreign tongue, or had been struck down with imbecility.

'Don't you understand? To remain in the city at a time like this might be to sign your own death warrant. If the plague has arrived, what chance do you think a priest, who's constantly visiting the sick and dying, has of remaining free of the disease? Go and save yourself. You owe nothing to the city of Narbonne.'

Father Pierre spoke as abruptly as if he were chiding a backsliding parishioner. What he said made complete sense, of course, on one level, yet how could I justify leaving at the very time when my services could be of most use?

'I must pray,' I replied. 'I can't make such a decision without asking for guidance from God. I'll stay here tonight, if you'll have me, and make my choice tomorrow.'

Pierre became more agitated than ever.

'Are you mad? Tomorrow may be too late. Look at me, I'm an old man, my life is of no value. But you're young, you have many years in front of you in which to do God's work. In what insane world can it make sense for you to remain? Just go. Now.'

I thought for a moment. 'I've made my decision. I'll stay tonight and pray to God to guide me. I take it that you won't deny me one night's lodging?'

He shook his head, threw his hands up and walked away, muttering under his breath.

For the rest of the day, we listened to the sound of wheels clattering across the cobbles outside. Some carts were heading towards the harbour, others in the opposite direction, presumably to find refuge inland. From time to time, groups of horsemen rode past, and we heard sounds of disorder, of weapons being drawn and cries of grief and agitation. Father Pierre spoke little. I suggested that we should go out into the city to see for ourselves what was actually happening, but he dismissed the idea as if I were an idiot. Whether the sounds we heard were of distress and fear or of looting, it was difficult to tell.

I found myself torn between my duty as a servant of God, and the desire to escape an unseen peril which might well be fatal. That night, I think I prayed more fervently than at any time in my life. The most powerful feeling in my heart was that I would be overcome by shame and guilt were I to take the opportunity to flee. At the same time, Father Pierre's words seemed to hold some validity: how much could I really achieve if I were to stay? No matter how fervent my prayers, no clear answer came back. I sank deeper and deeper into despair from feeling abandoned at my time of greatest need. At one point I fell into a restless sleep, but soon awoke again with my heart still in torment.

Dawn arrived, and I hauled myself to my feet. I discovered Father Pierre still sitting by the window; he had clearly not been to bed all night. My bag lay on the table, a loaf next to it. My flask had been refilled with water.

'You're right, Father Pierre,' I said. 'God has given me no sign that I should stay.'

'Go now,' he said quietly. 'Before it's too late.'

I retraced my steps back to the main north gate. Ahead, I could see a company of people dressed in expensive clothes who were taking with them several carts laden high with possessions, everything from their more valuable pieces of furniture to their dogs. They were passing through the gate as I joined the more impoverished group who straggled along behind, most taking with them only what they could carry on their backs. As we arrived at the gate, a number of them looked back over their shoulders, as if hesitant. What thoughts went through their mind? Some, perhaps, had left loved ones behind. I spoke to one man who seemed to be alone, and was clearly hesitating to take the momentous decision to leave the city.

'It's not a simple decision,' I said to him, stating a truth rather too obvious.

He hesitated for some moments, then said, 'I've left my aged father behind. It pains me to do so, but he's near death anyway. His fate is sealed whether I stay or leave.'

I was taken aback by his candour. What degree of fear could justify a crime of such magnitude?

'His neighbours are providing for his needs,' he said. 'My wife and children are staying with her parents at St Marcel. How will they survive if anything happens to me?'

Without waiting for my reply, he trudged forward and made his escape. He did not look back.

I stepped forward and, as I was about to pass through the gateway, could not resist asking a guard the identity of the wealthy group who had preceded us. To my surprise, he laughed in my face.

'Who do you think it was? To be that rich, you have to be an archbishop.'

The guard walked away, chuckling to himself. I stood open-mouthed. I was already aware that to hold episcopal office was in itself no guarantee of sainthood, and indeed had heard from Anna and Jean that the Archbishop of Narbonne was not a man of high principle, but that he should abandon the city and its inhabitants at a time of such distress seemed to me incomprehensible. I could still see the carts and their passengers disappearing into the distance, and a part of me wanted to run after it and berate the Archbishop for his negligence of duty. The guard looked back at me in what I felt to be a threatening manner, and I put the thought from my mind.

Somehow, my own decision to leave appeared in a different light. I held no office and had no specific responsibility towards the people of Narbonne, yet is an ordained man not in a sense responsible to all God's people? Was my decision so much less reprehensible than the Archbishop's?

I moved away from the gate and slumped down against the cold, hard stones of the city wall. I must confess that I began to curse my untimely arrival in a city of which I felt myself to be no part, and to bemoan the impossible dilemma which now faced me. How long I remained there I do not know, for in my misery I ceased to care about the passing of time. To leave the city, as I could well have done without censure, would, I knew, not ease the misery.

The stream of people heading through the gate showed no sign of diminishing. A commotion broke out as a young woman holding a baby came running forward, grasping at people in the crowd, searching desperately for someone. At last she let out a cry as she caught sight of a man a little way ahead of her. She called out his name, he turned around and saw her and began to quicken his pace, but she was already upon him. She threw herself to the ground at his feet, grasped his clothing and pleaded with him not to abandon her and the baby. The other refugees looked askance, and walked quickly past.

To my horror, the man kicked her away from him, cursed her loudly and threatened her with violence if she did not leave him. As they struggled, his shin struck her in the face and she was thrown to the ground, losing hold of the baby which fell sprawling in the dust and, after a few moments, began to cry loudly. The man showed no concern and ran out of the city as fast as his legs would take him. The woman, racked with sobs, crawled across and picked up her baby, wailing in her grief. One of the guards set off to move her away but the sergeant called him back, shaking his head.

Through her tears, the woman caught sight of me staring at her. I knew nothing of the situation between her and the man, but I could not see how any human being could have been unmoved by her entreaties. As she looked at me, she said nothing, but her eyes pleaded for help. The baby had become silent. She raised herself to her feet and shuffled back towards the city, her shoulders hunched. A guard spat on the ground.

My future, at least for the duration of the plague, had been decided by one incident which I had witnessed purely by chance. I thought of Jonah, the reluctant prophet sent by God to preach to the people of Nineveh, and the lengths to which he was prepared to go in order to evade the will of God. History would not record my experience as it had that of Jonah, but at least it was now clear that I had received a summons from which there could be no escape. A resolve began to form itself in my heart, to try to live up to my vocation and to prove myself worthy of the challenge to which God had summoned me.

Father Pierre remained seated where I had left him. He briefly raised his eyes as I entered, then motioned to the other chair. I slumped into it, and placed my head in my hands.

'I'm sorry,' he said in a low voice.

'God has spoken,' I replied without raising my head. 'The Lord gives and the Lord takes away. Blessed be the name of the Lord.'

'Would it be inappropriate for me to say that, in my heart of hearts, I'm glad that you'll be here to help me through this—this period of trial? I'm not anxious to give up this life, any more than you are to give up yours. But if God calls us, we can only answer, "I am here, Lord". Can't we?'

'Perhaps,' I said, 'the rumours of plague will turn out to be unfounded, or at least exaggerated. After all, sickness and suffering are part of the human condition.'

He gave me a weary look, then stood up and beckoned me to follow him. We left the house, walked along the street and stopped at a dilapidated house. An elderly woman came to the door. It was so warped that it took all her strength to open it.

'How is he?' Pierre asked.

The old woman began to weep on the doorstep. We walked past her and into the room. Inside, on a low cot, was an old man in terrible distress. He lay with his arms and legs spread-eagled, as if trying to keep them as far from his torso as possible. He was uncovered despite his high fever, and in his groin and armpits we could see large, suppurating swellings. On his body were dark stains, like huge bruises. As we watched, he turned on his side, which clearly caused him great agony, and coughed up blood onto the floor. The stench of decay and corruption was so overpowering I was forced to cover my mouth and nose with my sleeve.

'What do you think, Father?' she said.

'I think we must prepare for the worst,' Pierre replied. 'When the end is near, come and fetch me and I'll do what's necessary.'

She sniffed hard, and nodded. Pierre gestured to me that we should leave. As we walked back, I said to him:

'Believe it or not, I've never seen anyone suffering from the plague. Is it always as bad as that?'

'As bad, and worse.'

'I hope that I'll be up to the demands of this time,' I said.

He nodded. 'So do I. Let's both pray that our faith will be strong enough.'

The following morning, I heard a knock at the door. There was no sign of Pierre, so I opened it and found a girl about twelve years old waiting outside, holding a basket of vegetables. She was painfully thin, as children of that age often are, and her dark hair was unkempt, but she had curved red lips which smiled readily and attractively. Most striking were her eyes, bright and fiery. They flashed in the morning sunlight.

'I'm Madeleine,' she said. 'Who are you?'

'My name is Nicholas.'

'Are you a friend of Father Pierre?'

'Yes, I suppose I am now. How about you?'

'I look after him. I suppose I'm a bit like a daughter to him.'

Something about the girl's manner made me feel uncomfortable, as if I should apologise for my presence. She showed great poise and self-confidence for one of her youth. And she read my thoughts.

'Don't worry,' she said, 'Father Pierre has lots of visitors. I don't mind.'

So saying, she strode past me into the house as if I were a doorkeeper and she an illustrious guest. She went straight to the kitchen and began to busy herself preparing the vegetables.

Pierre came back into the house a short while later. Madeleine rushed up to him and placed her forehead towards his mouth. He kissed and embraced her, and then she returned to her domestic tasks with even greater alacrity.

'She's my angel on earth,' he said to me. 'I have no idea what I would do without Madeleine. Apart from live in squalor and starve, of course. She cooks and cleans for me better than any wife could ever do.'

'In that case,' I replied, 'I can see why you refer to her as an angel. Such a helper is a treasure without price.'

'Her father, Antoine, is a widower. Madeleine's mother died two years ago. He was going to send her away into service, but to be truthful I'd always been so fond of the girl that I couldn't bear to see her condemned to such a life. I pay her more than I have to, but I suppose Antoine needs all the help he can get.'

Madeleine carried out her work with such enthusiasm that she was the equivalent of two normal servants, if not more. It seemed to me that a diligent and hard-working girl of such intelligence deserved more than the life of child-bearing and drudgery which doubtless awaited her.

'Is there any news of the old man along the road?' I asked Pierre.

'I've just been to give him the Last Rites. He'll be dead in an hour or so, God willing. He's suffered enough.'

XVII

I DECIDED THAT, IF THE city of Narbonne was destined to be my home for an uncertain period of time, I might as well explore it and become better acquainted. Father Pierre, who had spent his whole life there, proved to be a fount of knowledge about its history. He was keen that I should understand that it was in some respects a shadow of its former self; its heyday had been in centuries past, when it was one of the major cities along that part of the coastline of the Mediterranean Sea. It had been founded by the Romans well over a century before the birth of Christ, hence the designation of the Roman province, of which it was the capital, as Gallia Narbonensis. The site was no doubt chosen for its strategic importance at the junction of the east-west Via Domitia and the Via Aquitania, leading to the great sea to the north-west.

Following the fall of the Roman Empire, Narbonne was successively occupied by Visigoths, Moors, and Franks. Pierre told me that in recent centuries its main claim to intellectual fame had been the number of outstanding scholars arising from within its substantial Jewish population. Perhaps not surprisingly, I was to discover that most of Narbonne's inhabitants knew nothing of this aspect of its past. However, its colourful history still lent it a vibrancy, even at the ill-fated time when I was there, which could not be matched by many cities in England, though coupled, as in the rest of the region, with a licentious attitude in certain matters of morality.

Narbonne was connected to the sea by the River Aude, but in the previous century this had become progressively shallower as deposits of silt built up. Indeed, I heard that the river had begun to change its course in order to find a more congenial channel to the sea, resulting in more frequent occurrences of flooding in low-lying areas. The consequence was that the role of Narbonne as a port diminished, since only smaller ships could now make their way up into the city's harbour. Its prosperity naturally suffered as a result, and over the course of time I formed the view that the consciousness of their reduced circumstances had rendered at least some of the city's people resentful and suspicious. Unlike in other areas through which I had travelled, their behaviour towards those they perceived as outsiders was not particularly friendly or welcoming. Violence in public places, often fuelled by an excess of the robust local wines, was not uncommon.

One symptom of this economic decline was that building works on Narbonne's otherwise fine cathedral of St Just had come to a halt, leaving the east end in an unsatisfactory condition. How unfortunate that a building designed to express the majesty of God should become a monument to the vagaries of mercantile trade. Notwithstanding, the city retained many fine structures from its distinguished past, some dating back to the age of the Roman Empire. Indeed, some of the Roman buildings seemed of such sound and robust construction that I suspected they would remain standing long after the demise of others of much more recent date.

Narbonne remained, nevertheless, a populous and crowded city, despite the hurried departure of a fair few of its citizens. I heard wildly varying estimates of its population, but it seemed that the number of inhabitants in normal times would be so great as to put it on a par even with Norwich. As a result the city was densely-occupied, nestling as it did within a cramped site with little room to expand its boundaries. This, I feared from the outset, would hamper attempts to halt the spread of the plague. The most rapid possible burial of the dead was clearly essential, but according to Pierre the city's cemeteries were already near the limits of their capacity before the plague struck. In all probability, therefore, it would soon be necessary to consecrate new areas to cope with what would surely be a growing number of victims, yet no obvious open spaces remained within the walls.

I found myself wondering why a large part of the city's people chose not to flee as soon as the presence of the plague was suspected. Father Pierre was equally puzzled, since he told me he made a point of interrogating some of them on this point as he made his rounds from house to house. The reasons given were invariably mundane and pragmatic rather than heroic. Most had no means of supporting themselves and their families other than to continue their established trade or business. Many had no doubt well-founded fears that their homes and possessions would not be safe if left for any period of time. On a more sinister note, some had been influenced by rumours circulating in Narbonne that groups who took the decision to leave had been ambushed and killed by armed men from neighbouring communities, who feared that those fleeing the city would infect them as they passed through. Whether there was truth in these rumours I had no way of knowing, but they raised doubts in many minds as to whether the dangers of remaining within the city were greater or less than those which might lurk outside. I found myself wondering if the Archbishop and his company had arranged an armed guard to ensure their safe passage.

It was in a reflective mood that I was walking with Father Pierre through the centre of the city one morning when we saw that a large crowd had gathered in the main square in front of the cathedral. We made our way through the mass of bystanders to find out the cause of this unexpected congregation. We could see little reason for it until a man of about thirty years, clad in a brown friar's robe, made his way onto the steps before the cathedral's west end, stood facing the crowd and placed a large, worn leather bag on the ground at his feet. We positioned ourselves close enough to be able to hear. A tall, wiry man moved up alongside Pierre.

'What are you doing here, you old scoundrel?' he said. 'Don't tell me you need to take lessons in preaching from friars?'

'Know your enemy,' Pierre replied. 'Let me introduce you to my young friend Nicholas. He's English. Nicholas, this is Esteban, he's a charlatan, excuse me, I mean a physician.'

'I will choose to ignore your barbs, as always,' Esteban said. 'Anyway, I thought you and the friars were supposed to be on the same side.'

'I'll tell you when we've heard him speak. Do you know anything about him?'

'Apparently he's a Franciscan. That's probably about all you need to know.'

The friar raised his arms to indicate that he was about to speak. The crowd took some time to fall silent. His plump face looked stern, expressing his obvious disapproval at their lack of respect.

'Brothers and sisters,' he began in a booming voice, 'we are living through troubled times.'

111

'You came here just to tell us that?' Pierre said under his breath.

'Troubled times indeed,' the friar continued. 'The angel of death hangs poised over this sinful city. He hangs poised over each and every one of you.'

He paused, seemingly waiting for a reaction from his listeners. There was none. He cleared his throat and continued in an even louder voice.

'The angel of death comes to bring you God's judgement. God's judgement on your sins, sins which would cause even the people of Sodom and Gomorrah to blush in shame.'

'Not in my house, sadly,' Esteban said. Several people standing nearby laughed.

'Sodom and Gomorrah were destroyed by the wrath of God, just as the city of Narbonne will be destroyed. Because you have failed to heed the signs. Signs and portents which, in His mercy, God showed you to give you a chance to repent and change your ways.'

As if he had arranged it in advance, a death cart piled with corpses passed by the square, its wooden wheels clattering on the cobbled street. One or two around us shivered. A voice from behind us called out, 'What signs and portents?'

'Ah. "What signs and portents?" I hear you cry. Can there be anyone who has not heard? Very well, I will detail them for you. Earthquakes and eruptions of volcanic fire have occurred in many parts of the world, too many to enumerate. Outside the walls of the holy city of Jerusalem itself, a ferocious dragon appeared, consuming all in its path. Monstrous showers of frogs and worms have fallen from the sky in Cathay, the most monstrous of such occurrences since the Lord visited plagues on Egypt in ancient times. In India fire fell from the sky, submerging the whole land, melting mountains and killing all who came near to the stench of its foul smoke. Were these not enough to warn you of the wrath to come?'

'How were we supposed to know about all those?' the same voice cried. 'They happened in other parts of the world.'

The friar, who had clearly anticipated this response, crossed his arms and nodded slowly, savouring the moment.

'You want evidence from closer to home? Very well, I'll give you evidence. In the latter months of last year, did you never look up to the sky?'

At this point, a murmuring began to spread through the crowd.

'I see that you know already to what I refer. A ghostly star, a comet, which remained in the sky over these parts for many weeks. Now, some sceptics will say, comets appear from time to time, we may not know they are coming, but they are a natural phenomenon. Am I right?'

To judge from the reaction, the crowd did indeed contain a number of sceptics. The friar, unlike the heavens, was unperturbed.

'You blind fools. Those with eyes to see and ears to hear could tell that it was no ordinary comet. The perceptive saw that it moved across the sky so quickly that its motion could be observed.'

'If it was moving that fast,' an arch-sceptic shouted, 'how could it stay in the sky for many weeks, like you said?'

The friar froze his antagonist with a stare.

'Some have eyes to see, some remain stubbornly blind. But don't take my word for it, my friend.' He turned his attention to his wider audience. 'Did not those of you with higher intelligence and more astute faculties actually hear the motion of the comet as a mighty rushing noise?'

He paused, and a few people around us began to shout, 'I did', and 'So did I, it was like thunder.' Pierre and I looked at one another with expressions of equal dismay. The friar was back in full cry.

'Then can there have been a clearer sign of the pestilence and death to come? Could God have made His warning any clearer to you? I see that some of you are now nodding your heads in agreement. But as if the comet were not enough, I saw with my own eyes a portent so ghastly, so hideous, that I shudder as I recall it. Indeed, I am not sure that I can bring myself to describe it to you.'

Needless to say, it was not long before some of his listeners demanded to know the details of this gruesome event. His head sank into his hands and he turned away, but the shouts became louder and louder. At last he turned around once more and raised his arms. This time the silence was immediate. His voice sank to a lower pitch, so much quieter that we had to strain to hear his every word.

'It was in this very city. I was called to see a woman who had just given birth, and who was in great distress. I could not see why someone who had safely given birth should not be feeling elation, but I went along nonetheless. What I saw there was a most hideous, devilish sight. Lying in a cot, next to the woman's bed, were twin girls, newly born. At first I still could not see the cause of her anxious state, until I pulled back the blanket which covered them, and saw that the two girls shared one body, from the neck of which their two heads grotesquely emerged. I gasped in horror, even more so when I saw that on the crown of their heads was inscribed none other than the Mark of the Beast. I quickly recited a prayer of exorcism to drive away the demon lurking within them. After I had prayed fervently for some time, I heard an unearthly scream, and saw a black demon rise up from the body and then vanish into smoke, still wailing bitterly.'

The friar sank to his knees, as if exhausted by the effort of recalling this horrendous event. A deep unease now communicated itself through the crowd, and people began to call out, 'What can we do? Tell us what to do.' As the sound became deafening, the friar rose once more, his eyes closed in silent prayer. At length he opened them and held out his hands in a pose of supplication.

'My friends, my brothers and sisters. There is a way to escape the scythe with which the angel of death prepares to cut you down and send you to the eternal fire. It is not too late to mend your ways. But you must pray most earnestly for God's forgiveness. Will you pray with me, here and now?'

As one, the congregation dropped to their knees. Pierre looked at me and Esteban in turn, and we lowered ourselves to the ground.

'O Lord, hear, we pray, the entreaties of this wretched, sinful people. Hear their cries of repentance, their cries of horror at the sins which they have committed, blatantly and nakedly, in your sight. Reprieve them from the horrors of your avenging angel, allow them to prove to you that they are a new people who have turned aside from their former ways.'

After a long pause, the penitents looked up one by one as they realised that the prayer had ended. The friar, however, stood in silence, his eyes firmly closed. When he opened them again, his listeners hung on his every word.

'I have a message to pass on to you,' he said. 'The Lord has heard your prayers. He believes that you sincerely wish to prove that you have changed your ways.'

'Yes, yes, tell us what we must do,' came the cries.

'The Lord has spent thousands of years listening to the pleas of sinful men and women who begged Him for mercy, then promptly forgot their promise to change their ways. He therefore wants you to show your love for Him by your support for His Church. For He knows which of you have been avoiding your tithes, pretending to poverty in order to escape from your sacred duty. Now He wants you to make up for your past errors. But our God is a just God. He does not expect something for nothing. He offers you a gift in return. He offers you the chance to acquire a sacred object which will always remind you of His grace, a relic of one of His holy saints, even, for those who wish to express their gratitude to the full and receive God's pardon in return, a sliver of the very cross on which Christ was crucified. In His mercy, God offers these to you in return for a token of your support for His holy Church.'

He picked up his bag from the ground.

'See, within this bag of relics I have with me a finger bone from the body of St Andrew, the very brother of Simon Peter, the leader of the apostles, the holy martyr who was crucified in Rome. And here, a lock from the head of none other than St Alban, the first Christian to be martyred among the Britons, taken from him immediately after his beheading. I have many more such holy relics, all guaranteed genuine, all holding the sanctity of the saint from whom they came, all powerful to absolve you from your dark sins. All I ask is that you show your repentance by your gifts to God's Church in return for these priceless objects. Come, who will be the first to show that he has forsaken sin and turned to the way of God?'

We were pushed and jostled mercilessly in the rush. I lost contact with Pierre and Esteban, swept along in the human tide. Out of curiosity, I made my way to the front for a closer view of the objects which the friar was offering. Surely he could not possibly have been able to carry enough relics to satisfy the demand of this large crowd, but his bag seemed to be bottomless. One after another they emerged, and as far as I could tell no-one went away unsatisfied.

Some time later I returned to Pierre's house to find him and Esteban deep in conversation, each nursing a large cup of wine. They stared at me as I walked in.

'We were wondering what delayed you,' Esteban said.

'Let me guess,' Pierre said, 'you've bought a fragment of the holy cross.'

'Better than that,' I said, and withdrew my hand from a pocket in my cloak. 'A quill pen used by St Augustine, rescued from his writing desk just before the Vandals sacked the city of Hippo.'

They gazed at me in disbelief.

'Have you lost your senses?' Pierre said. 'What makes you think that object was ever anywhere near St Augustine?'

'Faith moves mountains,' I replied.

'Anyway, never mind that. Esteban thinks we should protect ourselves when we visit plague victims.'

'Indeed,' the physician said. 'It's an established fact that sweet-smelling herbs and flowers can help to counteract the effects of poisoned air and other effluvia. I recommend angelica, camphor, myrrh and rose leaves. Keep them in front of your mouth and nose at all times when the plague is near. Oh, and drink plenty of wine to keep your blood pure.'

I said nothing, but my expression must have conveyed my scepticism.

'He may be a devilish fraudster,' Pierre said, 'but who knows what will and won't help at a time like this? His advice makes sense to me. Especially the last bit. Oh, and one more thing.'

He nodded towards the top of my head. I fingered my scalp, circling the area where my tonsure had long since grown over through neglect.

'If you're going to act as a priest, you'd better look like one.'

XVIII

FATHER PIERRE'S PARISH WAS FORMED of a densely-packed, and hence closely-knit, community of artisans, including weavers, carpenters and masons. Their houses were generally small and overcrowded. Pierre knew each and every one of them by name. They greeted him, not so much with enthusiasm, but as one who was simply a regular and accepted visitor. Not surprisingly, the only matter on their minds was the threat of the plague. Indeed, it seemed to me that, if or when the plague arrived in their area, the degree of overcrowding would make it all too easy for the sickness to spread quickly.

Although we had no official figures to which we could refer, there seemed little doubt that the number of the sick was rising day by day. We saw physicians scurrying through the streets, and after dark we heard the rattle of the death carts taking the victims to be buried. The ecclesiastical authorities had already decided that burials should take place at night, perhaps in the knowledge that they would attract less attention, perhaps in the hope that the cooler night air would reduce the spread of the contagion from the dead to the living. Whichever was the case, their aspirations proved to be unfounded.

As I walked the streets of the city, I sensed a tangible fear among the inhabitants. People walked quickly to their destination, avoided contact with others as far as they could, and often took circuitous routes to avoid areas they expected to be crowded. The market place, once a hub of commerce and human interaction, was largely deserted. In short, the everyday activities which lead to the pleasures of normal social intercourse were slowly coming to an end. It seemed as if, even at this stage, the plague was winding itself around Narbonne in the way that a snake coils itself around the body of its victim before constricting the life from it.

Before long, the demands of visiting the sick and dying prevented Pierre and me from going out together, as had formerly been our custom, and we were obliged to divide our forces. I was by now becoming familiar with the layout of the streets which formed his parish, and had few qualms about venturing out alone. Indeed, after all the years which I had spent observing unchanging rituals, it seemed almost exciting to be thrown into such frenetic, and unpredictable, activity, perverse though that may sound. The accompanying dangers only increased my sense that these were days which would live in my memory, at least for as long as I survived.

I had almost forgotten Esteban's advice on the use of herbs and flowers to counteract the plague, but decided that there was nothing to lose by trying his remedy. Madeleine accordingly made up a wonderfully-scented blend of the substances he had recommended, which I took to carrying around with me in a bag over my shoulder.

One day I paid a visit to the house of Bernard, a middle-aged weaver who, according to Pierre, was one of the least assiduous of his parishioners in the matter of fulfilling his religious obligations, yet one of the first to complain of anything he saw as a dereliction of duty on the part of any member or department of God's Church. I stuffed some of Madeleine's concoction into a kerchief, which I tied tightly around my nose and mouth, then knocked on the door. It was answered by a young woman whom I took to be his daughter, and behind whose skirts a small boy sheltered fearfully. She frowned at my impromptu mask, but said nothing.

Inside, an older woman, presumably Bernard's wife, sat sewing. He himself sat by the window, a cup of wine in his hand, staring out into the street. He seemed unaware of, or uninterested in, my arrival.

The presumed daughter looked me up and down.

'Where's Father Pierre?' she demanded.

'Father Pierre has duties elsewhere. The plague keeps priests busy, you know.'

'What?'

I started to repeat myself, but she held her hand up to stop me.

'I can't hear a word you're saying. You'll have to take that thing away from your mouth.'

The fragrant aroma from within my prophylactic could not disguise the fact that it made it very difficult to breathe. After momentary hesitation I removed it, with some relief. She led the way into a back room, where a young man lay under a blanket on a cot. I nodded to her, and she left without a word.

The young man was, I guessed, about twenty years of age. His dark hair was matted with sweat, and his features so contorted in pain that I could not begin to say whether he was of handsome appearance or not. The blanket was soaked with sweat, and from it rose a most unpleasant stench. I placed the bundle of herbs back under my nose and inhaled deeply. The man's eyes were closed, but he moaned constantly, muttering words which were inaudible, as if in a state of delirium. From my limited experience I found it difficult to tell what stage the sickness had reached. I went back out into the main room. Bernard's wife was still sewing, but this time he rose to his feet.

'Has he been seen by a physician?' I asked.

He narrowed his eyes and made a dismissive gesture with his hand. His voice was deep and rough.

'Where do you think we can get the money for a physician? We can barely feed ourselves. What are you priests for anyway? Can't you tell God to do something for him?'

It seemed curious that no member of the family had expressed any sense of grief or despair about the young man's condition. I returned to the back room. The young man was now doubled up, as if suffering agonies in his stomach or internal organs. His moaning had grown louder, and his breathing more rapid. I said a prayer for delivery from sickness, but knew in my heart of hearts that it would not be answered.

I began to look around the room, and saw to my surprise pieces of old vellum lying in untidy piles. It was of poor quality, the kind which at Croyland we would have used for rough drafts, but some of the documents showed evidence of a competent hand. How could such items have come into the possession of a doubtless illiterate family? They appeared to be items of a mercantile nature, bills of credit and such like. I noted that most were in the name of one Jacob, presumably a money-lender, but that the debtors were many and varied, all seemingly with Christian names. I cannot deny that my interest was more taken up with these documents than with the patient suffering a short distance away. Jacob had presumably suffered some undesirable fate, perhaps at the hands of members of this family, even of the young man who groaned alongside me.

I was about to leave when I came across something which intrigued me even more. It was a pen drawing, in black, brown and grey, of what seemed to be a tree bearing ten circles, presumably representing fruit. Inside each was a word in the Hebrew language, but sadly I had not developed my knowledge of this tongue sufficiently to work out their meanings. For some reason the picture fascinated me, and the longer I looked at it the more it seemed to draw me in. Clearly it could not be the property of Bernard or of any member of his family, so to remove it would not strictly be stealing. I secreted it inside my robe.

'I'll return to see him in the morning,' I said, taking my leave. 'Try to keep him cool. God will determine whether he'll recover.'

I felt Bernard's eyes boring into my back as I let myself out of the house. In the distance, a woman wailed hysterically.

XIX

THE DIAGRAM CONTINUED TO CAUSE me considerable anxiety. In all my years of study I had never seen anything quite like it, and began to suspect that it was not a Christian representation. It had been among the papers of a man I supposed to be a Jewish money-lender, but I knew little enough of their beliefs and practices. Could it even be somehow related to the Cathars? I finally decided to take my courage in my hands and show it to Father Pierre. He stared at it and then looked up at me, frowning.

'Where did you come by this?' he asked.

'It was in Bernard's house, in the room where his son lay dying. It was among a large number of papers strewn around at random.'

'What sort of papers?'

'Mostly bills of debt, as far as I could see. What he wanted with them I can't imagine.'

Pierre nodded. It seemed that this strange juxtaposition at least made some sense to him.

'So, what do you make of the diagram?' I asked. 'I'm sure that it doesn't illustrate any facet of Church teaching. Could it be something to do with the Cathars?'

Father Pierre lowered his voice as if to imply that I should have done the same.

'You're partly right,' he said. 'This has nothing to do with Catholic orthodoxy. Some would say, however, that it derives from a source even more sinister than the Cathars.'

He wandered across and looked out of the window, seemingly lost in thought. I was eager to know what he meant, but he was in no hurry to satisfy my curiosity. At length he said, still staring through the window:

'If you really must know more, there's someone you may wish to meet. But it will be better to wait until after dark. Make sure that no-one sees you. These are dangerous times.'

So it was that, after nightfall, I found myself stumbling down a narrow, vermin-ridden alleyway, my cloak wrapped tightly around me and my hood over my face like a common criminal. The upper storeys of the houses leaned out into the street towards each other, creating the effect that I was crawling through a tunnel. Several times I stopped and retreated into a doorway, asking myself whether I really felt strong enough to continue, but each time my curiosity drove me on.

When I reached the house which Pierre had indicated as my destination, I looked up and down to ensure that no-one had followed me, knocked on the door as loudly as I dared, then waited. For some time, nothing happened. I thought I heard footsteps on the other side, but it did not open. I knocked again, and whispered:

'My name is Nicholas. I've come in peace. I'm searching for Zacharias. Zacharias the Jew.'

The door creaked ajar, and I stepped back a pace. I could see no face within, but the hesitant, heavily-accented voice of an elderly man whispered back.

'I've never heard of you. What do you want?'

'I'm hoping to draw on your wisdom. I've been told that you may have the answer to my question.'

'Oh? And what is your question?'

'I have something to show you. May I come in?'

A skeletal head peered round the door and surveyed the alleyway, then nodded to me to enter. Within, the house was in darkness except for the light of a single candle by which it appeared Zacharias had been reading, though how his elderly eyes could have achieved the feat under such feeble illumination was a mystery to me. He resumed his seat and indicated a second chair, previously invisible in the shadows. I dragged it alongside until we were both huddled next to the candle. In the feeble light, I saw that his face was as furrowed as a ploughed field. His eyes were bright, however, and suggested that an intelligent spirit lay within. All my earlier training had taught me to exercise suspicion towards Jews, although I had never shared the intense hatred expressed by some of my fellows. Now that I was in the house of Zacharias, my old feelings would not disappear, but I determined to conceal them as best I could.

'May I thank you,' I began, 'for agreeing to talk to me, especially in these difficult times.'

'For you, difficult. For me and my people, unbearable.'

I was unsure what he was referring to, but he did not seem about to elaborate. He spoke in little more than a whisper.

'What did you say your name was?'

'Nicholas. Brother Nicholas of Croyland. In England.'

'Hmm. England, you say? What are you doing here then?'

'I've been travelling on—on business. By chance I had just arrived in Narbonne when the plague struck and the city gates were sealed.'

'A paradigm for our lives.' He chuckled at his own incomprehensible joke. 'You seem like an honest man,' he said. 'But hush, I am failing in my sacred duty to provide hospitality to a stranger. Would you like some wine?'

Zacharias did not wait for my reply before moving to a sideboard, taking a jug and pouring two large cups of wine. How he could see to do so, I have no idea. I had been apprehensive in the extreme when I set out, but I was already more curious than afraid. He handed me my cup and resumed his seat. Some instinct prompted me to wait until he sipped his wine before putting my cup to my lips.

'May I ask you,' I said, 'what you meant about life being unbearable?'

He stared back until I felt discomforted.

'Is that what you came here to ask me? Well, it doesn't matter now. What's done is done. My people are immune to suffering.'

'Your voice suggests otherwise. I detect a deep sadness.'

He frowned at me, and I began to wonder if I had pressed him too far. To my surprise, he leaned forward and placed his hand on my knee.

'How is it with the Jews of England?'

I hesitated, but he watched me eagerly. 'The Jews have been expelled from England,' I replied. 'Although we have suffered since for the lack of their, how shall I say, business acumen.'

'As money-lenders, you mean?' He leaned back in his chair, and stared into the candle-flame. 'I will tell you a story, young Nicholas. Have you ever been to Toulouse?'

'No, but perhaps it will form part of my itinerary.'

'And have you heard of the Pastoureaux?'

My encounter with this hostile group outside Paris while I was travelling with Vittorio remained fresh in my memory.

'I have had some contact with them,' I replied, 'although not in this region.'

'Then you are indeed fortunate. Do you know this? When they arrived at Paris, they demanded that the King lead them on a crusade to drive the Saracens from Palestine, but of course he saw through them and dispersed them. Having been driven from Paris, one contingent of the Pastoureaux headed south-west until eventually they reached the Toulousain, where they set to their Christian duty. By the time they left Castelsarrasin, over 150 Jews lay dead, slaughtered in cold blood. Nothing was sacred to these Pastoureaux, they even robbed churches and attacked priests. In fact they spread terror wherever they went. The Seneschal of Toulouse sent a force out to arrest them, and they were brought to the city as prisoners. A large crowd gathered to see the spectacle. I myself watched from a balcony overlooking the main square, relieved that at least they could cause no more trouble once they were in the prison behind bars. But some of the Pastoureaux started to shout out to the crowd that they were being persecuted because they wished to punish the enemies of Christ—God should have struck them down on the spot for their blasphemy—and before anyone could stop them, the crowd rushed forward and began to untie them.' Zacharias' head sank into his hands. 'What followed was a scene of madness and bloodlust.'

He waited, seemingly needing to regain his breath, or his strength, before continuing the story. He raised his head and stared into the candle flame, as if in its flickering he could see these very events replayed before his eyes.

'The escaped Pastoureaux began to shout that all Jews must be put to death, and the mob became inflamed. I fled in terror to my house, in a side street off the square, and barricaded myself in. Groups of insane men, and women too, rampaged through the area attacking anyone they suspected of not being a Christian, often without bothering to make sure one way or another. They stripped a man naked in the street to see if he was circumcised. They then took hold of another and demanded, on pain of death, that he point out the houses where Jews lived. He immediately pointed to mine, may God have mercy on him. They broke my door down and seized me, pinning me to the ground, and screaming that I must accept baptism or be killed.'

His eyes betrayed that the recounting of these events was taking a considerable toll on the old man. It was some moments before he felt able to continue.

'To my shame, I decided to save my life. I was dragged to the church of St Etienne, where two Christian priests were waiting. They themselves were trembling with fear, and confided that if I did not agree to be baptised, they would be unable to save me from the fury of the mob. They pointed out to me the bodies of others who had had more courage than I, lying on the floor soaked in blood, with terrible wounds to all parts of their bodies.

'I had not totally lost my wits, and decided to try to buy time in the hope that they would lose interest or that their bloodlust would dissipate. I stated that I was willing to be baptised, but that I would like a Dominican friend of mine, Jean l'Allemand, to stand as godfather. In truth I hoped that Jean would be able to turn them from their madness, for he was a man of some standing and widely respected. I left with one of the clerics to try to reach his house, but we were challenged by the mob in the streets, who demanded to know whether I had been baptised or not. I pleaded with the cleric to say that I had, but he would not do so, since he was as terrified of the mob as I. He dragged me back to the church, saying that it would be impossible to reach anywhere in the city that day.

'After we returned to St Etienne, I tried to stall once more, first by saying that I would like my sons to be present, then that I wanted the Seneschal's sergeant-at-arms to act as godfather. I did in fact know him, and I suppose I hoped that by some miracle he would be able to rescue me by force of arms. All this time, we could hear cries and screams from the streets outside as people were cruelly tortured and murdered, then the crackle of flames as their houses were burned. In the end I realised that there was no escape, and consented to be baptised, making my profession of faith with all the sincerity I did not feel.'

By this stage, it seemed clear that Zacharias was barely aware of my presence. It was as if he were dictating a memorandum for posterity.

'Afterwards, I wanted to go back to my house to see what, if anything, I could salvage, but the priests persuaded me that it was still too dangerous, so they took me to their own house and gave me some wine. I finally returned home under cover of darkness only to find, needless to say, that my house had been well-nigh destroyed and just about everything of any value taken. All my books had been thrown into the street and burned. I used the few possessions left to me to bribe an officer of the guard, who had been posted to protect the Jews in any case, for all the good it did, to secure me a safe passage out of Toulouse, and at first light I slipped away with the intention of heading for Montgiscard, along the road leading south-east from the city.

'My nightmare was not over. Another group of Pastoureaux was travelling that way, and demanded to know if I were a Jew. I replied in the German tongue that I was not, but my ruse failed, and they became more insistent. For some reason, perhaps shame at my cowardice on the previous day, I said that I was. In truth, it did not seem to me that my sham baptism could by any definition be considered valid, so in my heart my reply was truthful. I was locked up with other Jews overnight, with the open connivance of the civic authorities, then taken to Pamiers to be interviewed by the Bishop, Jacques Fournier.

'I knew of his fearsome reputation, but when I was taken before him I told him in detail what had happened to me, imagining that, like most educated Christians, he would be appalled at the behaviour of the Pastoureaux. However, he seemed most interested in the circumstances of my forced baptism. I pointed out that I had hardly been able to give my consent to being baptised and, indeed, that the act was carried out in such indecent haste that I was given no instruction as to the significance of the sacrament itself, or what part it played in the Christian faith. Bishop Fournier listened to my arguments with interest, but finally announced that he did not consider that I had been baptised against my will. He stated that those who profess Christianity but then renounce it are treated by the Church as heretics, and that there is only one sanction appropriate for use against heretics. I closed my eyes as I stood before him, and it seemed to me that I could smell the smoke of a burning pyre, see flames licking around my feet, and feel the unbearable heat roasting me from beneath.'

Zacharias' voice faded to nothing. Tears were trickling down his cheeks and, although his eyes reflected the candle's flickering light, the fire within them had gone out. I saw with dreadful clarity what he had meant by describing these times as unbearable. He looked more sad and weary than anyone I had ever seen. And yet he had taken it upon himself to relate the story to me, of his own free will. Could it be that this was the first time he had unburdened himself? I tried to find some words of comfort and reassurance, but my tongue froze when I considered that those who had persecuted Zacharias and his fellow Jews professed the same faith to which I held.

Whether he felt any comfort or relief for having been able to relate his story, it was difficult to tell. This was clearly no time to raise the matter which I had hoped to discuss with him.

'May I visit you again?' I asked.

Zacharias may have nodded slightly. I thanked him, gathered up the papers I had brought with me what seemed like a long time ago, drained my cup of wine, and closed the door behind me as quietly as I could.

XX

Over the following days, certain patterns began to emerge in regard to the spread of the plague. The number of victims increased relentlessly, to the extent that Pierre and I could not always be sure to reach them in time before their souls departed, a source of anguish both to ourselves and the families, and often the prompt for an outpouring of invective directed against the Church in general, and ourselves in particular. At first I felt greatly disheartened by this, given that we worked night and day to minister to the needs of Pierre's parishioners, but eventually decided that it was better for them to vent their anger against us, who stood before them in tangible form, rather than against God Himself.

Most distressing to me was the disproportionate number of children who were succumbing, and not just those already of a sickly disposition. Indeed, most victims I visited were either young or old, those in between seeming to be blessed with more resistance, although even so the very young, babies and infants, showed themselves unlikely to become victims. A particular paradox was the susceptibility of otherwise healthy young males, whom one might suppose to be the strongest members of the community. I made a mental note to ask Esteban if he could explain this phenomenon. In addition, I had expected that the wealthy and well-nourished would be less likely to fall ill than the poor and malnourished, but even this did not hold true. If anything, the rich seemed more likely to become victims than their impoverished neighbours. It was almost as if the plague were better able to feed on those who were themselves well-fed. All in all, I was confused by the path the disease was taking. Predicting its future behaviour seemed well-nigh impossible.

Madeleine continued to arrive every day without fail to minister to our worldly needs. She ignored me most of the time, but I found myself growing more and more curious about her. One day, I was in the kitchen while she prepared a meal for us.

'Where did you learn your domestic skills?' I asked.

'From my mother. She worked for us until the day she died.'

'You must miss her very much.'

She paused before replying. 'I don't think I'll ever stop missing her. My life seems empty without her. Do you have a family, Nicholas?'

'No. No, I don't.'

'What happened to them? Do you mind me asking?'

'Of course not, Madeleine. They all died in a fire when I was very young.'

'That must have been terrible. Who looked after you?'

'I suppose you could say that, from that moment on, the Church became my family.'

'How did the fire start?'

The lack of inhibition with which Madeleine asked the question took me aback, but for some reason I felt compelled to be truthful.

'I started it.'

'How?'

'To be honest, Madeleine, I still find that very painful to talk about.'

She stopped and turned around, wiping her hands on her dress. Her face was no longer that of a child.

'Then perhaps it's time you unburdened yourself, Nicholas. Why don't you tell me?'

Why not indeed? At that moment, I felt that God had sent Madeleine to me as a confessor.

'Will you sit down with me, Madeleine? I want to tell you something.'

She took the chair opposite me and leaned her elbows on the table, her chin resting on her hands. Her piercing eyes were fixed on me.

'I often have a dream, one which has haunted me since my childhood. I refer to it as a dream because I still see it in my sleep, but in reality it's a memory.

'I lie in bed in complete darkness, listening to the sounds of the night: owls screeching, foxes barking, bats, mice and other small creatures skittering through the thatch above me. I'm gripped by the grotesque fears of a child, I imagine that I hear the rustling of spiders as large as cats. My parents have taught me at these times to pray to God to grant me peace of mind and keep me safe from the dangers of the night. But my terror remains.

'When the darkness becomes unbearable, I rise and edge my way step by step towards the living area. My hands and feet are stinging with the cold. I kick something over, I can't tell what, and it clatters across the floor. I wait for my parents to leap from bed and turn their anger on me, but the house returns to silence. Even my two sisters, sleeping just a short distance away, stir but don't wake. At last, after much aimless groping, I discover the object of my search, the smooth waxy surface of a candle, and light it from the last embers of the fire in the kitchen hearth.

'Shading the flame both from draughts and from any eyes which may chance to open, I start to make my way back to my bed, but I trip and drop the candle. It rolls across the floor and lodges against the edge of a blanket which has been flung over an old wooden chest. Before I can retrieve it, the blanket begins to smoulder, then bursts into flame. Within moments the chest begins to crackle and the heat becomes intense, too great for me to have any chance of putting out the fire. The thought uppermost in my mind isn't that we're all in mortal danger, but that my parents will be furious when they discover how the fire started. I turn and run blindly out of the door into the cold night air.

'The fire spreads quickly. Before long the thatch is ablaze, and soon it collapses and sets the whole house alight. I watch the doorway, waiting for my parents and my sisters to rush out, but no-one appears. I think I hear screams above the roar of the flames, but can't be certain. Our neighbours are beginning to pour onto the street, dousing sparks, clearing away burning thatch blown into the street by the wind, doing everything they can to prevent the fire from spreading.

'Soon, there's little left of the house. When the flames have died down and the heat starts to diminish, a few brave souls venture into the smoking wreckage and, one by one, emerge with the charred bodies of my family, laying them on the ground side by side. Even in the darkness, I can see that they're burned beyond recognition. Women from the neighbouring houses take it in turns to embrace me, to tell me that I won't be left alone and helpless, but I'm too numb to care what they're saying, or fear what's in store for me.

'When, finally, the full reality of what I've done sinks in, I dissolve into uncontrollable weeping, as I have ever since, at the end of each dream.'

I wiped away tears from my eyes, too ashamed to look at Madeleine. She reached across, took my hand and grasped it tightly.

'It wasn't your fault was it, Nicholas? It was an accident.'

'I was still responsible for their deaths. If I'd been obedient and followed my parents' instructions—'

'I'm scared of the dark too. Do you know what I do sometimes when I can't bear it any more? I go outside and look up at the stars and imagine they're giant lanterns, and the longer I watch the brighter they seem to get.'

'And when it's cloudy?'

'In the dark, clouds seem to glow. Have you seen that? I try to stay outside until first light, but if father stops snoring I hurry back in case he's about to wake up. He'd thrash me if he found out I went out at night on my own. If I do have to go back inside, the house is like a trap or a pit, a dark prison.'

She released my hand, stood up and returned to her duties.

'Thank you for letting me talk to you, Madeleine.'

'That's all right. It's not good to burden yourself with secrets. You can talk to me at any time.'

I returned to see Bernard's son, only to discover that he had passed away minutes before. I expressed my regrets, and suggested that he allow me to sprinkle holy water on his corpse and commend his soul to God. I cannot deny that in the back of my mind lay the prospect of checking for any further documents related to the one I had taken on my previous visit. Bernard launched a tirade of foul abuse, some of which was beyond my understanding. He then spat in my face and slammed the door.

That night, Pierre and I sat in the courtyard of his house, unburdening ourselves of our anxieties with a bottle of wine, he having taken this part of Esteban's advice very much to heart. I was also finding increasing consolation in the fruit of the grape, since our lives were no longer our own, never knowing at what hour of the day or night we might be called out. The coolness of the air at that time also helped to calm our turbulent emotions.

Up to that point, we had simply been too busy to spend much time discussing our respective perceptions of the events going on around us, not to mention thanking God for allowing us to survive for at least one more day. Despite the length of time we had now spent under the same roof, I felt that, because of the pressures on us, I barely knew Pierre. I took the opportunity to try to rectify this.

'What do you say, Pierre, when people demand to know why a just God has deserted them, deserted this whole city?'

He stared into his cup, then took a deep draught before replying.

'I tell them that they have to choose what kind of a God they want to believe in. Everyone has to die, and some die earlier than others. Some die before they've even begun to live. That's been the case since the dawn of creation. It's always been the case that some die peacefully in their beds with their family at their side, while others die alone and in agony. In that sense, nothing has changed despite the plague.'

'And does that answer satisfy them?'

'Of course not. They want straightforward answers to deep mysteries. They want to know why three of their family have died while, just next door, their neighbours haven't been touched. They want to know if the plague is a punishment for sin, and if so, whose.'

'That's understandable,' I said. 'Surely people can be punished for their sins on earth, rather than waiting for the fires of hell after death.'

Pierre laughed. 'Wouldn't it be good to think so. But do you believe that God has struck down our Archbishop for abandoning his people to save his own skin?'

'We may never know.'

'Indeed. But even at your age you must have seen enough pain in this world to know that there's no direct connection between sin and suffering. With my own eyes, I've seen a thatched roof struck by lightning. It burst into flames and started falling into the house below, and within moments everyone inside was doomed. The whole place was consumed in a few minutes. And yet people believe that God sends us our weather.'

I shuddered. Pierre did not seem to notice.

'And what God does with the sinful after they die is His business, I'm pleased to say, not mine.'

We sat in silence for several minutes while I contemplated Pierre's unorthodox approach to these questions. At length he interrupted my reverie, clasping his hands.

'I was called to a house near the harbour today, Nicholas. It turned out that the plague victim I was visiting was old Father Gaston, one of the finest men it has ever been my privilege to know. All his life he's sought nothing but to serve others to the glory of God. His skin was covered in blotches and sores, he had a raging fever, in his delirium he kept mumbling about the fires of hell. I sat there and held his hand until mid-day, not caring if I were increasing my own chances of catching the sickness. I watched him die, and then I wept like a child, even though according to my faith I should have been rejoicing that he was at peace with God.'

He looked down, slowly shaking his head, then abruptly looked up.

'Tell me about yourself, Nicholas. I know virtually nothing about you. Talk to me about your parents, your family.'

This time, it was I who drank deeply before replying.

'My parents died when I was a child.'

'Ah, so were you brought up by grandparents?'

'No, by the Benedictine Order. I remember travelling on a cart to the gatehouse of Croyland and being taken inside. The world beyond the abbey walls seemed to disappear after that. I don't suppose I ever asked myself if there were other options.'

Pierre leaned back in his seat. 'Interesting. So you've not had to make choices about the path your life would follow, never having known anything else?'

'I suppose that's true. Until recently, anyway.'

'Once, I heard the voice of God calling me to serve Him. That was a long time ago now.'

The tone of Pierre's voice did not suggest that this memory filled him with warmth and renewed hope.

We turned around as one when we heard someone hammering insistently on the door.

'I'll go,' I said.

XXI

THE NEXT TIME I WENT to Zacharias' house, familiarity with the route had probably rendered me somewhat less cautious than on my first visit. I ignored the dark doorways and overhanging eaves, and indeed felt tempted to dismiss Father Pierre's initial warnings about the danger of making contact with the Jew. I knocked at the door more boldly than previously, but with the same result. It was only after confirming my identity and lack of companions that Zacharias consented to invite me inside.

After our initial exchange of pleasantries, including the pouring of wine, I wasted no time in showing him the tree diagram which had so puzzled me. He looked at it with obvious interest, then suddenly his mood changed.

'Why do you show me this? Where did you get it?'

'I found it in the house of a young man I visited a few days ago. It intrigues me. Father Pierre suggested that I should show it to you.'

'It is better that you leave. You should not have come here. Just go.'

I was so taken aback that for some moments I was speechless. When I recovered my voice, it was still hesitant and stuttering.

'But I assure you, I'm simply anxious to learn, to satisfy my no doubt vain curiosity. Why would I wish anything which could cause you harm?'

'You came here the other night and pretended to befriend me. You persuade me to trust you, then you trap me into saying something you can use against me. I know the tactics of the Inquisition's agents only too well.'

I gasped. 'The In—you surely can't think—I have nothing to do with the Inquisition. I'd never encountered it until I arrived on these shores.'

'But I know more about you than you think. I've discovered that you're travelling on the orders of the Pope, or more to the point those who control him.'

As far as I was aware, there was only one person in Narbonne apart from myself who knew this. Perhaps Pierre had mentioned it to Esteban, or Madeleine?

'I won't deny that, since you accuse me of dishonesty. I have orders from His Holiness. But investigating the activities of those who hold to the Jewish faith forms no part of them. It's Christians I'm here to find out about.'

Zacharias watched me, and I sensed from his eyes that he was tempted to believe me.

'I have nothing to hide from you, Zacharias. If I wanted to make trouble for you, I could simply make use of what you've already told me. But I returned because I wish to ask humbly for your help. I understand that you're suspicious because of what you've been through. But tell me honestly, do I seem to you anything like the men who caused you to suffer in Toulouse?'

He looked straight into my eyes.

'No. No, you do not. But neither for that matter did Bishop Fournier, and I have nothing to thank him for.'

'I have little in common with Bishop Fournier for that matter, apart from a desire to serve the one true God. Each of us in our own way.'

Zacharias stood up and walked to the other side of the room, disappearing into virtual darkness as he did so. I took a sip of my wine, wondering in what humour he would re-emerge into the candlelight. A voice finally came out of the shadows.

'It is the Tree of Life.'

'Excuse me?'

'The picture which you showed me.'

Zacharias emerged from the gloom and resumed his seat. 'Have you heard of the way of Qabbalah?'

'No.'

'Perhaps it has not reached England. Qabbalah is a system of thought amongst Jewish scholars and philosophers. It is knowledge. Secret knowledge which enables those who understand it to achieve spiritual enlightenment and become closer to God.'

'I dare say that all faiths have similar systems of thought,' I replied. 'Can you explain to me further?'

Zacharias returned to the diagram.

'The ten circles are spheres, the ten sefirot, singular sefirah. Each sefirah represents an emanation of the Godhead.'

'I'm sorry. I don't understand.'

'I'm not surprised,' he said. 'I'm simplifying to the point of absurdity. To understand these things takes many years of dedicated study. But let me put it to you like this. You Christians believe that there is one God, but that His nature can be expressed as a Trinity of Father, Son and Holy Spirit. Is that not so?'

'In essence, yes,' I replied, wondering if I were being led into a trap.

'And how many ordinary Christians truly understand the nature of this three-in-one God? How God can be one and yet three, all at the same time?'

'It is indeed a doctrine which causes confusion to the untutored. And even to some scholars.'

'Quite so. Hebrew scholars have refined their understanding of the nature of God even further, to the ten sefirot. I cannot begin to explain them to you, but they all represent aspects of God on which the devotee must meditate until he achieves full understanding.'

I looked back at the diagram. 'Explain, then, the Tree of Life.'

'The ten sefirot are graded in terms of their closeness to the realm of pure spirit in which the Godhead may be found. The devotee aspires to move upwards through the spheres, and finally attain—how can I put it—equality, consubstantiality, with God.'

I tried to conceal my horror at the implications of what Zacharias was telling me, but my efforts were unsuccessful.

'I see that you are taken aback by this,' he said. 'Does it shock you so much to think that we can attain that status? Is there not a particle, an atom, a wisp of God inside every man and woman? Perhaps inside every living thing?'

'Christian mystics have said similar things. Whether such insights were invariably inspired by God I'm not sure. How can God the creator share His essence with His own creation? How can the object created be of the same substance as the artist who created it?'

'Why not?' Zacharias said, as if it were the most obvious of deductions. 'When you listen to fine music devoted to God, or when you see a beautiful painting depicting some aspect of the life of Christ, you say that the artist has put some part of himself into the work. Perhaps you mean it as a metaphor, but in a real sense it is true. When you see a sapling growing beneath an oak tree, you know that it shares the same substance as the parent tree which produced the acorn from which it has grown. I believe that God could not have made us in His likeness, as the Book of Genesis teaches us that He did, without placing some part of Himself within us. After all, it was the very breath of God which brought Adam to life, was it not?'

For a few moments I had no idea how to reply to Zacharias. I searched for the obvious flaw in his arguments, but could not identify it.

'If what you say is true,' I said, 'then what ground is there for us to worship God, since we share His nature and have the potential to be equal to Him?'

'Let me turn that question around,' he replied. 'Imagine an island so remote that the inhabitants know neither the Jewish nor the Christian faith. Do you suppose that they will feel a natural instinct to worship God?'

'I believe so, yes. Even if they've not received the true faith, they may still see the works of God all around them and recognise that the world must have a creator and that the creator must be so powerful that he should be worshipped.'

'Indeed. Or they may see the handiwork of a number of deities, just as the ancient Greeks and Romans had a god or goddess for every area of life and every aspect of the physical world.'

'Perhaps,' I replied, again with some hesitation. 'But the beliefs of the Greeks and Romans were primitive. In their wilfulness they refused to recognise that there is only one God.'

'And how do we know that there is only one God? No, please, it is a serious question. What makes us so confident that we are correct and that the ancients were mistaken?'

'Because Holy Scripture makes it perfectly clear. When the Lord came down to appear to Moses on Mount Sinai, He instructed him to tell the Israelites that they should worship no other god but Him.'

'And does that very injunction not imply that there were other gods who could be worshipped, but that the Israelites must reject them?'

'Is that what you believe, Zacharias? That there are other gods?'

'No. But I believe that, in the time of Moses, the Israelites believed in the existence of deities other than the one who had revealed Himself to them. And who can blame them? After all, when God decided to create Adam and Eve, did He not say, "Let *us* make man in *our* own image and likeness"? To whom was God referring when He used the plural form?'

I had never even considered this question. By now my thoughts were racing.

'I assume, to His threefold nature as Trinity of Father, Son and Holy Spirit.'

'Perhaps. Or perhaps many of the words of the Scriptures are too profound to be read as they appear. Many centuries ago, one of our wise men told a story about God dictating the Law, the Torah, to Moses. When he came to the passage which I have just referred to, Moses complained to God and asked him why He chose to make His words so difficult to understand, and so easy to misinterpret. Do you know what God replied? "Just write!"'

'I imagine, Zacharias, that you're building up towards telling me that the path of Qabbalah is the way to understand these secret meanings embedded in Holy Scripture.'

'At last, Nicholas, you are beginning to understand. Qabbalah draws on ancient teachings, in some cases so ancient that their origins are lost in time. For instance, are you familiar with the name of Lilith?'

'I know this,' I replied, 'only as the name of a she-demon, some say a succubus.'

'Indeed. This is how she is widely known. But did you know that her reputation has been defamed over the centuries, and that she was in fact the first wife of Adam?'

'How fascinating. I was under the impression that we were engaged in a serious discussion.'

'Listen, Nicholas. Nowhere will you find this in the Book of Genesis, but a story just as ancient tells that Lilith was married to

Adam before he met Eve. However, they disagreed and she left him. Do you know why?'

'I have a feeling that I will never rest again until you tell me the answer.'

'Adam insisted that, during intercourse, he should lie on top, since it was appropriate that the man should express his dominance over the woman in this way. Lilith advised him that in that case he would need to find a woman less proud and more compliant. She has since been taking her vengeance on men. She visits them during the night and mates with them, causing them to soil their bedding. Adam, of course, subsequently took Eve to wife because she was prepared to be subservient. There, what do you think of that?'

'I think,' I said, 'that I'm far from surprised that Moses didn't see fit to include this story in the Book of Genesis.'

Zacharias, it turned out, was not done with me yet. He seemed to be enjoying himself.

'Tell me, young man, since you have such a thirst for knowledge, why did God forbid Adam and Eve to eat the fruit of the tree of knowledge of good and evil?'

'The answer is in the second chapter of Genesis. God warned them that if they did so they would die.'

'But they defied God's warning and did eat, and they did not die. God had been lying to them.'

'Not so. Eating the fruit caused the death of their innocence and of their former relationship with God and the rest of creation. That was death in a very real sense.'

'Indeed. But the aftermath of this story is interesting. God, who like you or I is walking in the garden to enjoy the cool of the evening, has to call out to Adam to find out where he is. When God discovers that he and Eve have eaten the fruit of the tree of knowledge of good and evil, what is His reaction? He is afraid.'

'God? Afraid?' Now I began to wonder if Zacharias was losing his sanity.

'Well, what does God say? "The man has become like one of us, knowing good and evil; what if he now reaches out his hand and takes fruit from the tree of life also, eats it and lives for ever?" Because God fears that Adam and Eve will themselves become like gods, He drives them from the Garden of Eden.'

I sipped from my wine cup and reflected on what Zacharias had said. I could not fault his recollection of the words of Genesis, which I had read many, many times in my life. Why had I never thought to ask myself the same questions? Why did God consistently refer to Himself in the plural? Why did He seem to behave, if you looked at the words in their literal sense, as the jealous protector of His divine status against the threat posed by Adam and Eve? Or had Zacharias succeeded in sowing some infernally-inspired seed of doubt in my mind? He saw my confusion.

'I am sorry, Nicholas. Perhaps it was unfair to throw all this at you. But now you see why it was so difficult for me to explain to you about the Tree of Life and the ten sefirot. And why it is so difficult for you to grasp the way in which we interpret the sacred writings. Let me try to illustrate. No, please bear with me just a little longer. What was the universal language of this earth before the building of the Tower of Babel and God's sowing of a confusion of languages?'

'Our philosophers assert that it was Hebrew,' I replied.

'Indeed. So it must have been the Hebrew language that God used when He spoke directly to the early patriarchs?'

'Yes. I suppose so.'

'That is why, to us, the very letters of the Hebrew language are sacred. Not only that, but each of them is endowed with a profound meaning, a hidden secret which has to be unlocked by means of study and meditation.'

'The way of Qabbalah, you mean?'

'Precisely.'

'Zacharias, I see that a huge gulf exists between us. My mind has indeed been challenged, not to say disturbed, by what you've said tonight. I won't pretend that I have accepted, or even understood, all that you've told me. But I do warrant that I shall think and pray for a deeper understanding of these matters.'

'In that case,' he replied, 'you have already taken the first step on the path of Qabbalah.'

XXII

I was afflicted by strange thoughts on leaving the house of Zacharias. I walked back along the alleyway outside with my mind seemingly in two compartments. One side had been stimulated by our discussion of the nature of God and of the inherent difficulties in interpreting the Scriptures. Indeed, I had discussed these matters often with teachers at Croyland, and had rarely felt challenged in the way I had on that night. And yet, the other side of my mind saw the potential of Zacharias' beliefs to encourage heretical views, particularly on the part of the unlearned. The purpose of Qabbalah, to enable devotees to attain a realm of pure spirit, to share the very nature of God, sounded uncomfortably like Father Robert's description of the beliefs of the Cathars.

I was deep in these thoughts when it became clear that I was being followed. I looked over my shoulder, and could just make out two figures lurking in deep shadow with hoods over their heads. I hesitated, wondering whether to pretend indifference or to run for my life. The decision was taken out of my hands when, at the next corner, two more figures appeared as if from nowhere and grabbed my arms. Those who had been following ran to catch up and, before I even had time to cry out, one placed his hand over my mouth from behind. At the same time I felt what appeared to be a knife pressed into my back, and a sack was placed over my head. They forced me in this way to obey their will, and dragged me for some distance into a house which, if my sense of direction had not completely deserted me, lay in the merchant quarter of the city.

I was pushed through a doorway and into an inner room, then forced to stand in the middle of the floor. The sack was pulled from my head, the coarse fabric rasping across my face, and I blinked as I took in my surroundings. In front of me was a table, behind which sat three men wearing cloth masks with crude eye-holes slit into them. Those who had dragged me there released me and retreated to the edges of the room. The man in the centre of the

141

three, presumably the most senior in some respect, then spoke to me in a deep voice, but no mouth-holes had been cut in the masks, presumably to disguise the voices of those involved, so the result was that every word he said was incomprehensible. For a moment the scene struck me as comical, and I burst out laughing. At this one of the men who had brought me there stepped forward and struck me hard across the face. My interlocutor spoke again, and still each word came out as a muffled mumbling noise. For some reason I felt a sense of bravado which was hardly justified by my predicament, and which proved to be misguided in the extreme.

'I'm sorry,' I said. 'Your voice is too heavily masked by the, er, mask. I can't understand what you're saying.'

He looked from side to side, and his companions nodded. He lifted the bottom of his mask, at the same time tilting his head down, presumably in an attempt to prevent me from seeing too much of his face. Once again I was struck by the absurdity of these events, but this time resisted the temptation to make my feelings obvious. By now the master of the proceedings was speaking again, his voice middle-aged and, I suspected, made deeper to disguise its true identity.

'State your name,' the voice said in a menacing tone.

'Tell me to whom I'm speaking, and I will confirm my identity.'

'We will ask the questions, and you will answer.'

The voice did not come across as one which was accustomed to speaking with authority or, indeed, to commanding obedience. I felt my anxiety at my situation being replaced by frustration and anger.

'I will tell you nothing,' I replied. 'I demand that you release me. I am on business from his Holiness Pope John, and it will be the worse for you if you do not do as I say.'

The boldness of my response rather took me by surprise. Indeed, I immediately feared that this had not been a wise thing to say and that, far from intimidating my captors, the reference to my mission might have the opposite effect. The three men in front of me began to whisper together. The man on the left of the three now lifted his mask and took over.

'You are the Englishman, Nicholas, are you not?'

'If you know this, why do you waste time asking me to confirm it?'

'What were you doing at the house of the Jew Zacharias?'

'That is no concern of yours,' I said. 'I am under no compulsion to tell you my business.'

The man sat back in his chair, and I had the feeling that he was looking at me gravely.

'Nicholas, it is only fair to warn you that we have the power of life and death over you. Doubtless you have heard of us. We are the People's Inquisition.'

The People's Inquisition? What madness was this?

'I've never heard of such a body,' I replied. 'As far as I'm concerned, you're kidnappers and ruffians.'

'Then you have a great deal to learn, Nicholas. The ordinary people of this city can no longer trust the so-called authorities, civic or ecclesiastical, to guard our interests and keep us safe. We are now the enforcers of the law.'

'And what law allows you to snatch men from the streets and drag them away against their will?'

'We make the laws now, and we do whatever is necessary to protect good Catholic people.'

'I am a good Catholic,' I replied, 'and I most certainly do not accept your right to speak or act on behalf of me.'

There was silence for a few moments. My hands were sweating profusely and the strength beginning to drain away from my legs. I began a silent recital of the *Pater noster*, but was only half-way through when the third man spoke for the first time. He was younger, and his voice well-educated.

'You are not a good Catholic, Nicholas, because you consort with Jews.'

I took a deep breath. 'I've already told you that I am here on business from the Pope in Avignon. I presume you would not wish to tell his Holiness that he's not a good Catholic.'

He paused, and I felt even through his mask a jet of malevolence.

'If the Pope ever dared to emerge from behind his high walls, I would tell him precisely that. He aspires to the leadership of all Christendom, yet he's corrupt and treacherous. He pretends devotion to the cause of freeing the Holy Land from the infidels, while he sits in luxury surrounded by sycophants and does nothing. He conspires with Jews and Saracens, and shelters heretics. The fact that you associate yourself with him seals your fate in our eyes.'

The whole drama now appeared so outrageous that I was surely in the midst of a dream. It was impossible to believe that the insane ranting of these men could form any part of the real world. I stood there blinking and wondering to what further absurdities the scene could descend. The third man was speaking again.

'You have one more chance to answer. What matters were you and the Jew Zacharias discussing?'

'Nothing more sinister or conspiratorial than the nature of God and the difficulties of interpreting certain passages of Holy Scripture.'

The first speaker, the man in the centre of this triumvirate, decided to resume the attack.

'And it was your choice to visit a Jew to learn of these things? Can you not find satisfactory answers in the writings and teachings of the Christian Church?'

I sensed that the way in which I answered this question could be decisive to the outcome. I decided to equivocate.

'I am devoted to the Scriptures and to the writings of the Fathers. In fact I have with me a copy of—'

'We will ask once more. What was it that you were seeking to learn from a Jew? Or are you in fact a part of their conspiracy? What reward have they promised you for your co-operation? Wealth? Power? What part are you expected to take? Speak now.'

'I have no idea what you're talking about,' I replied. 'I—wait, I've just recognised your voice. I know who you are. You're Bernard—'

'Silence!' he screamed back at me. 'Tonight you have committed a grave crime against the Christian people of Narbonne. It is our judgement that the only outcome which will cleanse this city of your filth is death.'

In my childhood, I experienced a recurring nightmare in which I was awaiting execution for an unknown crime. No-one, friends or guards, could tell me the offence of which I had been convicted. Indeed, no-one seemed to consider it of any importance that I was innocent. As I looked at my hooded interrogators in that stuffy room, my terror of that nightmare came sweeping back. I closed my eyes and then opened them again. The same scene lay before me. I tried to speak, but could form no words. My mouth hung open.

'The sentence of death will be carried out forthwith. But it won't be yours. Your sentence is to watch the death of another. Take him outside.'

My original kidnappers dragged me back out into the street. I saw immediately opposite the figure of Zacharias. He was trussed hand and foot, and lay on the ground arched backwards, his face towards me. Our eyes met in shared horror. In my outrage, I rediscovered my voice.

'What has this man done wrong? I went to see him, not he to see me. We met at my instigation. He has committed no crime. If you must have blood, take mine.'

A voice behind me replied: 'He has committed the greatest crime of all. He and his kind murdered our Lord Jesus Christ. They all deserve to die. Your punishment is to know that you've condemned him.'

Zacharias began to cry out, then to beg for mercy. His futile pleading chilled my blood. Despite the commotion, not a soul emerged from the surrounding houses to intervene, or even to investigate out of curiosity. Were people really so fearful of the power of these insane murderers?

As Zacharias lay helpless on the ground, two of the men began to place tinder and firewood around him. He screamed with a violence which did not seem possible from his frail frame. I struggled like an animal to free myself, but my captors had no intention of releasing their grip. One of them struck me over the head, stunning me, then another set fire to the wood, and the flames began to lick around the helpless body of the Jew. Through the smoke I saw that he had stopped moving, as if frozen by terror. Then, as the fire caught his clothes and his hair, he began to scream with all his might. I had read reports of judicial burnings of heretics, but I had never imagined what it would be like to watch someone consumed by fire, and to feel utterly powerless to help. I closed my eyes and for a moment the smoke was flavoured with the smell of burning thatch.

Within a short time Zacharias stopped struggling, and I knew that his fate was sealed. Mercifully, the fire took hold with great

145

rapidity, and his death must have come quickly. As I watched his lifeless body burn, an overpowering anger came over me. It made me feel that, could I but free myself, I would take vengeance on these murderers with my own hands. But no sooner had this feeling surfaced than it was transformed into a helpless exhaustion. My legs gave way and I slumped to the ground, and the men restraining me released their grip. I lay there in a heap, my misery more profound than I would have believed possible. When I finally looked up, my captors had all melted into the night. From out of the shadows came a group of four men, by their uniforms episcopal guards. One of them poked with his sword the smouldering remains of what had been Zacharias, stared across at me with a look of naked contempt, then they all turned and strolled away.

I remained there for some time, too stunned to move. Christ's words on the cross came into my mind: 'Father, forgive them, for they know not what they do.' But in my heart there lay no wish for forgiveness for this atrocity, only for punishment and vengeance. In my exhaustion I passed out, my unconscious state punctuated by horrific visions, not just of my own childhood crime, but of a forest of funeral pyres, the screaming victim on each one bearing a remarkable resemblance to myself. It felt as if all the demons of hell had clawed their way into my mind. When eventually I came round, a small crowd of people had ventured out onto the street. As they passed by the burned and mutilated body, some stopped to stare out of curiosity, while others hurried away making the sign of the cross.

When they had dispersed, I hauled myself to my feet and walked across the street. Zacharias was barely recognisable, his flesh blackened, his few teeth standing out from his charred face, his mouth still seemingly frozen in a last cry of agony. Had he prayed to God with his dying breath? I had no idea what to do next, but somewhere inside me I knew that it would be intolerable to leave his body lying in the street for birds and dogs and flies to pick over. Taking a deep breath, I took hold of his arm, which was still warm, and tried to lift him from the ground. What my intention was God alone knows, but as I pulled, the arm detached itself from the torso. I dropped it in horror, and turned and ran with all my remaining strength.

XXIII

WHEN I REACHED HOME, PIERRE was in bed asleep. I spent what was left of the night in a chair, trembling. I prayed to God for strength and composure, but the horror remained. Each time I closed my eyes, I heard Zacharias' screams, and saw the terror and agony on his face as the flames took hold. Worst of all, I knew that I bore some responsibility for his death, simply by drawing attention to his presence. I tried to pray for the souls of those who carried out the ghastly murder, but the words would not come. The only feelings in my heart were of loathing and hatred.

Next morning, I awoke after a short period of uneasy sleep, still in my chair. Pierre was standing over me, Madeleine sweeping the floor behind him.

'Are you all right, Nicholas? Did you find out what you wanted from Zacharias?'

'No. Yes. That is . . . something happened.'

My face must have conveyed that I was still in shock. Pierre sat down next to me.

'Do you want to tell me about it?'

I thought for a moment. 'Yes, I think I do. But what I have to say is not fit for a child's ears.'

Pierre glanced over his shoulder. Madeleine stopped sweeping and looked up. Had she been older, I would say that she glared disdainfully.

'You needn't worry about Madeleine,' Pierre said. 'If she decides that she doesn't want to hear any more, she'll leave.'

I related everything which occurred from the moment I left the house of Zacharias, never lifting my eyes from the floor. At several points, my voice threatened to give way. When I came to the end of my account, Madeleine turned away and carried on sweeping. Pierre sat back.

'I did warn you that you'd be in danger if you visited Zacharias.'

'I'd be in danger? All that happened to me was that my emotions were shaken. What did that poor man do to deserve the death he suffered?'

'Anti-Jewish feeling has been growing here,' Pierre said. 'The Jews always get the blame when things go wrong. Isn't it the same in England?'

I clasped my hands. 'There are no Jews left in England. They were expelled, by royal decree.'

'Hmm. Well that's one way of saving their lives, I suppose. To be honest, I don't know why the Jews don't all go to Granada, or some land where the Turks are rulers. They'd be much better treated there. There's no-one more anti-Jewish than an uneducated Christian.'

'But Pierre, you must have known Zacharias, otherwise you wouldn't have advised me to go and see him.'

'I put it forward as a suggestion, Nicholas, if you were really determined to pursue this Qabbalah nonsense.'

'But doesn't what happened to him mean anything to you? An innocent man was brutally murdered.'

Pierre leaned forward.

'Just recently, I've watched several times a day while innocent people, or as innocent as they can be, died in torment. So have you. How do we know why it happens to one person and not another? Until God chooses to explain His mysterious ways to me, which I suspect won't be in the near future, I'll get on with my work. You may want to consider doing the same.'

After a period of reflection, I resolved that the threats of those like Zacharias' murderers must not intimidate me from carrying out my duties as before. Pierre and I were both kept so busy that we had very little time to talk. After hearing his response to the Jew's death, I was grateful for this.

By the time the plague had raged for a few weeks, supplies of basic commodities such as meat and flour no longer arrived in the city. I noted, however, that in the houses of the well-to-do, stocks remained more than adequate. In those of the poor, hunger and malnourishment were commonplace. More often than not, the latter blamed not the rich, who were clearly hoarding at their expense, but the Jews.

One night, as I lay in bed, rain began to play upon the roof. I welcomed it as a means of washing away some of the insanitary remains which lay in the streets, dead rats, uncleared refuse and such like. In fact, I have always found the dull thud of raindrops soporific, and it soon lulled me into a peaceful sleep.

Next morning, the rain was still falling, but more heavily. The mixture of humidity and the oppressive heat of high summer made any exertion debilitating, and I found my pace slowing each time I walked through the streets. When I arrived at the house of one Jacqueline, a seamstress with a plague-stricken daughter, she looked out at the lead-grey sky.

'God really must be punishing us for something. What do you suppose we've done to displease Him?'

'I really can't say. I only arrived at the same time as the plague.'

'Do you think it's because we've let the Jews stay here? That's what I heard one of our magistrates say.'

'Well, who knows? The Lord works in mysterious ways. Now, perhaps you could show me to your daughter.'

'What? Oh, she's through there. But it won't do any good. Father Pierre has already prayed over her, and she's got no better. If anything, she's worse.'

I gritted my teeth. 'Well, in that case, what are you expecting me to do that Father Pierre has not already done?'

.'Oh, I don't know, but it can't do any harm, can it? Maybe God will listen to you.'

'Look, if you think—'

'Hang on.' Jacqueline's eyes widened and her lower jaw dropped. 'Did you say you arrived at the same time as the plague? Perhaps you brought it with you, did you think of that? I think you'd better go after all. I'll leave my daughter's fate to God, thank you very much.'

The rain continued as heavily as ever, until the streets were awash. One by one, people emerged from their houses and began to dance and revel, carousing and generally behaving as if suffering from some delirium. I went up to a group and asked why they were in such high spirits, given the death and suffering still going on around them.

'It's obvious, isn't it?' one said. 'The rain will wash away the plague. We've survived. It's a miracle. Praise be to God.'

'Wait. What makes you think that rain can remove the plague?'

'It stands to reason. The plague's caused by putrid vapours, a physician told me. All of a sudden, the air smells fresh and clean. Here, my friend, have a drink with us.'

My way home took me across the River Aude. I stood on a bridge and saw that the water was rising rapidly. It was still some way from overflowing the banks but perhaps, in the chaotic conditions of the plague, no-one was operating the gates upstream which normally regulated the flow of water through the city. I looked up, blinking as raindrops struck my eyes, and tried to estimate how many more hours of precipitation would be needed to bring about a catastrophe.

When I reached Pierre's house, he was sitting and staring through the window. Outside, people were still celebrating, apparently oblivious to the new threat they faced. Despite the heat, Pierre had lit a fire, or more likely Madeleine had, in order to counteract the dampness which had soaked into everything. I stood before it, steam rising from my clothes.

'I'm afraid,' I said, 'that unless the rain stops soon, the river's going to burst its banks. As if the people need any further calamity.'

Pierre sat nursing a cup of wine, his face downcast. He looked more wretched than I had seen him.

'Let's hope it sweeps the whole city away, and us with it.'

I had not been asleep long when the first anguished cries began to ring through the streets. Pierre and I arrived at the door at the same moment. We could see very little in the darkness, but could hardly fail to hear the sounds of fear and chaos. We headed towards the river, but did not have to go far before it became clear that many houses near its banks, most of which were of one storey, had been inundated. Rain was still falling, and even if it were to cease immediately the level would continue to rise for some time.

We helped those few families who were trying to load their worldly belongings onto carts, although where they were planning to take them I suspect even they had no idea. Most families, however, stood dazed among the sodden wreckage, seemingly lacking any initiative to help themselves. It was as if the plague had robbed them of self-will, had trapped them within a paralysing fatalism.

As the water continued to rise, we were forced to move back, and I began to fear for Pierre's own house. The rain began to ease just as the first rays of sun crept over the eastern horizon, and within about an hour ceased completely. As the light grew stronger, we were shocked to see that not only Narbonne's human population was displaced by the flood. From drains and crevices in all directions, rats were emerging, whole families escaping from the water which had doubtless also submerged their homes. We leapt back as they streamed past us, although in their panic they seemed barely conscious of our presence. They headed uphill, away from the river, many making for areas of the city which so far had been little touched by the plague. I surmised that some less fortunate creatures must have been swept downriver by the flood. Should they have survived, and I had heard that they were strong swimmers, this made it possible that they would carry the plague to areas outside the city.

In the full light of day, the extent of the devastation became clear. Every house within sight of the river, it seemed, had been inundated. Many people wept and wailed in the streets. I looked on helpless as an old woman waded to where the river bank had previously been, looked to the heavens, raised her arms to her sides, then slowly toppled forward into the swollen river. She floated downstream in the rapid current, face down, without any hint of a struggle. Pierre and I watched in exhausted silence until she drifted out of view.

'Where's your precious God now?' The voice emanated from a young man standing nearby. 'Not in this city, is He? Maybe He escaped with the Archbishop.'

Through my weariness I managed to say, 'God never abandons His people.'

'Unlike the Archbishop,' Pierre added.

We turned to go, but the young man had not finished with us.

'I don't know why you priests didn't all leave as well. We'd be better off without you. You can't save us from disaster, nothing can. The best thing we can do is to drown all the Jews, and after them you lot can be next on the list.'

Having threatened us with death, he then proceeded to kick floodwater at us. Pierre and I trudged homewards.

When we arrived back at the house, the river was half-way across the street outside. We were too exhausted to care whether it came any closer. Around mid-day when we arose, it was lapping against the threshold. Madeleine appeared from the kitchen and joined us at the door.

'It's been there for a while,' she said. 'It seems to have stopped rising.'

XXIV

THAT DAY WAS THE HOTTEST of the summer so far, but merely the forerunner, as it turned out, of a succession of such days. So intense was the heat that it became painful to remain out of the shade for any period of time. Although the flooded houses quickly began to dry, the elemental combination of heat and humidity proved too much for the flimsy construction of many, so that they either collapsed of their own volition, or became too dangerous for their former occupants to re-enter. For many, homelessness was thus added to the litany of miseries which Narbonne's people had already suffered.

Even worse, the innocent optimism of those who believed the rain would stem the spread of the plague quickly proved misplaced. Pierre and I estimated that we had each visited several hundred plague victims since the start of the outbreak. Across the city as a whole, the death toll must now run into many thousands. We gave up any pretence that we could reach every bedside before the moment of death, and resigned ourselves to praying posthumously for the salvation of many souls.

The streets were now thick with the stench of death. As I walked through them it seemed to cling like a viscous fluid. Even after I arrived home its overpowering odour refused to dissipate, as if it had permeated my clothes, my hair and my skin. Inside many of the houses the smell was almost unbearable, particularly those where the victim had been dead for some hours. This being not many weeks after the summer solstice, there were not enough hours of darkness to bury all the dead at night, so the authorities took certain unspecified measures to dispose of bodies in other ways. Perhaps by coincidence, perhaps not, we began to see a number of corpses floating downriver.

One morning, Pierre rose early and retired to the small room which he had adopted as his study. Concerned after a while that he might be ill, I found him sitting at his desk with pen in hand.

On the surface were small scraps of parchment on which, as far as I could see, he had scribbled a random selection of words and phrases.

'Are you all right, Pierre?'

He put the pen down and rubbed his eyes.

'Yes, Nicholas. I'm going to do something I should have done a while ago.'

'Would you care to be more specific?'

He turned towards me with a peculiar look in his eyes, as if I had spoken to him in an incomprehensible language. After a few moments, his expression softened.

'You know, the people are right in a way. We have failed them.'

'The Archbishop has failed them. As far as I can see, ordinary priests are fully occupied in trying to minister to their needs.'

'In one way, yes. But don't you see, the people believe that either there are answers, which we're keeping secret for our own nefarious reasons, or else that we're just as ignorant as they are. Either way, it's not surprising they're turning so hostile towards us.'

'So what do you intend to do?'

'As I said, what I should have done a long time ago. I'm going to tell them the truth, in simple words they can understand.'

'The truth about what, Pierre?'

'Follow me and find out.'

He strode past me, out the front door and into the street. After a moment's hesitation I decided that I had better do as he suggested, and went after him. For a man of his age he could still show a remarkable turn of pace when the occasion demanded. Although I had not noticed him pick it up, he carried with him a hand bell which from time to time he rang vigorously. People came out to investigate the source of the disturbance and, seeing who was responsible, followed behind in curiosity. By the time we reached the main square a sizeable crowd was in attendance, with more joining all the time. Pierre ran up the main steps of the cathedral and turned to face the crowd. He beckoned me to join him, which I did, to be honest, with some trepidation.

'Don't you need some sort of authority to do this?' I asked behind my hand.

'From whom? Our Archbishop?'

He waited until the whole crowd pressed forward within hearing distance, then raised his arms to still the hubbub.

'My friends, you are all God's people, never forget that. God certainly doesn't, even if it may seem that at this moment He's not paying much attention.'

The crowd responded with murmurs of approval, presumably of the second part of Pierre's opening statement.

'Some have told you that the plague which has cursed Narbonne has been sent by God as a punishment for the exceptional sinfulness of its people. Do you believe that?'

A number of his listeners replied in the affirmative.

'There are those who argue that the plague is somehow the work of the Jews. Do you believe that?'

A considerably louder roar provided the response to this question. It took some time to restore silence.

'I don't blame you for looking for reasons to explain the misery which has befallen us. You wouldn't be human if you didn't. So far, the Church hasn't provided you with any answers. And those who are supposed to be experts in medicine have no more idea how to cure someone suffering from the plague than the rest of us.'

At that moment I happened to catch sight of Esteban the physician at the back of the crowd. Not surprisingly, he was frowning. Pierre was warming to his theme.

'Well, today I'm going to start putting that right. And I'll begin with a couple of important truths, things which I have to tell you before I can help you to understand.

'I've travelled extensively throughout this land, as has my young colleague Nicholas here, and on one thing we agree. The people of this city are, on the whole, no more and no less sinful than those of any other. There are people carrying a heavier burden of sin than you in the Papal Palace at Avignon.'

He paused to allow the import of his words to sink in. The crowd seemed stunned.

'So, why was Narbonne singled out to suffer in this way? Why not Béziers, why not Carcassonne? I'll tell you why. Because God does not work in that way. He does not punish whole cities for the wrongdoings of their inhabitants. Oh, I grant you, He may have done so in Old Testament times, at least that's what we read. But if you imagine that God spends His days keeping watch over us like a gaoler observing his prisoners, then you've understood nothing of what your priests have been teaching you for all these years.

'So, if it's not a punishment from God, then there must be a more down-to-earth explanation, mustn't there? Perhaps it is the Jews, as many of you seem to think. But if so, there's just one thing which troubles me. If they knew in advance that the plague was coming, why didn't they all get out before it started? As far as I can see, the Jewish quarter remains fully occupied, and they've been just as likely to get sick as the rest of us.'

'We should still kick them out,' a voice called out.

'Kill them. Kill them all.'

These interjections were met with a roar of acclaim. Pierre crossed his arms, and waited for it to run its course. I shuddered as I recalled the fate of poor Zacharias, and became concerned that Pierre had inadvertently incited the crowd to vent their anger on the rest of Narbonne's Jews. Pierre knew his people better than I did.

'Enough. Just listen to yourselves. Driven mad by fear and anger, and determined to take it out on anyone you can lay hands on. You're like a pack of wolves. Haven't you listened to a word I've said?

'Tell me something. Were the people whose misery was compounded by losing everything they owned in the flood even more sinful than the rest of you? Of course they weren't. They suffered because, by chance or by choice since their livelihood was there, they lived next to the river. Or do you imagine the Jews were responsible for causing the river to burst its banks as well? I could have sworn it was the fault of the men who failed to operate the flood gates upriver.

'Don't you see what you're doing? You're blaming God or the Jews or anyone else you can think of for misfortunes which we ourselves could have avoided. We could have prevented the flood by dredging the river to increase its flow and, incidentally, improve our trade by allowing ships to reach our harbour more easily, but the city's authorities kept putting it off because no-one wanted to pay for it. We wouldn't have so many rats if we didn't fill our streets with stinking, decaying refuse. We could do things to help ourselves, but we prefer to sit back and blame God or the Jews.'

Some of the audience were looking down at their feet. Esteban was smiling.

'I could advise you to repent of your sins, which are many, or give money to the Church. But any passing friar could tell you that, and for all your failings you deserve better. God is inscrutable, I'll give you that. I've been studying His workings for over fifty years, and sometimes I feel that I've learned nothing, that I can learn nothing. But think of the example of our Lord, Jesus Christ. He was God's own son. Yet still on the cross he could cry out to his father, "My God, my God, why have You forsaken me?" Unlike us, Jesus was sinless, and he suffered far greater injustices than you at the hands of those who hated him. When you see someone tormented by the agonies of the plague, think of the agony of Jesus Christ nailed to the cross, the crown of thorns biting into his head, the nails burning into his hands and feet, feeling his life-blood draining from his cruel wounds. And when you have contemplated that for a good long time, then you can come and tell me how unjust God is.'

Without waiting for the reaction to these words, Pierre turned and marched through the west door of the cathedral. Many of the crowd stared at me, as if I had been left to continue and complete Pierre's message. At the back of the crowd, Esteban slowly walked away. I followed Pierre into the cathedral.

XXV

Someone was hammering on the door. I rubbed my eyes, hauled myself out of bed and found outside a young woman pacing up and down in some agitation.

'I need Father Pierre,' she said.

'Father Pierre's away on his duties. I work alongside him.'

'Then you'll have to do. It's my father. Come with me, quickly.'

She led me to a house in the street of carpenters, outside which a crowd had gathered. At an upstairs window stood an old man, totally naked. When he saw me approaching, he pointed and shrieked.

'Get away from me, priest. This is no place for a man of God. This is the house of the devil.'

'My friend,' I said, 'I'm sure there is no devil in your house, but I'll come and check if you like.'

'No, it's too late. I'm doomed. He wants my soul, and I'm going to give it to him.'

'I can assure you that the fate of your soul is in the hands of God, not the devil.'

The man placed one foot on the frame of the window as if preparing to jump. I turned to the woman who had led me there.

'How long has he been like this?'

'My father's been getting more and more deranged for the last week. He's convinced he's got the plague, even though he hasn't. He believes he's damned.'

From the corner of my eye I saw a dark shape plunge towards the ground. The old man lay spread-eagled face down, motionless. The crowd rushed forward, then drew back having presumably satisfied themselves that he was indeed dead. A pool of blood was forming around his head. His daughter began to weep uncontrollably. I made the sign of the cross, and one of the bystanders produced a blanket with which to cover him.

His daughter clutched my sleeve, still trembling. I allowed her to weep into my shoulder.

'I'm afraid,' I said, 'that many more in this city will be gripped by insanity before the plague releases its hold on us. At least your father is at rest.'

'Will God punish him for taking his own life?' she asked through her sobs.

Strangely, this aspect of his untimely death had not even occurred to me.

'God's mercy is infinite.' Hopefully, I might have added, but bit my tongue.

Over the following days, several similar incidents took place. It seemed that men were more likely to lose their minds than women, for reasons which were not altogether clear. I saw smoke rising from one house, and at the door a man holding a blazing torch. If anyone approached to try to drag him away, he held them at bay by brandishing the torch at them. He stood in the doorway, silent and resolute, while the house was consumed. As the flames took hold of his clothing, and soon afterwards his flesh, he showed no emotion, did not cry out in pain. When the fire finally burned itself out, the charred remains of his children, apparently bound by ropes, were discovered inside. An equally charred dog was lying across one of them. I crouched in the smoking ruins with the ashes scorching my feet, not daring to close my eyes.

Pierre told me of an equally harrowing case which he witnessed. A man dragged his screaming wife onto the main bridge across the Aude, holding at bay with a knife anyone who tried to intervene. The woman held something in her arms. With the knife at her throat, he forced her onto the parapet, then climbed up alongside and pushed her into the water. Moments later, he followed. As she screamed and struggled in the current, he grabbed her by the hair and held her under until her struggles ceased. He himself then disappeared beneath the surface, and was not seen again. When their bodies were washed ashore later, it transpired that the bundle in the woman's arms was a new-born baby.

The question of how God would treat the souls of those guilty of these deranged acts of suicide and murder now began to exercise me greatly. That they committed mortal crimes was beyond dispute, and yet so extreme had conditions in the city become, and so great the anxiety of its inhabitants, that some had clearly lost the ability to make reasoned decisions. I prayed for their souls, and hoped that God in His mercy would take some account of the circumstances in which their crimes were committed. Surely they had even more reason to consider their lives intolerable than Brother John, and I had pleaded with God to have mercy on his soul.

But if these events constituted an unexpected effect of the extraordinary suffering of the city and its people, another was becoming all too predictable.

I was walking home from the centre of the city when I heard a commotion in the distance, the yelling of angry voices. A few moments later, a group of about twenty people, men, women and children, all Jewish to judge from their appearance, came running across the square in front of the cathedral. Hot in pursuit was a mob of about a hundred men and a few women, some waving cudgels, all calling for blood. The Jews were heading for the west door of the cathedral, the men now carrying the younger children, and reached it just as the mob began to ascend the steps.

I ran through a side door and saw the Jews huddled together next to the altar, the adults wide-eyed with fear, the children weeping, whilst several of the cathedral canons stood between them and the mob. I thought of Zacharias and, after a moment's hesitation, realised that I could not stand aside whatever the outcome, so I moved forward and joined the canons, who seemed paralysed by what was happening in front of them. Those at the front of the mob were shrieking for us to stand aside.

'Wait,' I cried with as much resolution as I could muster. 'These people have claimed the sanctuary of God's altar. How dare you threaten to profane it? Go now, leave the house of God.'

For a moment there was silence, then a man in the forefront of the mob thrust his cudgel towards me and said, 'Get out of our way, or we'll kill you too.'

There was a cry of acclaim from behind him.

'What are you accusing them of? What's their crime?'

'Being Jewish, you fool. Now stand aside, we're coming to take them.'

He walked forward and I put my hands out in front of me. He struck me on the arm and then, as I sank to my knees, my head.

I fell to the ground, lying helpless as the crowd surged over and around me. A violent kick landed in my ribs. As my head throbbed, somewhere in the distance the Jews were screaming for mercy.

It seemed that I lost consciousness for a while. When I was able to drag myself to my feet, the cathedral was empty. I made my way to the west door, lurching from pillar to pillar, and emerged into the open just in time to see the Jews being dragged towards the river. I limped after and arrived at the river bank in time to see them, now gagged and bound hand and foot, thrown one by one into the current, to cheers from the mob. Their desperate struggles were to no avail, and my fellow Christians laughed as they drowned, especially the children.

When their sport was over, the crowd drifted away. One man walked directly towards me, and I recognised him as the kidnapper who had struck me across the face when I was hauled before the so-called People's Inquisition. As he walked past, he grinned and spat at my feet.

When they had all dispersed, I saw a diminutive figure standing on the bank, staring down into the murky water. I shuffled forward and placed my hand on her shoulder, wincing as pain shot up my arm.

'This is no place for you, Madeleine. No-one of your age should have to witness evil like this.'

She looked up, and I could read no emotion in her eyes.

'Apparently,' she said, 'the Jews were all together because they were mourning the death of a child from the plague. That's not a crime, is it?'

'In the eyes of some, the Jews will always be guilty of the greatest of crimes even when they've done nothing wrong. I'm sorry you had to see this at first hand. Sometimes it's hard to understand how people can descend to such evil.'

She tilted her head so that it rested on my hand.

'I already know about the evil of this world, Nicholas. Sometimes I think death must be a welcome release from it.'

'A girl of twelve shouldn't be saying such a thing. You've got many years of life ahead of you. You'll have a husband and children. You'll find there's beauty and goodness in this world too.'

We watched as the last of the bodies of the drowned Jews disappeared from our view downriver.

'Not in Narbonne,' she said.

I walked her home and we talked no more. The pain in my ribs made me struggle for breath. From time to time Madeleine looked up, but said nothing. When we reached her house, she stopped at the door.

'Will the people who killed the Jews go to hell?' she asked.

'That's up to God, who sees inside all our hearts. But unless they genuinely repent of their crime and ask for His forgiveness, I fear that they'll be punished at the Last Judgement.'

'I sometimes think we push God's forgiveness too far,' she said, and went inside.

XXVI

WHEN I GOT HOME, PIERRE and Esteban were deep in discussion, a wine bottle on the table between them. Esteban was sporting a bruised eye. They looked up as I eased myself gingerly into a chair.

'Before you ask,' I said, 'I'll be all right, and I haven't got the plague.'

'What happened to you?' Pierre asked, pouring me some wine.

I related my experience, wincing and grimacing as Esteban established that I had not, as I feared, suffered any broken ribs.

'It was foolish of you to intervene,' Pierre said. 'You can't reason with a mob. All they know is blind hatred.'

'Would you have just stood back and watched, like the cathedral canons?'

'What were they supposed to do? Ask an angry, violent crowd to sit down and have a reasoned discussion? You've seen for yourself that they'd think no more of killing us than killing Jews.' Pierre took a deep breath and leaned forward, resting his forearms on his knees. 'You're a good man, Nicholas, you always want to do what's right. Maybe in that respect you're a better priest than I am. But I'm afraid you're getting out of your depth. This is the second time that you could have lost your life because you intervened on behalf of Jews. Just have a care. Our chances of surviving this plague are slim enough as it is.'

'Speaking of which,' Esteban added, 'I hear that the city authorities have given up trying to arrange any kind of decent burial for plague victims. All the cemeteries are full, so they're digging a huge pit outside the western boundary of the city. From now on, bodies will just be tipped into it, then covered with lime and earth.'

'I've heard nothing of this,' Pierre said.

'What do you expect them to do, send a crier to announce it through the streets? All the people care about is keeping the bodies as far from themselves as possible. No-one's going to ask any questions.'

'Are you any nearer,' I asked Esteban, 'to finding a cure for the plague?'

'No.'

'Or any measures to help prevent its spread? When the plague first appeared—'

'Yes, I know what I said when it first appeared. Now I don't know. Every time the plague breaks out in a new area, it seems to be different, as if it's one step ahead of us, anticipating our every move. Historic remedies which have been used in previous outbreaks are now totally ineffective. As physicians, we're working in the dark, making it up as we go along.'

'But just supposing,' I said, glancing at Pierre, 'if it actually is a punishment from God, then it's hardly surprising that our best efforts are confounded.'

Esteban glared. 'Those things are for you priests to sort out. All I know is that people are becoming sick, and they expect physicians to make them better. If they want a bone set or a hernia fixed, it's not a problem. But if they succumb to something that's going to kill them, they just want someone to make it right, otherwise they'll take it out on whoever's around.' He pointed to his bruised eye, then turned to Pierre. 'You were right when you gave your open-air sermon the other day. You and I are equally helpless, and the people hate us for it. They want someone to take charge and make it all go away. When no-one does, they turn on the nearest available scapegoat. And before long, when they've run out of Jews, that could be us.'

At dawn the next morning, nursing my aching body, I walked out to the western wall of the city to see the new repository for the bodies of plague victims which Esteban told us about. My nose discovered it before my eyes, a colossal hole in the ground which, judging from the stench which reached even the city walls, might as well have descended all the way to hell. I covered my nose and mouth and wished I still had one of Madeleine's nosegays of flowers and herbs. The covering of the bodies had been perfunctory, and even in the cool morning air I could not bear the smell for long. I stayed just long enough to say a short prayer for the souls of those whose mortal remains had been disposed of in such ignominious manner.

As I walked back through one of the more prosperous areas of Narbonne, I saw that several streets had been turned into open-air markets. Traders were selling from carts in the middle of the roadway, fruit, cheeses, wines and other foodstuffs, and what were now luxury items such as pottery and clothing. I wondered at the amount of money changing hands, and compared the situation here with the dearth of even the most basic necessities which afflicted the city's poorer households. The merchants had presumably smuggled their goods in by boat or bribed the guards to open the gates for them, deciding that the risk of contracting the plague was worth the large and quick profit which they could make from these transactions. For the first time it occurred to me that on numerous occasions money had no doubt changed hands at the gates under cover of darkness to allow passage in the opposite direction. My presence began to attract a number of hostile glances, and I decided to leave.

The sun was already burning my skin, and I knew that the families of plague victims would be calling to demand the presence of a priest. Nevertheless, I felt unbearably weary in both mind and body, and needed time to collect myself. Walking on a little further, I sat in the shade at the foot of a huge plane tree.

For the first time since my arrival in Avignon, I felt a pressing need to collect my thoughts about the experiences which seemed about to overwhelm me. Father Simon had suggested that I led too sheltered a life in Croyland, that my faith needed to be tested in the crucible of all that the outside world could send to challenge it. Surely even he in his wisdom could not have foreseen how far his words would be borne out by events.

St Augustine had concluded from his reading of St Paul and from his own experience that we are born carrying a burden of sin which, however hard we try, we cannot shake off through our own unaided efforts. Even when we try to do what is good, we are unable to escape from the power of our own desires and our own needs. In recent weeks, I had seen instances of savage cruelty which I would not have believed possible in my former life at Croyland. In that sense, my Abbot had been proved right. Yet my own outlook on the eternal battle between good and evil had, I recognised, undergone some changes.

I found myself reflecting upon my encounter with Esclarmonde at the start of my journey, a girl whom, at one time, I would have considered steeped in sin. And yet my memories of her were fond ones; she had little choice but to live the life she did, given the circumstances in which she found herself. I now saw that she had spoken truthfully when she implied that the rich and the powerful, who generally dictate the situation of the poor and the powerless, have a great deal more to answer for.

Inevitably, my thoughts moved to Madeleine. Pierre said that her father had determined to sell her into service, and the cold reality was that this would probably have condemned her to a fate similar to that of Esclarmonde. I felt powerless to argue against the conclusions of St Augustine, a man clearly much closer to God than I, but it now seemed to me that men and women were constrained by worldly factors limiting the degree of control they could exercise over their own lives. If a man were ordered by his lord to take up arms against the innocent, what choice would he have? If a serving-girl were instructed to act as a whore, would she really have the option of protecting her virtue by refusing to comply?

I leaned back against the tree's cool, smooth trunk and closed my eyes. Above all, I felt exhaustion like I had never known. It could be many months before the plague ran its course, and it seemed certain that further acts of murder, insanity and suicide would take place. So far, my faith in God's goodness had been damaged but not broken. Everything I believed in depended on sustaining that faith. In the classroom at Croyland, when asked why a benign, loving God allowed evil and suffering to flourish on the earth, I had always known to reply that these were the consequences of man's own sinfulness, as epitomised by the fall of Adam and Eve in the Garden of Eden. In Narbonne, where death and pain were the daily reality for every inhabitant, that reply fell on deaf ears.

I was roused from my thoughts by an irritated voice.

'Hey, priest, you should be saying prayers for the dead, not wasting time sleeping.'

I lacked the strength or the will to open my eyes.

'In the words of our Lord: "Leave the dead to bury the dead."'

XXVII

IN THE RELENTLESS HEAT OF summer, with the plague refusing to relinquish its grip, the days seemed to merge with one another to the extent that we ceased to recognise any kind of calendar. The anger and violence which characterised the early period had, if anything, died down a little, to be replaced by a sullen indifference. The rattling of the plague cart no longer attracted any attention. Most forms of gainful employment were impossible, so people resigned themselves to getting by as best they could and waiting for the end, however long, and whatever form, that might take.

I arrived at one house just as Esteban was leaving. I asked him why, despite his advice to us, he seemed to have taken no measures to protect himself against the spread of the plague.

'Physicians who took every precaution they could have died just like those who took none at all. Priests who stopped visiting the sick because they were afraid have still died. We may as well be honest, Nicholas, there's nothing we can do. We're either going to die or we're not. Maybe God knows, I certainly don't.'

Inside the house was a boy in whom the disease was well advanced. He had a high fever, dark blotches all over his body and large, hard swellings in his armpits and groin. As always, the very air smelled infected.

I was about to begin the words of Extreme Unction when something on a table in the corner of the room caught my eye. I walked over and discovered a crude wax carving which, in a certain light, could have been an attempted depiction of the boy. I noted that his parents shrank back when I held it out to them and asked them to explain it.

'A young man came to our door,' the father said after some hesitation. 'He said he was the seventh son of a seventh son, he'd heard we had a sick child and he wanted to do something to help. He carved this in front of us, then said some words we couldn't understand. He said the image would slowly draw the sickness out of him, but it wouldn't happen at once. We have to be patient.'

I looked at the boy, then back at them.

'I hope for your son's sake that it doesn't take much longer. How much did you pay this young man?'

'Everything we had.'

At that moment I didn't know whether to be more angry with the couple for their foolishness, or with the charlatan who had taken advantage of them.

'So, if you've already placed your faith in this—this object, why have you asked me to come?'

The woman cast down her eyes. 'Just in case.'

Later in the day, I saw a youth emerge from a house with a rough hemp bag slung over his shoulder. He looked both ways along the street before he moved off. I walked after him.

'Slow down, friend,' I called out. 'You seem to be in a great hurry in this heat.'

He stopped and looked me up and down.

'What's it to you?'

'I just want to offer some friendly advice. That bag looks heavy.'

'I can manage it, thanks for your concern.'

'Why don't you let me carry it for you a little way.'

'No. Get away from me.'

He turned on his heel, but I grabbed him by the shoulder.

'What have you got in there? Not something you've stolen, I hope.'

'None of your business.'

He tried to elbow me in the stomach, but I twisted away and managed to grab the bag from his shoulder, emptying out the contents as I did so. He stopped in his tracks. There on the ground were a number of wax candles, some already shaped into the crudest semblance of human form.

The youth swung his fists at me and I leapt backwards, but he stumbled as his foot slipped on the candles. I grabbed him by the throat and forced him to the edge of the street, pinning him against a tree.

'I'm taking a good look at your face, and if I ever see you again, I will take your head from your shoulders and worry about asking for God's forgiveness afterwards. Do you understand me?'

His lips trembled, but he was unable to form any reply. The fear in his eyes was real enough. I released my grip, and when he had recovered his breath he ran with all his strength.

The commotion had drawn some of the street's residents out to watch. I replaced the candles in the bag and asked one of them to fetch me a torch. When he had done so, I set fire to the bag and watched the melting contents spread across the ground. I walked away, sensing several sets of confused eyes watching my back.

That night, after Madeleine had prepared our supper and left, Pierre and I sat outside as the air began to cool. The city was silent, but it was a silence born of unease and fear rather than peace and rest. Or so I felt. Pierre seemed to have noticed nothing, in fact by this stage of our confinement within the city he rarely showed any emotion about or towards anything or anyone, apart from Madeleine.

After we had sat for some time without speaking, I said to him:

'I wonder how you keep going, Pierre. For me, this is a nightmare interlude in my life: either I'll wake up when it's all over, or I'll be dead. For you, Narbonne is all there is. You've nowhere to escape to.'

'What's your point?'

'My point is, you don't seem to be moved by anything. When people die, you say some words over them, then move on to the next house. Whether they're old or young, it's all the same. Whatever the city's thrown at you, at the end of the day you sit here with some wine and then prepare to do it all over again.'

'And what else do you suggest I do?'

Pierre stared hard, waiting for an answer.

'I'd like to tell you something,' I said. 'Earlier today, I caught a man using deceit to persuade the parents of sick children to part with money, by selling them a candle carved into the rough shape of a child and then reciting some nonsense over it. I lost my temper with him and threatened to kill him.'

'At least he'll think twice before trying that one again.'

'Hopefully, but that's not the point. I'm telling this to you as my confessor. For a minute or so, I completely lost control of myself. I, a man of God's Church.'

Pierre drained his cup. 'Perhaps, but you also saved a lot of poor people from parting with money they can't afford. In the end, you did some good. Anyway, this situation is slowly driving us all crazy. We'll probably both have done worse things than that before it's over.'

'But you manage to stay calm.'

'Do I? Let me tell you something, Nicholas. Since the plague arrived, there hasn't been a day when I haven't wished it had turned up somewhere else and killed the people of some other city. But here we are, both of us, caught in the wrong place at the wrong time, so we just get on with what needs to be done. What else is there?'

I refilled my cup. Pierre held out his.

'Tell me something, Pierre. Do you still believe in the same God you did before all this happened?'

'You mean, as opposed to the God of some other religion? The Saracens, maybe?'

'You know exactly what I mean.'

He sank back in his chair and stared up at the sky.

'All right. If you want an honest answer, I've pushed consideration of such matters to one side. I'll return to it when all this is over, if I'm still alive.' He looked out towards the city. 'People like us will never be proclaimed saints, Nicholas. Those who sit at God's right hand in Avignon don't even know that we exist. Well, that I exist. But our faith is tested every day in the fires of hell. We know more about the nature of God than all the theologians in Paris or Oxford. We see His works in all their glory before our eyes, and sometimes we hate what we see.'

XXVIII

THE CITY HELD ITS BREATH as the suffocating days of summer drew to a close. Although reliable figures were hard to come by, with the advent of the cooler winds of early autumn came the first tantalising signs that the number of new victims was no longer growing, perhaps even starting to fall away. Not that Pierre and I saw any diminution in our workload, but a few people began to clean and repair their houses, clear weeds from their vegetable patch, or mend their clothes. It was as if, for the first time in months, the people of Narbonne began to see that they might have a future.

One morning, Madeleine arrived earlier than usual.

'Father has fallen ill,' she said. I expected her to burst into tears but she remained calm, as if she had told us that he had a slight headache. 'Perhaps you could call round later, Father Pierre.'

'My child,' he said, 'I'll come straight away.'

'There's no need,' she said. 'It's the plague. His condition won't change for hours, perhaps days.'

She went through to the kitchen and began preparing breakfast. Pierre followed her, avoiding my gaze.

When I returned later in the day, Pierre was sitting with Madeleine.

'How is your father?' I asked her.

Pierre gave her no opportunity to reply. 'Antoine is weakening. I've told Madeleine that she will always have a home here, for as long as she needs it.'

Given that he had just pronounced the imminent death of her father, the girl still seemed strangely unmoved.

'Of course,' I said. 'Madeleine is almost a member of the family already. It will be like having a daughter.'

'And I'm looking forward to having a new father,' she said, and threw her arms around Pierre's neck. He saw my puzzled frown and, almost imperceptibly, shook his head. To my greater surprise, he went on to say that he had arranged for Madeleine to move in immediately to reduce the risk of her catching the disease from her father. Pierre himself would look after Antoine for whatever time remained. I offered to give up my room, but he insisted that he would make up a bed for her in his own.

That night, while Pierre was out ministering to Antoine, Madeleine and I sat in front of the fire, the first lit in that hearth since the flood.

'You must be very worried about your father, Madeleine.'

She shrugged. 'There's not much point worrying. He'll be dead soon anyway.'

'There are rumours circulating that one or two people in the city who seemed to be dying have actually recovered. It's possible that the plague is beginning to lose some of its force.'

'Perhaps. But my father's going to die. Father Pierre won't let him suffer.'

I repeated her words in my mind to make sure that I had heard correctly. Her face showed not a line of anxiety.

Pierre did not return that night, and I slept fitfully. I could hear Madeleine turning over and over, at times crying out in her sleep. At dawn the front door opened, and I found Pierre looking as if it were he himself at death's door. Blood-red eyes were sunken into an ashen face. Without a word, he went to the kitchen and poured himself some wine. We sat in silence for some time. His hands were shaking.

'Is Antoine dead?' I asked.

He nodded, his eyes fixed upon the table.

'Then he died remarkably quickly. God in His mercy ensured that he didn't suffer for too long.'

'Is Madeleine still sleeping?'

'I believe so. Not surprisingly, she's had a restless night. Now you need to get some rest, Pierre. I'll break the news to her when she wakes.'

Pierre, for the first time since I met him, looked weary beyond endurance. He finished his wine and, without a word, collapsed into a chair near the remnants of the fire. I covered him with a blanket and left him.

When Madeleine started to move around, I waited a few minutes, then went into her room. She was stretching, looking out of the window.

'I have some bad news, Madeleine. Your father has died.'

She kept her back to me. 'Yes. I know.'

'I'll pray for his soul.'

'If you like.'

'Is there anything you want me to do, Madeleine? Are there other family members who need to know?'

'No, there's no-one. But thank you.'

I walked across and stood alongside her. She was watching the death cart make its way back from its macabre night's work.

'You don't seem very distressed by your father's death. Perhaps it'll take time to sink in.'

She turned around to look at me, smiling. 'Yes. I expect it will.'

I went to close the door behind me, then paused.

'Madeleine, how did you already know that your father was dead?'

'I heard Father Pierre return.'

In the ensuing days, word spread that the plague was receding, even though the numbers dying each day were still as high as in the early weeks of its ravages. People began to appear on the streets in small groups rather than as furtive individuals, sometimes smiling and laughing together. One paradoxical consequence of the slow decline in the number of new victims was that the family of those who did succumb would feel an even greater sense of injustice. It reminded me of the plight of soldiers who, days after the battle is won, discover that the wound they received on the field has proved to be a mortal one.

Although I continued to recite the rite of Extreme Unction with monotonous frequency, still it was hard not to feel a glimmer of hope that the end of Narbonne's ordeal might be in sight. And yet within myself I felt a strange ambivalence. I had long since given up wondering whether any particular day might be my last, and continued to give no thought to my own future, but I could look back and see that my experiences during the plague had shaped and changed me as a person, that indeed, strange to relate, I had never felt more truly alive. Despite the misery all around, my life would surely never be so rich again.

After the death of Madeleine's father, I found myself avoiding the company of Pierre. He soon recovered from his vigil on that fateful night, and was characteristically unmoved by the wider sense of optimism at the plague's apparent diminution. Some instinct told me that I had on occasions revealed a little too much of myself, and that it would be wise to be more circumspect in his presence. In any case, he was very much preoccupied by the now constant presence of Madeleine, and it was all too easy to leave them to their obvious enjoyment of one another's company.

Increasingly, I took solace in the words and wisdom of St Augustine. The book of his *Confessions* regularly seemed to fall open at one particular passage, recounting the saint's grief after the death of a dear friend:

> *What can be the source of the sweet fruit which we pluck from the bitterness of life while we mourn and weep and sigh? Does it arise from the hope that we can make You hear us? This is so when we are at prayer, since the purpose of prayer is to reach You. But can it also be true when we are in grief and sorrow for what we have lost? Or is weeping itself a bitter thing in which we find solace only when we turn against what we formerly held dear?*

At that point, I felt that the fruit of life's bitter crop held little sweetness for me, increasingly isolated as I was both within Pierre's household and as an outsider within the city. While the gates remained shut, we were all in the position of condemned prisoners, the power to determine our own lives removed from us, clinging to the hope that we might yet be saved by some act of mercy. Once the city re-opened, our condition would change in a moment. We would be faced with a stark choice: whether to return to our old life, or to consider the salvation unexpectedly bestowed on us as a kind of re-birth, an opportunity to follow a different path. With growing certainty, I now felt clear in which direction God was leading me.

XXIX

NEXT MORNING, AFTER PIERRE LEFT on his rounds and Madeleine went to visit friends, I found myself succumbing to the general atmosphere of forward-looking optimism, and began the task of summarising my findings so far for Cardinal de Savigny, one which I had had no time to embark on since my arrival. I sat down at Pierre's desk, but before I managed to write a word began to feel unwell, struggling to swallow and wiping sweat from my brow even though the day was cool. It soon became clear that I could not continue, and I lay down on my bed.

During the ensuing hours, my condition worsened. My head throbbed and a raging thirst, such as I had never known, consumed me. I struggled to my feet but my legs buckled under me, and it was only with the greatest difficulty that I managed to crawl back onto the bed. My mind, however, remained lucid. I well recall contemplating the likely outcome, picturing myself in the wretched pose of all the plague victims whose end I had witnessed. For some reason a strange calm took over; I plucked up the courage to feel under my arms, and discovered that the swellings had not yet appeared. I drifted in and out of sleep and, it seemed, in and out of sanity.

Over the years, my memories of my family had faded to the point where I had difficulty in summoning up their faces. What would my sisters look like had their lives not been prematurely terminated? They would doubtless be married and raising children, at the same time keeping an eye on my ageing parents who, like all those attaining that stage of life, would dote on their grandchildren to the point of wondering why their own offspring had not been as enjoyable at the same age.

My only clear memory was of a journey I made on foot with my elder sister Matilda. Being some three years older, she was considerably taller and could walk much faster. I could not recall our destination, but it was clearly an undesirable one as I hung back and wandered off at every opportunity. Finally her patience snapped.

'Look,' she said, 'if you don't hurry up we won't get there before dark.'

'Don't care,' I replied in the surly manner which only young children can deliver effectively. 'Don't care if we never get there.'

She stopped ahead of me, placed her hands on her hips and glared.

'You know what they say about little boys who don't care? One day God will make them care, and then they'll be sorry. They'll have their fingernails ripped out by demons, and their eyes poked out by evil black creatures with animal heads. Then they'll be dipped in boiling oil until they scream.'

Whether Matilda was describing a Doom painting she had seen, or was conjuring these details from her fervid imagination, I could not be sure, but either way the effect was powerful enough. I ran forward, grabbed her hand and began to cry.

'I hate you,' she said. 'I wish you'd never been born.'

My eyes still blurred by tears, I replied: 'One day I'm going to kill you. I'm going to kill you dead.'

Pierre did not return home until evening. I heard him moving around the house, and realised that there was no reason for him to assume that I was there. A little later, Madeleine arrived back, and I heard her ask where I was. Soon after, I somehow knew that Pierre was standing over me, even though I did not have the strength to open my eyes. He hesitated for some time before walking away, returning with a cup of water which he helped me to drink, holding up my head. I drank greedily even though my throat had almost sealed itself up.

'I'll go and fetch Esteban,' he said. 'He'll know what to do.'

I shook my head, and the pain felt as if it would crack my skull.

'Take me away. Mustn't stay here. Madeleine.'

'The only place we can take you is to one of the plague hospices. They're nothing but corpse warehouses. You don't want to end your days there.'

'Have to.'

There was a long pause. 'Well, if you're sure that's what you really want.'

'No.' The voice was that of Madeleine, who was standing in the doorway. 'Let Nicholas stay here. We can look after him.'

I wanted to remonstrate, but had exhausted my strength.

'Nicholas is only concerned for you,' Pierre said to her. 'He doesn't want you to become infected.'

'Whether I become infected is up to God,' she replied. 'Isn't that what you've been preaching? We can't know why He strikes down some and not others, you say, we just have to accept that our lives are always in His hands. And the man who cowers on the edge of the battlefield is most likely to catch a stray arrow.'

I lost track of the passage of time as day merged into night. The fever was at its worst shortly after sunset, and I drifted in and out of consciousness throughout the hours of darkness. At length, with the sun streaming in through the window, I awoke with a dull ache in my head and a dry, rasping throat. I forced open my eyes to find Madeleine sitting next to my bed.

'Nicholas,' she said, smiling broadly, 'you're still alive. I'll go and tell Father Pierre.'

A few moments later, Pierre entered the room and once again helped me to drink some water.

'So, it seems you're one of those favoured by God,' he said. 'He must see something in you.'

'Thank you for your optimism, Pierre. But we've both seen this before. The plague relents in the morning only to return more fiercely the next night.'

'Do you have swellings in your armpits and groin?'

I checked. 'No. Not yet.'

'Blotches on your skin?'

I shrugged. He pulled back the blanket and inspected me.

'Well, you stink like a plague victim, but you don't have the critical symptoms. Let's stay hopeful. Madeleine has been praying for you ceaselessly.'

Even in my weakened condition, it occurred to me that Pierre had said nothing about doing so himself.

A little later, Madeleine brought me some clear and, to me, tasteless soup, but I consumed it without complaint.

'Would you like me to read to you?' she asked.

'You can read?'

'Of course. Father Pierre taught me many years ago. He has books of poetry, if you'd like to hear from those.'

The books to which she referred turned out to be books of troubadour love poetry, which in certain cases would have caused me to blush had my face not already been heated by the fever. Many of the poets showed what seemed to me an unhealthy interest in female anatomy. Madeleine's voice never wavered while she read them to me.

As it drew towards evening once more, I expected the worst. Madeleine's face grew anxious too, and I wondered if she had overheard my conversation with Pierre that morning. As the sun went down, Pierre arrived and ushered her away.

'We'll soon know one way or another,' he said. 'This could be a long night.'

'The longest of my life. Or perhaps not.'

The fever returned with full force. I now lacked the courage to check my own body for the tell-tale signs of plague, and resigned myself to my fate, whatever that might be. I resolved to spend the night, or as much of it as possible, in prayer but found that, beyond the opening lines, even the prayers which had brought me most comfort throughout my life now slipped from my memory. It crossed my mind to ask Pierre to pray for me. I decided to trust in God's mercy.

As the fever raged, strange visions infected my mind. I saw my childhood home burning to the ground, but on this occasion my parents and my sisters came rushing out of the door one by one, in flames and screaming in their agony. My younger sister rushed up and threw herself against me, pleading for help, until I could feel the heat from her poor body burning my own. I awoke with a start and tried to yell, but no cry emerged from my swollen throat.

The sounds of the night broke into my room: a dog howling in a distant yard, a cockerel's call, the incoherent song of a drunkard staggering past. I watched through my window for the first faint glow of dawn, and the sky remained resolutely dark.

Some hours later, a hand on my shoulder brought me round with a start. I looked up to find the room full of light, Pierre and Madeleine next to my bed.

'How do you feel?' Pierre said.

I thought for a moment, tried to swallow, felt under my arms. 'Better. Perhaps. No worse, anyway.'

Their faces broke into a relieved smile.

'I should give thanks to God,' I said.

'You should give thanks to Madeleine,' Pierre said. 'Give thanks for her faith.'

XXX

IT WAS SOME DAYS BEFORE I felt strong enough to resume my duties, even though I felt guilty at leaving Pierre with a greatly increased workload. I reflected on what seemed to have been my reprieve, and had to acknowledge that there were times when I feared the prospect of death, in curious contrast to the two recent occasions when I had found myself unexpectedly in mortal peril. I prayed to God to give me greater strength should I have to undergo such an ordeal again.

I resumed the task of visiting the sick and dying as soon as possible, but found that fatigue set in much more quickly than before. On one occasion, I was praying over the corpse of an old woman when the sound of celebration began to filter into the house from out in the street, voices screaming and laughing, some clearly drunk. I went outside to find a great throng dancing and singing. I asked the nearest man what was the cause.

'Haven't you heard? It's over. No-one's got sick today. We've all survived.'

I started to tell him that a recently deceased plague victim lay in the very house outside which he was revelling, but he was already skipping down the street in joyous abandon. As I made my way across the town, I saw similar scenes everywhere.

'Who told you the plague was over?' I asked one woman.

'What? Who cares? Come and have a dance.'

I hurried home and found Pierre in agitated mood.

'What the hell's going on?' he said as soon as I walked in the door. 'The fools think it's all over. If I catch the person who started this rumour—'

He stopped when he realised that I was looking over his shoulder at Madeleine, standing in the kitchen doorway.

'It'll burn itself out, like other such rumours,' I said. 'I suppose you can't blame people for clutching at any fragment of good news. They must feel as if a siege has been lifted.'

There was no immediate reduction in the cases we had to visit, but over the next week we noticed for the first time the numbers tailing off. New infections seemed to have become rarer, and even the normally pessimistic Pierre began to concede that the end might well be in sight. Out in the streets, the mood of celebration showed no sign of abating.

The day finally arrived when neither Pierre nor myself was called out to a new plague victim. People began to speculate openly on when the authorities would re-open the city to the outside world. Once more, the city held its breath.

I had long since ceased to wonder at the apparently limitless extent of Pierre's wine cellar, but that night he emerged with a bottle which even I could tell was of exceptional vintage. He opened it with great care, and produced from a cupboard three exquisite glasses which glinted like diamonds in reflected candle-light. Why he had kept them hidden up to that point I could only surmise. He wiped off the dust, poured the wine as if it were the very blood of Christ, and handed a glass each to myself and to Madeleine. He passed his own glass under his nose, and smiled as the aroma infiltrated his olfactory organ.

'Here's to the survivors,' he said.

'Thanks be to God,' I said.

'Thanks be to the two of you,' Madeleine said.

We drank deeply, and seated ourselves before the fire. I think each of us felt that it would be wrong to spoil the moment with words. At length, however, I could hold back no longer.

'Why do you think we've been spared, Pierre? As a reward for our efforts?'

He wrinkled his nose. 'Four priests have died of the plague. I knew them all, they were every bit as conscientious, but God didn't spare them. What's the point in trying to make sense of it? And don't tell me God works in mysterious ways. We've no more of a clue than we ever did what God is like and how He operates. Perhaps He rolls dice to decide who lives and who dies.'

I watched the effect of Pierre's words on Madeleine, but she did not seem surprised. Given the number of years she had known him, perhaps she had heard him express such sentiments many times before. She sipped her wine with clear enjoyment.

'What are you going to tell your parishioners?' I asked.

'The truth. For God's sake drink up, both of you. Now I've opened it, this bottle has to be finished.'

For some days, the people of Narbonne waited for an official announcement that the emergency plague measures were to be lifted, but none came. The mood of euphoria slowly changed to one of tension, and sporadic outbreaks of violence showed the effect that this was having. As if to emphasise how misplaced the previous celebrations had been, the weather began to deteriorate. It became unusually cold, with flurries of snow and sleet driven on a high wind. People began to suspect that, in one way or another, more misery was on the way.

Just as it seemed that the inhabitants of Narbonne were about to lose hope once more, a herald came riding through the streets early one morning to summon all the townspeople to the main square for an official announcement. We could not find Madeleine, but Pierre and I followed the crowd. When it seemed that most of the surviving population had squeezed their way within hearing distance, the herald mounted the steps and called for silence.

He began his announcement with a meaningless preamble reminding everyone who the town's surviving magistrates and civic officials were, and recalling what a difficult period the town had been through in recent months, as if we were not only too well aware of this. Just as the crowd's restiveness threatened to transform itself into something more sinister, he made the statement that all had come to hear: the city's authorities considered the state of emergency made necessary by the plague to be drawing to a close, and as of the eleventh hour the following morning the gates would be re-opened and normal commerce could resume.

Even though people had anticipated that this would be the herald's message, the final announcement was greeted by an eerie silence. Once it was clear that the message had been unequivocal, a wave of hysterical cheering erupted, complete strangers embraced, and the main square of Narbonne became the scene of uninhibited joy. I was swept along in a human tide and lost contact with Pierre.

After some time, sheer exhaustion caused the celebrants to lose some of their initial vigour, though not before I had witnessed a number of acts of outright lewdness, their nature too shameful to relate, committed in full view even of children. It seemed, however, that no-one wanted to leave the square, as if from fear that they would wake up from a dream if they did so. I noticed that many eyes had turned back to the cathedral steps from which the now-departed herald made his proclamation. There, with his arms raised, was Pierre. My heart sank.

'People of Narbonne,' he began, 'today is a momentous day. You are entitled to feel joyful and relieved. God in His mercy has brought you out of the desert of Sinai into the Promised Land. But for many of you, He did not bring your parents, your grandparents, your children, your friends and loved ones.

'You celebrate because you yourselves are still alive. Why aren't you mourning those who perished in agony in front of your eyes? Let their fate be a warning to you.

'Even as I moved among you, I heard many say that things will never be the same again, that you have seen the error of your ways, that your reprieve from death has made you determined to live your lives differently from now on. And so you should. But I say to you that you are lying to yourselves. Your memories are short, and you will soon forget the way you feel at this moment. Once the pits where the dead were thrown in their thousands have grass growing over them, once children start to be born again, once your lusts and your greed return to their former levels—when the plague starts to become a distant memory, then you will go back to your old ways. And you will have learned nothing.

'King Belshazzar of the Babylonians held a great feast, and during that feast a ghostly hand appeared and began to write on the wall opposite the king. Only the prophet Daniel was able to interpret the words, and he told Belshazzar this: "You have been weighed in the balance and found wanting." That very night, Belshazzar died. For some months, a moving finger has been writing on the walls of Narbonne in the blood and the pus secreted by the plague's victims. Do you need another Daniel to interpret its words for you?

'Go back to your old ways, if you must, cheat, lie, fornicate, just like you always did. In a brief moment of contrition, you'll come to me and confess your sins, then immediately go out and commit them again. Do you think perhaps you'll be able to make everything all right with God by repenting on your death-bed? I don't suppose those whose bodies now lie in deep pits covered with lime were in any fit state to do so. What makes you think you'll be more fortunate?

'Each one of you has, for reasons known only to God, been given a second chance. How will you make use of it? Go on a pilgrimage? Resolve to give alms more regularly? By all means do those things, they're worthy enough, but don't think they'll be enough to save you. I see into your hearts, and they're as black as the putrid tongue of a plague victim. Try looking there yourself some time.

'Why God has chosen to allow you to live while many thousands no more sinful than you have died, I cannot answer. No-one can. But I tell you this. The suffering and the torments of the plague will be as nothing by comparison with what awaits you if you don't change your ways. Read the writing on the wall. Your fate is in your own hands.'

Pierre descended the steps and walked through the crowd. They parted before him like the Red Sea parting for the Israelites. Once he had passed out of view, they drifted away in silence.

I meandered home, trying to postpone the hour when I would meet Pierre again. What had made him choose that of all moments to take the people to task? Doubtless they needed to change their ways, but he himself had previously pointed out that Narbonne's men and women were no more sinful than those of any other. If they had not brought the plague on their own heads, then surely they were entitled to celebrate its end? I began to despair of ever truly understanding what Pierre believed.

I returned home early in the afternoon to find him pacing the floor. Before I could say a word, he beckoned me to follow him to his bedroom. Madeleine lay on her bed, her face red and covered in sweat, twisting her head from side to side, mumbling in some form of delirium.

'Perhaps,' I said, 'it's the same fever I had. It can't be the plague, not now.'

He lifted her arm. In her armpit was an ominous swelling. I could find no words, and knelt next to the bed and lowered my forehead onto the backs of my hands, praying as earnestly as I had ever prayed in my life. Before long, my hands were wet with tears.

When I looked up, Pierre was staring at Madeleine in apparent disbelief.

'Do you think I should fetch Esteban?' he said. His voice sounded weak and confused. The contrast with his strident and didactic tone of a few hours earlier could not have been more complete now that he was facing the death of the one person in the world he loved. My reply was perhaps more terse than it should have been.

'To do what? Physicians have never had an answer to the plague. Some cut open the swellings to release the pus, and the patient died. Others used herbs and tinctures to restore the balance of the body's humours, and the patient died. Madeleine's life is in God's hands now. You of all people must know that.'

Pierre rose to his feet and left the room, looking deeply sad and, for the first time I could remember, old and tired. The combative Pierre of just this morning had retreated into a melancholy shell. Much as I shared his distress at the condition of the child who lay suffering before us, I also found myself angered by the rapid change which had come over him since the plague had imposed itself on his own life, as if he could not bring himself to consume the medicine of resignation which he so freely prescribed to others.

He returned with a bowl of water and bathed Madeleine's face.

'Do you know,' he said, 'I'd sacrifice my life for hers here and now if God were listening.'

'Perhaps God doesn't want your life. And I don't think He appreciates it that much when we try to bargain with Him.'

'I just feel so helpless in the face of this evil disease.'

'Perhaps you should have thought of that before—'

I stopped myself just in time from completing the sentence. Pierre no doubt supplied the remaining words for himself. He gave a sigh which rose from the depths of his soul.

'Perhaps you're right. But please, let's not argue, not in front of Madeleine.'

'She can't hear us.'

Madeleine lay very still, so still that Pierre checked for continuing signs of life.

'Let's leave her to rest,' I said. 'We'll have a long night to get through.'

Pierre left the house. I checked on Madeleine every hour or so, but there was no change in her condition. An angry drunk came hammering on the door demanding to see Pierre, having apparently decided after a considerable amount of wine that he did not care for what Pierre had said that morning. Despite being told that the person he sought was not at home, he refused to leave until I threatened to remove his head from his shoulders, at which he staggered away with a parting volley of curses.

Pierre did not return until several hours later. He did not say where he had been, and I declined to ask. He seemed reassured that Madeleine's condition had not changed.

At the end of the afternoon we lit candles, and I could not help feeling that the house was already taking on the air of a mortuary chapel. We resumed our places beside Madeleine's bed, less because we thought it would bring the girl comfort than because we did not know what else to do. Grief was etched in Pierre's face. I retrieved my Gospel book and began to read.

'How can you read at a time like this?' he said.

'How will it help her if I don't?'

His face threatened to form itself into a scowl, then subsided once more. He tried to persuade Madeleine to drink some water, but she coughed it back out. We settled ourselves to watch her young life slip away.

XXXI

As the evening drew on, Madeleine's suffering increased. At times she cried out in her agony, breathing rapidly, occasionally thrashing her head from side to side. Pierre stared at her, his mouth open, his eyes wide.

'Her condition's not likely to change for some hours,' I said. 'Perhaps we should take it in turns to get some rest.'

Pierre replied that he would remain at her side. I lay on my bed for a while but, despite my weariness, found sleep elusive. I listened for any sound from the neighbouring room; Pierre muttered now and again, presumably comforting words to Madeleine. Her cries had ceased. I finally drifted into a dream-ridden sleep, and when I awoke, the first rays of light were creeping upwards from the horizon.

I walked into the room where Pierre maintained his vigil with Madeleine, and saw that her condition had deteriorated to the point where her passing could not be more than a few hours away. Her eyes were open, staring upwards but appearing to see nothing. Each time she tried to move her body in the slightest degree, she winced in pain. She tried to speak, but her voice was too faint for us to make any sense of her words.

Pierre was slumped in his chair, and I gestured to him that he should take some rest, but he shook his head wearily. We watched the sky brightening outside, and heard the first sounds of the city stirring. Madeleine closed her eyes and subsided into a deep sleep, if that word can be appropriate to describe a senseless state prefiguring the eternal sleep of death. Her breathing became shallow and erratic, as if her body were closing itself down organ by organ. Pierre and I did not exchange a word.

She remained in this condition for several hours. We did not need to look outside in order to sense the growing excitement in the streets as the hour of the city's release approached. Madeleine gave a deep, rattling sigh. Pierre put his hand in front of her mouth, waited some moments, then looked at me and, with tears in his eyes, shook his head. In the distance, the bells of Narbonne's half-finished cathedral rang out to signify that the eleventh hour had arrived.

'Thank God that she's at peace now,' I said.

Pierre subsided to his knees, took Madeleine's hand, buried his head in her blanket and sobbed. I withdrew to allow them some last moments together. When I looked in later, he had fallen asleep where he knelt, his head resting on the bed, Madeleine's lifeless hand still in his.

'You realise we can't let anyone know that she died of the plague,' I said later. 'Not just when they all think—'

'I'll make all the necessary arrangements,' Pierre said. His voice was flat and devoid of emotion. 'Esteban will certify that she died of something else. He owes that to me.'

We stood at the window and watched the noisy and colourful celebrations in the street outside. Narbonne was enjoying one grand carnival.

'You should leave the city,' he said. 'Without delay.'

'Pierre, I've only ever known Narbonne as a city under siege. I've only seen its people frightened and angry. I'd like to stay and watch it return to normal.'

He thought long, as if slowed by the weight of his own grief.

'How can you say that either condition is normal or abnormal? Each one of us in our own life is besieged, whether we realise it or not. Including you, by your memories of what you did in childhood.'

'Madeleine told you—'

'She told me out of concern for you, Nicholas. Anyway, what does that matter now? If you stay here any longer, you won't find it a joyous experience, I can promise you that.' He looked at me, and the sadness in his eyes was for more than just Madeleine. 'It somehow suited God to bring you here as the plague set in, and I'll be eternally grateful that He did. These months would have been much harder to bear without you. But He's released you now, in a more profound way than any of those thousands of fools out there.'

A group sauntering past, clearly the worse for drink, caught sight of us at the window and waved. A woman blew kisses.

'Listen to me, Pierre. I will pray to God that He never tests me again by putting me through an experience such as this. But I can look back now and recognise that I've never had such a strong sense of purpose as in these last months. I knew what my duty was, and I had no choice but to get on and do it. Now that I can see an open-ended future stretching in front of me, I feel self-doubt and fear. I don't want to leave Narbonne yet because I've no idea where to go or why.'

'What about the Cardinal's mission?'

'He wanted me to come to Narbonne because he had some idea that it was a hotbed of heresy, Cathars and so forth. He didn't specify where I should go after leaving here.'

Pierre shook his head. 'Cardinal de Savigny knows perfectly well that there have been no Cathars in Narbonne for many years. Whatever he really wanted from you, it had nothing to do with Cathars.'

'Then perhaps I should return to Avignon and ask for further instructions.'

'Nicholas, can't you see? The Cardinal doesn't want you back in Avignon any more than your Abbot wants you back in England. Look, I can't tell you what to do, but if my advice is of any value whatsoever—'

'Pierre, please.'

'All right. If de Savigny still cares about whatever the real reason for your mission is, and if it hasn't been overtaken by other events, he'll find you wherever you are. He'll already know that Narbonne has re-opened for business.'

'Isn't that an even stronger reason for staying here and waiting on further developments?'

'That rather depends how you look at it. If you like, you can finish your report here, I'll make sure that it gets back to Avignon. After that, it's up to you. Become a missionary, go on a pilgrimage, whatever you want. You're young and strong and a great deal wiser than you were. Embrace the life you've got ahead of you.'

'And what about you, Pierre? The city will be a very different place for you, too.'

He paused. 'I know. I've been thinking about that. I had Madeleine with me for such a short time, and now she's gone there's a deep ugly pit at the centre of my life. Perhaps it's time for me to move on, too. The Abbot of Fontfroide owes me a favour. Don't ask. I'm sure he won't turn an old friend away.'

'You're going to leave Narbonne?'

'Fontfroide is not too far. What have I got to stay here for now?'

Outside, the revels were already beginning to die down. Pierre turned and dragged his feet towards the door.

'Where are you going?' I asked.

'To fetch Esteban.'

I spent the rest of the day at Pierre's writing desk, often struggling to keep sleep at bay. Pierre returned with Esteban, and shortly afterwards they carried Madeleine's body from the house in a winding-sheet. I surmised that the physician had brought some form of transportation, but was not invited to play a part in whatever arrangements they were making for her interment. I knew they would ensure that she received full funeral rites and a respectful burial, even if the mourners numbered only two.

As the hours passed, I reflected on what Pierre had said, and began to feel a greater sense of optimism about the path, or paths, which lay in front of me. As I wrote the last sentences of my report, they seemed to represent the closing of a chapter of my life. It was of no importance whether the report would be considered of any value. I pictured myself striding out of the house onto the street for the last time, and heading out of the city gate which had closed in my face, metaphorically at least, so long before.

Next morning, I gathered together my meagre belongings. Pierre filled one flask with water for me and a second with wine, claiming that it was the last of his once-ample stock, though a wry smile did seem to play on his lips as he spoke. I was about to embrace him for the last time when the door shook from the impact of a violent hammering from outside. I opened it to find two thick-set uniformed men, the foremost having a prominent sword-scar across his cheek. His companion stood behind him with arms folded.

'Are you Nicholas?'

'I am. Who is asking?'

'You need to come with us.'

'Why?'

'Your presence is required at the palace.'

'Has the Archbishop returned?'

'No.'

'Then who requires my presence?'

'If you come with us, you'll find out, won't you?'

Both men were armed with swords, which they made little effort to conceal beneath their cloaks.

'In that case, I suppose you leave me no choice.'

'Wait,' Pierre said, disappearing into his study. He returned with my report. 'I have a strange feeling you'll need this.'

XXXII

The palace turned out to be a grand house a few streets from the cathedral. Around the main door, the frames were splintered as if the house had until recently been boarded up. Inside were high ceilings and large fireplaces on all sides, but of furnishings and ornamentation very little remained. The former occupants had performed a thorough job of vacating it.

My escorts showed me into a small room with a blazing fire which spat and crackled in a hearth opposite the window. At the far end, behind a table, I was not surprised to see the figure of Cardinal Bertrand de Savigny. This time, he looked up as soon as I entered, rose to his feet and smiled. With a wave of his arm, he directed me to a chair in front of him.

'I'm afraid I can't be quite as hospitable this time, Nicholas. As you see, our facilities here are somewhat limited. Oh, and I'm sorry for the armed escort. I hope it didn't alarm you, but there are rumours of strange goings-on. I didn't want to take any chances with your safety.'

He looked over my shoulder and gave a dismissive wave of his hand. I turned to see the two guards, who had positioned themselves either side of the door, give the most insignificant of bows and close it behind them as they left. The Cardinal relaxed back into his chair.

'To be honest, Nicholas, I feel a little guilty. I specifically asked you to spend some time finding out what you could in Narbonne, never imagining that it would be under such circumstances. Praise God that He's kept you alive.'

'I pray for those He didn't. But it has been, how shall I say, a life-changing experience.'

The Cardinal nodded. 'I'm sure. Sometimes it's only in the crucible of misfortune and disaster that we find our true strength. Sadly, our esteemed Archbishop didn't take the opportunity to put his to the test.'

'It caused great resentment among the people. Do you know where he fled to?'

'Oh yes. He is, let's say, being kept safe.' I saw a brief flash of a smile, but it died on his lips. 'It is, of course, vital that he be prevented from returning to his archdiocese.'

'That, I'm sure, will be a relief to the people of Narbonne,' I said. 'What will happen to him?'

He steepled his fingers. 'That's not for me to say. Unfortunately the Archbishop has some rather powerful acquaintances. I fear that it won't be easy to inflict on him the punishment he so clearly deserves. That's why I was keen to meet you as soon as possible.'

As I listened to these words, it occurred to me for the first time that the Cardinal must have travelled at full speed to arrive here so soon after the re-opening of the city. The thought caused a shiver to pass up my spine. He glanced at the roll of coarse parchment which had been in my hand since leaving Pierre's house.

'I realise that you've had little time to collect your thoughts, and that you've had other preoccupations. But I do need your report as quickly as possible. I need to know what you discovered here.'

'Will it help you to punish the Archbishop?'

The Cardinal frowned and looked at me askance, perhaps assessing whether my question had strayed into the realm of impertinence.

'That rather depends on what you've written, Nicholas.'

He held out his hand, and I passed the report to him. He opened it without taking his eyes from me. It did not take him long to read it.

'This is it?'

'As you yourself pointed out, your Eminence, I've had other pressing duties since my arrival here.'

'I'm not referring to its brevity. Have you forgotten the specific terms of the mission which I gave you? Which his Holiness gave you? You haven't told me what I need to know.'

'With respect, I can only tell you what I've discovered with my own eyes and ears.'

'Which is nothing. What have you told me? There are charlatan friars who will exploit any opportunity to make money. When people want an easy scapegoat, Jews are hunted down like vermin. Suffering can bring out the best in people as well as the worst. Lowly parish priests are often more wedded to their duties than bishops. Quod erat demonstrandum. You haven't told me anything I don't already know.'

Cardinal de Savigny exhaled loudly, and stared at the ceiling. Was his anger genuine or synthetic?

'Surely,' I said, 'the fact that the Archbishop fled like a coward instead of ministering to the needs of the people of his diocese is reason enough to strip him of his position.'

After what seemed like an eternity, he leaned forward and placed his forearms on the table. His voice was quiet, its tone controlled.

'You have absolutely no idea how the world works, do you, Nicholas? This matter needs to be resolved immediately, before he has a chance to return to Narbonne and demand his archdiocese back. Now, I want you to re-write your report. I want you to give me the information I need to make sure that this diocese has a new Archbishop worthy of the name. In particular, I need you to confirm for me that heresy flourishes in Narbonne, unchecked by its Archbishop. Soon to be former Archbishop. Is that clear?'

'But it's not true.'

'Then you'll have to dig deeper into your memory, won't you? The memory can play tricks on us, can't it, Nicholas? Looking back, particularly over a period as dreadful as you've lived through, can almost make us believe that whatever we want to be true, is true. Can't it?'

'One of the Ten Commandments says, You shall not bear false witness.'

He smashed his fist on the table with startling violence. 'Don't try to teach me the Bible, you upstart. Who in the devil's name do you think you are?'

The door creaked open behind me. The Cardinal screamed at whoever was responsible to get out. His voice dropped in a moment to little more than a whisper.

'Let me try to explain to you one more time, Nicholas. The Archbishop of Narbonne, as both you and I know, is not fit to resume his duties, in so far as he ever fulfilled them. The people of Narbonne deserve to have an Archbishop who takes his duties seriously and is worthy of his role. I am trying to find a way to get rid of the current Archbishop, despite his connections in high places. If you can't bring yourself to help me to do that, then you will have to answer to the people of this city who, as you yourself pointed out, deeply resent the failures of the present incumbent. Have I made sufficiently clear the appalling consequences of any failure on your part to co-operate?'

All I could think of was my need to escape from the presence of a very powerful and very angry man. My voice trembled as I gave my reply.

'I'll do as you ask. Give me until this time tomorrow.'

Cardinal de Savigny leaned back in his chair, trying to prevent a smile from creeping across his lips.

'Good. I knew you were an intelligent man, Nicholas. And an astute one. The people of Narbonne are counting on you. And I'll be waiting for you.'

I rose, bowed and was about to make my escape when, as if to compensate for my failure of courage moments before, I found it within me to ask one final question.

'Do you have a better candidate already in mind to be the next Archbishop of Narbonne?'

The Cardinal stared at me for long enough to revive my fears before deciding to answer.

'Yes, as it happens. Why do you want to know?'

'Do you mind if I ask his name?'

'He's no-one you would know.'

'In which case, will you grant me one last request? Please indulge my curiosity.'

He tilted his head and drummed his fingers on the desk. 'Well, I suppose it doesn't matter. His name is Raymond. Raymond de Savigny.'

As I closed the door behind me, a man hurrying past barged into me, knocking me to the floor, and told me in no uncertain terms to watch where I was going. When I picked myself up, I found myself face to face with none other than Vittorio di Collini. I am not sure which of us was the more astonished. He smiled, but as so often during our earlier encounter it was difficult to judge exactly what this gesture conveyed.

'Nicholas,' he said, 'what a pleasant surprise. Come with me, you must tell me all about—'

Without bothering to finish the sentence, he gripped me firmly by the shoulder and steered me out of the main door into the open air, glancing from side to side as he did so. He spoke even more rapidly than usual.

'My young friend, you must be very careful. I must not say too much. But you will need eyes in every corner of your head. Do you understand what I am saying?'

'I understand that the Cardinal is not a man to be trifled with.'

Vittorio began to laugh, then quickly silenced himself.

'More than that. De Savigny is a man who does not take no for an answer. I don't know what he wants from you, and I don't want you to tell me, but I advise you to give it to him. You cannot argue with him. And he has a long memory.'

'But what he's asked me to do offends the very principle of truth. It would be sinful.'

'Then ask for forgiveness afterwards. God will understand that you can't refuse the will of de Savigny.' He grasped my shoulder again, and looked around as if alert for possible assailants. 'You're a likeable young man, Nicholas, and a good man. I've been around people like the Cardinal for too long, it's too late for me. But this is not your world. Do as he asks and then get as far away as possible. For your own sake. Before he thinks of another use for you.'

XXXIII

PIERRE SPENT A GREAT DEAL of time tutting and shaking his head. In the end, my already frayed nerves snapped.

'If you can't say anything helpful, can't you at least leave me in peace to think.'

He seemed unperturbed. 'I'm sorry, I didn't realise you were waiting for me to speak. If you're looking for my advice, you should have said so.'

I prayed hard for patience and tolerance. 'Pierre, if there is any helpful advice you can give me, I would be grateful to hear it.'

He stroked his chin with his thumb and forefinger. 'On one level, of course, your friend Vittorio is right. You can't outwit a man like Cardinal de Savigny, nor can you overcome him in a battle of wills. Most men would simply follow his instructions, however unpalatable. After all, if the end result is that the cowardly and self-seeking Archbishop of Narbonne is replaced, then some good will come out of it anyway.'

'And on another level?'

'On another level, you're a man of principle, unlike the Cardinal. You can espouse a particularly pointless martyrdom by openly refusing him, or you can take the simpler option.'

He waited, determined to make me ask. I gave in.

'Which is?'

'Run away.'

'Run away?'

'Run away. Make your escape.'

'And what will Cardinal de Savigny do if he doesn't get my falsified report?'

'What do you think? He'll fabricate one. Oh, I'm sure he'd rather you carried out his dirty work for him, but if necessary he won't hesitate to have your report forged. After all, you're hardly going to stand up in public and call him a liar, are you?'

'And how can I possibly escape? He's probably having the house watched to prevent exactly that eventuality.'

'Ah. Well, that's where I may be able to help.'

'Don't tell me, you're going to smuggle me out of the house in the guise of a corpse.'

I bit my tongue, regretting the indelicacy of this tasteless remark. Pierre seemed not to have noticed.

'No need for such desperate measures, my boy. I don't have a large cellar for nothing, you know.'

We waited until it was nearly dark, then Pierre opened a hatchway and we descended a flight of narrow and dilapidated wooden stairs, he preceding me with a torch. We arrived in what seemed more a corridor than a cellar. As he swept the torch from side to side, I saw that the walls were lined with racks which still contained, despite his protestations to the contrary, a considerable number of bottles of wine. How he had managed to acquire so many on a priest's income I could not imagine, and it was too late to ask now.

In the darkness there was no way of knowing how far we walked, but the cellar must have extended a long way beyond the foundations of the house.

'Do you know why this passageway was built?' I asked.

'Many years ago, Cathars lived in this house. They built it as an escape tunnel in case any friendly Catholics came to pay a visit. Ironic, isn't it?'

We came to a wall in the middle of which was a door. Pierre cleared away years of decaying cobwebs, then pushed it open with his shoulder. Beyond was another staircase, if anything in even worse condition than the first.

'Don't forget what I told you,' Pierre said. 'When you get to Carcassonne, you need to ask for Roger in the street of the lawyers. Don't let his profession put you off, he's an honest man. I have a feeling you'll get on well with him.'

'Pierre, you realise the Cardinal's men will come looking for me tomorrow.'

'I'll think of something, don't worry. I haven't been a priest all this time without knowing how to explain away unwelcome truths.'

We embraced until the torch began to singe my hair.

'Before I go,' I said, 'I have one last confession to make.'

'I hardly think this is the time. How grave a sin can it be?'

'I'm not actually a priest.'

'Nicholas, I'm not in the mood for jokes.'

'I'm not joking. At Croyland, I was never ordained beyond the order of deacon. I should have told you at the outset but, well, there didn't seem to be a right time.'

Pierre stared hard, then threw his head back and laughed loud and free. I had never heard such unrestrained mirth pass his lips.

'When they consider the kind of men who can be appointed as bishops and cardinals these days, I'm sure the people of Narbonne will be thankful that you exercised the responsibilities of a priest, even if one or two technicalities have been overlooked.'

We grasped each other for a final time, then I ascended the rickety staircase. At the top was a trap-door. I put my shoulder against it, but it was unwilling to yield.

'Earth will have drifted over it since it was last opened,' Pierre said. 'You'll have to push harder.'

Just as I began to doubt that I possessed enough strength, the trap-door moved with a jolt. Soil fell through the opening onto my face and into my eyes. I spat mud. When I could see again, I pushed harder and the trap-door fell wide open, landing on the ground with a loud thud. I waited, but could hear no sign of movement outside. Raising my eyes above ground level, I saw that I was about to emerge into a large garden or orchard, still within the city, but close to its outer perimeter. I looked down and could see only the torch below. I waved towards its bearer, then closed the trap-door behind me.

The ground was uneven, causing me to stumble with painful consequences for my ankles. I threaded my way between two houses and emerged onto a narrow street. At one end was one of the smaller city gates. I approached cautiously but it seemed that, in the general mood of liberation, the watchmen had decided that it was no longer necessary to man their post at all times. I slipped out of the city and made my way towards the main road to Carcassonne.

After some hours I rested in an old barn, but did not allow myself to sleep for too long as I wanted to put as much distance as possible between myself and the city before sunrise. Once it began to get light, I moved off the road and followed the line of a ridge which ran to the west, still keeping the road in view, but hopefully not visible from it.

At around mid-day I came to a farmhouse where the farmer's wife offered me simple but welcome fare, bread, cheese and olives. When she asked me the reason for my journey, I told her, God forgive me, that I was on a mission from the city's authorities, but because of its delicate nature could not go into details. She looked me up and down, clearly unconvinced, but in all truthfulness did not seem very interested anyway. She gave me a loaf for the journey and filled my water-bottle, and I pushed onwards.

During the afternoon I crouched down while a group of riders passed at some speed in the direction of Carcassonne. I walked on, debating whether it might no longer be safe to make for that city, but my anxieties were relieved when, a few hours later, they rode back towards Narbonne with equal haste. I thought of Pierre, and wondered how he would fare under interrogation from the Cardinal's men. He was resolute and resourceful, but in the end he owed me nothing. I hoped that he would not put himself at undue risk.

After dark, I returned to the road and tried to make up for the time I had lost travelling across country, but it was an overcast night, and a stinging rain began to set in. By the time the rain eased I was feeling unutterably weary, but some inner strength, fuelled by what I have no idea, unless it was the last of Pierre's wine, seemed to drive me on. As dawn broke I entered a barn, out of use but still smelling strongly of its former bestial occupants. I climbed to its upper storey, chased away a large colony of mice and lay down to sleep on some filthy straw.

I had intended to rest for a few hours, but when I awoke it was clear from the sun's position that it was well into the afternoon. I looked outside and saw a group of labourers working a short distance away. Perhaps it was hunger which brought into my mind the Gospel story of Jesus' escape from a group of men sent to arrest him by simply walking unchallenged through their midst, as if invisible. I passed the labourers without acknowledgement and continued on my way. None of them hailed me. I did not look back to see if they were watching.

A little later, on mounting the breast of a hill, I saw across the plain in the distance the high and formidable walls of Carcassonne, coloured a fiery ochre by the setting sun. I fell to my knees and gave thanks to God.

It was several hours after dark by the time I arrived at the city gates. I waited for the changing of the watch, and saw that the new watchman appeared to be already very drunk, walking unsteadily and singing a ribald song some of whose words were unfamiliar to me. As I had hoped, before long he sank to the ground with his back against the inner wall, and was soon snoring. I slipped past him and into the city.

I had no idea where to look for the street of the lawyers, but guessed that it would not be in one of the more impoverished areas. Sure enough, by concentrating my search on the quarter containing the largest houses, I soon came to a street many of whose houses boasted a plaque to proclaim their owners' profession as that of lawyer. I knocked at the most modest door I could see and waited. After some time, it opened slightly without allowing me to see who was behind.

'I apologise for troubling you, my friend. I'm looking for Roger.'

A male voice, still youthful, replied. 'Why?'

'I've been sent by a mutual friend, a priest in Narbonne.'

'What's his name?'

'Pierre. Why do you ask?'

The door opened wider, and in the dim light I could just make make out the features of an open-faced young man.

'Then you'd better come in. I'm Roger.'

XXXIV

ROGER'S HOUSE WAS SIMPLY BUT comfortably furnished. Just about every wall was given over to shelves of books. He appeared with a jug of wine and two goblets, rather finer than the surroundings would have led me to expect. He noticed that I was staring at them.

'These are one of my few indulgences,' he said. 'Pierre and I may argue like dogs, but on one thing we agree, as you see.'

We sat beside the fire. His wine was indeed of the finest quality.

'I'm sorry for the wary reception just now,' he said. 'We've learned to ask questions first, I'm afraid. These are not the safest of times. Sometimes I wish I could learn to keep my mouth shut.'

He raised his goblet, encouraging me to drink, which I did with gusto. My stomach was so empty that I soon felt the effect.

'I don't suppose there's any chance . . .'

Roger gasped. 'What am I thinking of? You must be starving. Wait here.'

Within moments, he returned with a tray of bread and meats. I could barely restrain my eagerness within the bounds of politeness. The meat was not of the best cuts, and the bread had lost its youthful freshness, but to me it was as if I were already dining in the Kingdom of Heaven. When I could manage no more, I placed the tray on the floor and washed down my meal with a long draught of wine. I could not remember the last time I had felt so contented and secure.

I sniffed at my clothes. 'I'm sorry to arrive in this state. I've been travelling across country on foot.'

'Not to worry. I'll sort out some clothing for you in the morning, as long as you don't mind looking like an ordinary artisan.'

'I have a feeling that would be a good idea. Father Pierre tells me you're that rarest of beasts, an honest lawyer.'

'Honest lawyers, virtuous priests, they're both supposed to be as rare as snakes' legs. I don't claim to be a saint, but some of my clients are not exactly people of means, put it that way. I tell my fellow advocates that one day, in the far-distant future, the law will give people of all estates the means to protect themselves against arbitrary injustice.'

'They must find that highly amusing.'

'They laugh like men besotted. "How can we make any money from acting for poor people?" they say. To which, of course, there's no answer, except that one day maybe not all lawyers will be as greedy and grasping as them.'

'It sounds to me as if you're looking beyond the confines of this age,' I said.

Roger smiled. 'No, I leave that to you people.'

I looked into the flames, and for once saw nothing but burning wood.

'I gather you're from England,' Roger said.

'Yes, from Croyland in Lincolnshire.'

'Can't say I've heard of it, I'm afraid. What brought you to this region?'

Whether it was purely the effect of the wine, I will never know, but I already felt sufficient trust in Roger to tell him the whole story of my commission from Cardinal de Savigny, and of my adventures to date. When I reached the last part of my tale, he began to frown.

'You need to be cautious, my friend. You've made a dangerous enemy. Pierre can look after himself, and I suspect that at his age he's past caring what they do to him. But a man like de Savigny can extend his tentacles far and wide.'

'That's certainly true enough, but God has preserved me this far.' I thought Roger winced at these words, but could not be sure. 'Anyway, I suspect that my future lies outside this region. Pierre was anxious for me to get as far away as possible. But before I move on, there's one mystery I'd like to clear up if I can.'

'Which is?'

'I'm still puzzled about the Cathars. Heretics they may have been, but the enormous effort, military as well as spiritual, which went into wiping them out during the last century seems—I don't know, disproportionate. Everyone tells me they've as good as disappeared, yet there seems to be a lingering fear of them even now, as if they may be lying in hiding, planning some kind of conspiracy. Our Church leaders still seem afraid of them.'

'Church leaders see conspiracies everywhere,' Roger said. 'And don't forget that the history of the crusade against the Cathars has only been told by the Catholic victors. Anyway, you must be weary. I'll prepare a bed for you. Sleep as long as you want, I have the morning free.'

'Perhaps then you can show me some of the sights of your fine city.'

'I can do better than that. If you really want to know about the Cathars, there's someone I think you'll want to meet. Someone who can tell you a lot more about the crusade than I ever could. But we have to keep this secret. No-one must know.'

I awoke earlier than expected after the most restful sleep I could remember for a long time: since, I thought, the night I spent in the company of Esclarmonde all those months before. A clean set of clothing lay at the foot of my bed.

Roger was working at a lectern, surrounded by untrimmed sheets of rough vellum, some of which he had already used, and on which he had scribbled notes in all directions, often overlapping one another. We breakfasted heartily, and then Roger appeared with our outer cloaks.

'I'm going to take you to the house of a man called Guilabert. He has a remarkable story to tell, but don't be surprised if he takes a while to learn to trust you. He has more reason to be fearful than you and I, so you'll need to be patient. Oh, and when we're outside I advise you to put your hood over your head.'

He led me in silence through a warren of narrow streets. At times I felt sure that we were re-crossing parts of our earlier route. At length we arrived at what must have been one of the most ramshackle houses in Carcassonne.

'You'll have to make allowances,' Roger said. 'Guilabert's said to be about ninety years old. He's blind, though his mind is still sharp, all things considered.'

As I stooped to enter through the low doorway, it struck me how stuffy the tiny house was. There were few furnishings to speak of: all I could see was a small table, two chairs and some bedding spread out on the floor. In the opposite corner, in Stygian gloom,

I discerned Guilabert. He was seated on the floor, propped against a wall, dressed in threadbare old clothing. His emaciated body seemed at first sight too small to support his head. By his side was a bowl of soup which had not been touched.

'Does he know I'm here?' I whispered.

'He knows.'

We moved closer and sat next to the old man. He made no acknowledgement of our presence, and I began to wonder if perhaps he were also deaf. His cloudy eyes stared straight ahead, and his lips moved soundlessly. It was as if, being unable to perceive directly what goes on in this world, he had retreated into another, a world accessible only to him. I looked at Roger. He nodded.

'Hello, Guilabert. My name is Nicholas,' I began. 'I would like to talk to you.'

Guilabert turned his head towards me, and appeared to stare so hard that I had to remind myself firmly that he was unable to see me. I shivered, perhaps not just from the cold.

'I've been told,' I continued, 'that you have seen many extraordinary things in your life. I would like to talk to you about some of them. My friend Roger here—'

'Yes, I know,' he replied. Despite the infirmity of his body, his voice was strong.

'Are you happy to talk to my friend Nicholas?' Roger asked.

'What about?'

'About your early life. And your beliefs. You can trust Nicholas, I'll vouch for him. He's English, and he's interested to know about the crusade from the point of view of the Cathars.'

Guilabert stared at me again. His unseeing eyes were deeply unnerving. He took a long time to reply.

'Montségur. You should know about Montségur. The world must never forget.'

I looked at Roger again, raising my eyebrows. He placed his finger to his lips. Guilabert picked up the bowl of soup and drank noisily from it. As he lowered it to the floor with shaking hands, he said:

'I was there. I was there when the crusaders captured Montségur.'

'But I've heard,' I said, 'that the siege of Montségur ended well over seventy years ago. Can you remember clearly events from so long ago?'

Even in the gloom I fancied that there were tears welling up in Guilabert's eyes.

'As if it were yesterday. It happens, you know. The curse of old age.'

He shifted position and, with immense effort, sat cross-legged.

'Montségur,' he said, 'perched in all its glory on top of a high pinnacle. The sides were sheer, there was only one path by which it could be reached, and that with difficulty. It was the nearest thing to an impregnable fortress you will ever see. As the net cast by the crusaders, or should I say the bloody murderers, closed in on us over the preceding years, the fortifications had been strengthened several times, especially on the west wall of the keep, since we considered the eastern approach so precipitous as to be unscalable. When you approached Montségur at ground level from the south, if you were lucky enough to catch sight of it at dawn or dusk on a clear day, the battlements seemed to catch fire from the rays of the sun.'

Guilabert picked up his soup bowl and drank again. I was impatient for him to resume but he was determined to tell the story at his own pace.

'By the year—when did you say it was?'

'According to the chroniclers,' Roger said, 'the siege began in the year of our Lord twelve hundred and forty-three.'

'Ah yes. By then, the Catholic Church and its Inquisitors had persecuted and burned us so relentlessly that Montségur was one of the very few places where we could remain in safety.'

'By we,' I said, 'you mean you and your fellow Cathars.'

He fell silent, and I began to fear that my interruption had brought our conversation to a premature end. Roger looked at me and shook his head.

'My friend wishes you no ill will,' he said to Guilabert. 'He's a simple seeker after truth.'

Guilabert seemed to weigh this up, and apparently felt reassured.

'My parents moved to Montségur from Albi thinking that we would all be safe. For a while it seemed that they were right. A number of distinguished perfecti had made their home there over the years, and Montségur had hosted several assemblies of Cathar dignitaries. But a few years before its fall, the Inquisitors returned and began to persecute those in the surrounding area suspected of Cathar sympathies. One by one, the remaining Cathar strongholds fell. More and more families fled to the safety of Montségur, and when it became overcrowded they dug out caves in the rock face just below the walls. At last only Montségur and Quéribus remained unconquered. By this time, there must have been about five hundred souls crammed into our narrow fortress.'

Guilabert stopped once again and breathed deeply. I could sense how much his retelling of these events, still vivid in his mind after so many years, was exhausting him. He finished his soup and took another deep breath.

'A couple of years before the fall of Montségur, Raymond the Seventh, the Count of Toulouse, a man with no convictions of his own but no wish to make enemies, decided to show his loyalty to the Catholic Church by besieging the fortress. From the timing of his arrival, in autumn, we doubted that he intended to make a serious attempt to capture it, and in any case we had plenty of food and water in reserve. Even though his army looked formidable, a number of men within its ranks were more sympathetic to our cause than to Raymond's. By the end of the year the onset of winter had driven him to raise the siege. Our belief in our invincibility was reinforced still further.'

I marvelled at the articulate way the old man recounted these events. At times he seemed almost to be reading from a book, so little hesitancy was there in his voice, although of course he must have been asked to recall the story many times over the years. I resolved to cause no further interruption. To be truthful, I was finding myself drawn deeply into this tale of unrepentant heretics.

'I had a close friend, a boy named Ramon, who was about five years older than I. We used to look down from the tower and think that the army of the Holy Roman Emperor himself could never take the place. The fortress was always kept well-stocked in case someone should be fool enough to try to besiege us, and we had many friends in the surrounding region, some Cathar sympathisers, others who simply hated the northern lords who had arrived to take part in the campaign of persecution in the hope of rich pickings for themselves.

'As I said, the Inquisitors had returned to the region, and the year before the final siege began, at the end of May, four Inquisitors from Toulouse arrived in the town of Avignonet, on the road between Carcassonne and Toulouse. Their leader was a man we detested, Guillaume Arnaud, a man of ruthless cruelty, totally devoid of any human feeling. The Governor of Avignonet, Hugh of Alfaro, a man of fiercely independent mind and no friend of the Inquisition, sent a messenger to alert us and our commander, Pierre-Roger of Mirepoix, set off immediately with a large, heavily-armed force of knights. When they arrived at Avignonet the following night, a sympathiser let them into the citadel where the Inquisitors were sleeping. They killed them and destroyed their accursed depositions and the records of their hearings. It was said that Guillaume Arnaud died with the *Te deum* on his lips before a sword pierced his heart, but I doubt it. When they found him, his head had been smashed against the stone floor. I hope God had mercy on his soul. I certainly wouldn't have.'

Guilabert spat on the ground, whether in disgust at the recollection of Guillaume Arnaud or merely to clear his throat, I could not tell. He closed his eyes as if to compose himself before continuing.

'The leaders of the Catholic clergy had never trusted Count Raymond of Toulouse, and suspected him of organising the murders, although in reality of course he had played no part. Nevertheless, he was excommunicated, and part of the price he had to pay to be accepted back into the Church was to take decisive action against us. But of course the Catholics didn't trust him to lead another expedition; instead, they gave the job to a man of more determined character called Hugh d'Arcis, the Seneschal of this very city. He arrived at Montségur with an army in the late spring of—twelve hundred and forty three, did you say?—and we watched as he made his preparations way below us. But even he did not have enough troops to invest the fortress completely, and reinforcements regularly arrived to increase our garrison, simply by-passing his lines. Not only that, but a number of Hugh's men, like Raymond's before, did not have their hearts in the campaign.

Our deacons went back and forth at will to minister to those Cathars who remained in the surrounding villages.

'Messages of support reached us from other Cathar communities, even from as far away as Cremona. Many of the garrison at Montségur were not Cathars, but they wanted the region to remain free from outside control, especially from the King of France and his northern lords. Even some loyal Catholics hated the Inquisition. We knew we simply had to wait for the arrival of winter, and then Hugh's army would melt away as its predecessors had done. Ramon and I used to stand on the ramparts and throw rocks down on them. I'm sure we never caused any serious injuries, but it was our own gesture of defiance.

'There were a few skirmishes outside the walls, but nothing of any consequence happened through the summer. Our women played as large a part as the men, not only treating the wounded but operating catapults and other engines. Life settled into a routine for us, as I'm sure it did for the men in the besieging army. The fortress remained well-stocked with grain and water, and we knew that time was on our side.

'By the time the first snows arrived, Hugh's army had achieved virtually nothing. We waited for them to disperse like Raymond's before, but instead they dug in for the winter. This was something we hadn't expected, but even so we were convinced that Hugh's army would not be able to last through months of snow and freezing conditions. Then in November, Durand, the Bishop of Albi, arrived with reinforcements from his diocese. To our misfortune, he was also an accomplished siege engineer.'

'A siege engineer? The Bishop?'

My eagerness to ensure that I had heard him correctly had forced me to go back on my resolution to make no further interruptions. Guilabert simply smiled at my incredulity. By now he was looking extremely weary, and I asked him if he would prefer to rest. He shook his head. If anything, a new fire seemed to burn inside him.

'Bishop Durand succeeded in setting up a powerful trebuchet on the eastern face of the rock, which we had largely ignored because, as I said, we considered it to be insurmountable. The trebuchet, however, was able to cause considerable damage to the east tower. Our commander took the decision to withdraw the defenders from that side, trusting to our natural defences on that flank. This turned out to be a fatal miscalculation.

'In January, a group of Basques succeeded in climbing the eastern escarpment at night. Heaven alone knows how they managed it. I heard that when they looked down in daylight, they were horrified at what they had done. They killed the sentinels and took possession of the eastern barbican, and though they made little impression on the main keep, we knew from that moment that Montségur's days were numbered.

'I was still a small boy, and became deeply afraid. My parents tried to reassure me that help was already on its way. They told me that the Count of Toulouse, the King of England, the Emperor Frederick, even Prester John himself, was coming to relieve the siege. I wanted so much to believe them, but even at my young age I could see in their eyes that they knew these were mere fables. Ramon and I would huddle on the battlements and watch as the army below made preparations for a final assault. Although they must have suffered appalling deprivations through the winter, Hugh and his men now knew that the end was inevitable.

'Pierre-Roger led a final attempt to dislodge the Basques from the eastern barbican, but it failed. After that, the garrison concluded that there was no point in continuing, and the fortress was surrendered. I feel that the Cathars would have fought on to the death—after all, what did we have to lose?—but the Catholic members of the garrison felt that there was no point in throwing their lives away on a lost cause. I don't blame them for that.

'At the beginning of March, the garrison surrendered. We had resisted for nine months against a formidable army. All in all, the besiegers were merciful, in their own terms. Those who agreed to abjure their Cathar beliefs were allowed to depart with only light penances from the Inquisition. They even allowed the perpetrators of the murders at Avignonet to leave with their lives.'

I noted that Guilabert said nothing of the fate of those who remained true to their beliefs to the end. I waited, and saw that there were now tears trickling down his cheeks. It was unclear whether he had decided to end at that point. His voice had become more frail as he reached his account of the garrison's surrender. I took his hand and he feebly grasped mine.

'I thank you from the bottom of my heart, Guilabert. It has meant a great deal to me to hear these words from the lips of one who witnessed these momentous events. But there is something which I am sure you have been asked many times, and which you have not so far mentioned.'

He sat up and stretched his legs out in front of him.

'Ah,' he said, 'so you are just like all the others. You are searching for the treasure.'

I had no idea what he was talking about. Roger intervened.

'Nicholas is not interested in any treasure. What I think he means is that some have speculated that the inhabitants of Montségur knew the whereabouts of the Holy Grail.' He glanced at me and I nodded. 'Some even believe that it was concealed at Montségur for safe keeping, perhaps by the Knights Templar. Can you shed any light on these tales?'

'I will tell you all I know,' Guilabert said. 'Many treasure-hunters have visited the place, some doubtless searching for the Holy Grail, whatever it is or was, and there were indeed riches at Montségur. We had to be able to pay our way when we needed to. There is a story that a couple of months before the surrender, Pierre-Roger arranged for two deacons to leave the castle by night and hide the contents of our treasury in a cave. This seems credible to me, for when the fortress was surrendered, the besiegers found little of value. What had been in the treasury, I do not know. But it was also said that, the night before the fortress was handed over, Pierre-Roger, who had concealed three or four Cathars in his own quarters, let them out by night. They made their escape by descending the rock-face and in due course retrieved the treasure. What became of them or it thereafter, no-one seems to know.'

'And did no-one in the fortress ever speak of the Grail?' I asked.

'Not that I can recall. But I was only a child, I have already made that clear.'

There was no point in pressing him further, but at the same time I was anxious to know how his account would have ended had I not interrupted him.

'Guilabert, I apologise for my unnecessary diversion. Is there anything else you wish to add to your account?'

He rubbed his eyes and took a deep breath. 'There is one more thing to tell,' he said. 'Without it you cannot understand what I have already told you.

'For some reason which I still do not understand, Hugh d'Arcis allowed those remaining in the fortress some fifteen days after its surrender before they were to hand themselves over. Perhaps he hoped that this would allow time for even the most determined to repent of their errors, as he saw it, but I will never know. Suffice it to say that the delay had the opposite effect. Most spent the time listening to increasingly emotional sermons and indulging in a frenzy of self-mortification. A number of novice Cathars received the *consolamentum*, the equivalent of what you would call baptism into the faith, in full knowledge that they were thereby condemning themselves to death. A few who had not been adherents at all pledged themselves to the Cathar faith, including my friend Ramon, even though I pleaded with him not to. A fever took over the fortress, like nothing I have ever experienced in my life. My mother and father remained steadfast, although there were often tears in their eyes when they looked at me, knowing that in a matter of days they would see me for the last time. Their faces haunt me to this day, and will do so until the moment of my death.

'On the day when the last occupants of the garrison were to give themselves up, those who had remained faithful to their beliefs were manacled and led out to meet Hugh d'Arcis and leading members of the Inquisition. Children like myself were not chained, and I walked along holding my mother's arm as tears poured down her face. The besiegers, including Hugh himself and the Inquisitors, begged the captives to change their minds even then and recant, but not one did so. We children were led away, although not before seeing that a huge pyre had been prepared on the open ground below the battlements.

'I do not know how many perished on that day. I would guess the number must have been at least two hundred. The other children and I were taken into a tent and made to sit down with our hands over our ears and our eyes closed. I removed one hand just enough to hear the crackling of the pyre and the sound of screaming. I opened one eye and saw that several of our captors, hardened soldiers though they were, were weeping uncontrollably.'

Guilabert's voice finally gave way and he too began to sob. Roger took my arm and gestured that I should rise. As he led me out of the door, I looked back over my shoulder and saw that Guilabert had buried his face in his hands.

XXXV

Roger led the way to an inn where we sat in a dark corner. He ordered wine, bread, fruit and cheese. I was grateful for the wine, but had no stomach for food.

'Have you heard Guilabert's story before?' I asked.

Roger clasped his hands on the table. 'Almost to the word.'

'You think he's made it up? He's just retelling a fable, like a troubadour?'

'No. On the contrary. I think that every day he relives what he's just told you. The story doesn't change because his memory doesn't.'

I gazed at the bubbles dispersing on the surface of my wine.

'When Guilabert dies,' I said, 'which can't be long delayed, there'll no longer be any account of the siege at Montségur, or probably the whole crusade, from the point of view of the defeated side.'

'Chronicles are written by the victors, so it's said. Anyway, I thought you and your masters wanted all memory of the Cathars erased. Why should you care?'

I thought for some moments. On one level, Roger of course had a point.

'Guilabert told a very moving tale,' I said. 'If human suffering and courage have any meaning in this world, perhaps it's a tale which should be retold, however mistaken the beliefs of those concerned.'

Roger lowered his voice. 'Be careful the Cardinal's spies don't hear you say that.'

'Yes, I know.' I leaned across the table. 'But listening to Guilabert I could understand why even the Inquisitors begged the Cathars not to throw their lives away. In fact I can hardly believe I'm saying this, but I feel a grudging admiration for those who were prepared to face the pyre rather than renounce their beliefs. And it seems regrettable that there'll be no record of their heroism from their own side.'

'Then why not write it down?' Roger said.

'What? Are you mad?'

'You're a scholar of some kind, presumably. Guilabert's testimony is still fresh in your mind. Who better than you?'

'What if the Inquisition or the Cardinal's men find it?'

Roger leaned back and shook his head. 'Have you no imagination, Nicholas? You just say you wrote it down the better to denounce him, then had second thoughts because of his great age and decided that it would serve no purpose.'

'I suppose you're right.'

Our meal arrived, and I found that I had regained something of my appetite. The bread was dry, the fruit over-ripe and the cheese hard, so we decided to wash them down with more wine, purely to render them digestible. My spirits were lifting by the moment, until I noticed that Roger was staring at me. He had been drinking rather more quickly than I.

'You're a strange one, Nicholas. What in the name of all Satan's acolytes did someone as astute as de Savigny think he was going to get out of you? It doesn't make sense.'

'I'm not sure whether to be flattered or insulted by that.'

'Think about it. You have nothing in common with the people who work for him. I know you've had quite an education since you arrived on these shores, but you're still a simpleton when it comes to the ways of the world. Please don't take offence. But most of all, you're a man of principle. You choose to put your own life at risk rather than give de Savigny the lies he wants, even though, for all you know, the outcome of his scheme might have been for the best for the people of Narbonne.'

'Pierre thinks de Savigny will just make up his own lies. Which seems likely, I must admit. But do you really think my life's in danger?'

'Who knows? Better to be on the safe side. How long are you planning to stay in Carcassonne?'

'I don't know. I suppose I'm waiting for God to tell me. In the same way He told me He didn't want me to leave Narbonne.'

'Either God, or an unfortunate accident of timing.'

We stared at one another for some time. I took a draught of my wine.

'What do you believe, Roger?'

'About what?'

'You know perfectly well about what.'

He glanced from side to side, then leaned forward.

'All right. I don't believe in a God who sits remote in His heaven like a celestial engineer or timekeeper. I don't believe in a God who rewards the pure with happiness and good fortune, and punishes the wicked with plagues. And I don't believe in a God who puts kings and popes on thrones and tells us we have to obey them because He appointed them. There. Does that shock you?'

'You've only told me what you don't believe.'

'That's the easy part, for me anyway. To say what you do believe is easy for you: *Credo in unum deum, patrem omnipotentem*, et cetera. But I'm not convinced you can reduce belief to a form of words. Words are created by human beings. Yes, yes, I know God recited the words of the Law for Moses to write down, but that was a long time ago and a long way away. For me the fundamental question is, does human life have a meaning for its own sake, rather than just in terms of serving God? Because if it has no meaning, then it has no value, and we might as well all just open a vein and have done with it, and that I can't accept. But I don't happen to feel that anyone can just hand the answer to us, whether priest or pope or theologian or philosopher. If we haven't worked it out in our own lives, our own experience, we'll never understand. Life is a quest, Nicholas, or it's nothing.'

'I don't take issue with you on that. St Augustine wrestled with the questions which disturbed him until the end of his life. But for most people, life allows little space for grappling with fundamental issues. They're too busy just trying to keep themselves and their families alive. They look to the Church to provide them with a framework of beliefs. If you took that away, they'd have nothing.'

'Good. All the better.'

'All the better? You actually want to leave people believing that the world is chaotic, that there's no order or meaning?'

Roger was unmoved. 'Look, in the distant past, our ancestors worshipped their own gods. The sun, the moon, the earth, the seasons, fertility, birth, death—all these were tinged with the divine because there were gods and goddesses responsible for them, to whom people could turn for help.'

'Your point being?'

'They didn't believe because priests told them to. They believed because they opened their souls to the divine all around them, and they felt it, worshipped it, celebrated it. I happen to believe that all people have the capacity to do that, not just educated, well-spoken people like us.'

'You're beginning to sound like the Cathars.'

'Some of the Cathars' beliefs were ridiculous. But look into your heart. Does any man have the right to burn another to death because of what he sincerely believes?'

'Yes,' I said, 'if the one on the pyre would otherwise have led the gullible astray and placed their souls in eternal jeopardy.'

Roger glared at me, drained his cup and slammed it down on the table.

'Let's go,' he said and, without waiting for me, stood up and strode out of the door. I was so taken aback that it was some moments before it occurred to me that I did not know the way home.

A few days later, our theological disagreements apparently forgotten or at least suppressed, Roger and I were enjoying a time of quiet reading and meditation when the door burst open and a young man I had not seen before rushed into the house, his eyes wide.

'It's true! It's true! The great Inquisitor Bernard Gui has confirmed it!'

Roger put his book down on the table next to him with exaggerated slowness.

'Anton,' he said quietly, 'what in the name of the devil's testicles are you talking about?'

'They're trying to kill us all,' the young man replied. 'Come to the market place, quickly. The whole town's assembling there. The Seneschal's going to address us.'

We followed him as he raced out and along the street, stopping anyone he found going about their normal business and insisting they make their way to the square. A few pushed him away. Most followed, like us, out of curiosity.

On the back of a cart, as he was not a tall man, stood the Seneschal, looking as if this were the day he had waited for all his life. He smiled in, I thought, a notably smug manner, his fat jowls vibrating as his head moved slowly up and down in satisfaction at the sight of the arriving mass. Roger and I pushed our way to the front of the crowd, which by now was extensive, and when the Seneschal was satisfied that his audience had reached its greatest extent, he cleared his throat dramatically and called for attention. He waited until every eye was on him, then raised an official-looking document.

'I, Aymery de Cros, Seneschal of Carcassonne,' he began in a ponderous tone, extending every syllable to its maximum length, 'have in my hand a decree from—none other than King Philip himself.'

He paused, but the crowd were unimpressed by mention of the royal author, simply wanting him to get to the point of his address. He raised the document once more as if to read from it, then seemed to change his mind.

'The decree is written in legal terms too complex for you to understand, so I will summarise it in words more familiar to you simple folk.'

Open dissent was now breaking out in sections of the crowd, and the Seneschal began to look alarmed. He wisely decided to hurry on with his address.

'King Philip says that he has received confirmation of a most sinister conspiracy, not against his august person, but against all the people of this land.'

He now had his audience's full attention. Learning from his previous mistake, he continued without delay.

'The conspiracy involves a plot to contaminate in a most foul way all the wells and water-courses on which we depend for our drinking water, so that we will die a most foul and horrible death. Following this, the perpetrators of the plot will seize our property and make themselves the lords and rulers of this land. Indeed, they have already apportioned to themselves in advance every estate, every position of power and authority in France.'

Roger's right eye was twitching nervously. He turned to me and soundlessly mouthed 'The Jews', drawing his finger across his throat. The Seneschal was already in full flow once more.

'Some of the perpetrators have confessed to their evil crimes, although such is the depth of their deceit that they were only forced to do so after the application of torture. King Philip gives every assurance that it is only a matter of time before all of them are captured and punished in the only way appropriate to crimes of such magnitude.'

He had made a point of not so far identifying the culprits, holding back this vital piece of information for dramatic effect. Some of the crowd had already drawn their own conclusions.

'It's the Jews. Tell us it's the Jews.'

'It's always the Jews. They hate us all.'

'Let's go and burn the synagogue.'

Aymery de Cros raised his hands for silence. It took some time to achieve his objective. He did not resume until the crowd were stilled.

'Those who have confessed have confirmed that the conspiracy has been hatched by—the lepers of France.'

There was a stunned silence, people staring at one another in confusion. Roger could not contain himself and burst out laughing. I was afraid that this had been an injudicious response, but soon laughter began to break out throughout the crowd. It was as if a huge weight of apprehension had been removed, and required some emotional response to rush in and replace the vacuum. Before long I found myself joining in the general mood of mirth. The Seneschal, on the other hand, was furious that his finest moment had ended in farce. He leapt down from the cart, almost falling on his face as he landed, and hurried away with servants and guards trailing in his wake.

As Roger and I walked home, there was something of a festive mood in the streets.

'I'd never appreciated that our King possesses such a well-developed sense of mischief,' Roger said. 'I wish all his decrees were as entertaining.'

'So what's all this about? No-one could seriously expect people to believe such nonsense.'

Before Roger could answer, we found ourselves face to face with a bald, enraged priest who clearly did not share our amusement. His face resembled the sky before a thunderstorm.

'It's outrageous,' he fumed. 'If I knew the identity of the idiot who provoked that outbreak of mirth, I'd strike him down right here and now.'

I looked at Roger, whose face no longer reflected amusement.

'I suppose,' I said to the priest, 'that the Seneschal's momentous revelation took everyone by surprise. After all, the lepers are not usually supposed to be conspiratorial, and surely don't have any organisation capable of bringing about such a disaster.'

'How do we know? How do we know? Do we suppose that our King hurls such accusations around for fun? I tell you here and now, I intend to investigate this matter further.'

'In what way, Father Tomas?' Roger asked.

'Bishop Arnaud will be here tomorrow, and we'll interrogate the lepers of this city and we'll get to the bottom of this conspiracy, as God is my judge.'

Father Tomas stormed off, still fuelled by righteous anger. Roger, to my surprise, looked alarmed, and we walked the rest of the way home in silence.

That night, I spent several sleepless hours musing over our encounter with the irate Father Tomas. From what I had heard Bishop Arnaud was no fool, but whatever his true feelings on the matter, he could hardly say outright that he did not believe what King Philip had said. On the contrary, if he valued his position, which doubtless he did, he would wish to be seen as the most eager of all bishops to pursue prosecutions against the supposed vile conspirators. And if Father Tomas wanted interrogations, which doubtless meant torture, then he would find Aymery de Cros a willing participant in rounding up Carcassonne's lepers, who had the misfortune, like the Jews, to be a highly visible minority, and one which engendered a widespread sense of mistrust, if not outright fear.

XXXVI

THE NEXT MORNING I WOKE later than is my normal custom, and the sun was already up when Roger came to rouse me.

'My friend,' he said, 'events have moved more quickly than I expected. We need to be on our way as soon as possible.'

I dressed and breakfasted hastily and with a heavy heart, since I could well imagine what these sudden developments might be. About mid-morning we set off for the church in company with a good number of the townspeople, most of whom, unlike us, were still in jovial mood after the previous night's unexpected entertainment. We arrived to find the nave already packed. Roger led me back out and around to the north transept and hammered on a small side door. One of the Seneschal's guards opened it and scowled.

'Well let us in you fool,' Roger said, 'or answer to the Bishop for holding us up.'

The guard looked us up and down, considered for a moment, then opened the door just wide enough for us to squeeze through one after the other. No doubt the act of causing us this modicum of discomfort was sufficient to satisfy his injured pride. Once inside, we found ourselves standing in line with, though a little distance from, the table where Bishop Arnaud, grey-haired, austere, and stately in his episcopal robes, was about to preside. Father Tomas, seated alongside him, looked round at us and scowled. The hubbub amongst the crowd in the nave was an uneasy one; there was a palpable sense of expectation, but also apprehension now that the proceedings were about to get under way. The festive feelings left over from last night had dissipated in anticipation of what the crowd now realised could be, quite literally, a life and death struggle.

The Bishop hammered on the table to bring the assembly to order. I expected him to open the proceedings with a prayer, a call for truthfulness and integrity, but it seemed he had no time for preliminaries.

'Bring forward the first witness.'

There was a collective gasp as two of the guards dragged from the darkness behind a man of middle age who had clearly already been subjected to the rigours of what Tomas referred to as interrogation. Blood flowing down his right cheek had dried onto his skin, and his left eye was nearly closed by bruising. Paler patches of skin on his neck and hands represented the only visible sign that he might be suffering from leprosy. He was dragged, manacled, to a position at the side of the Bishop, turned so that the crowd could see his expression as he gave his answers. Even at the distance from which Roger and I watched, he was visibly shaking with fright.

'What is your name?' Bishop Arnaud asked him. The man stammered and gibbered and failed to make any comprehensible response. The Bishop tried again.

'Is your name Philippe?'

The man continued to tremble uncontrollably. He opened his mouth as if to reply, but no audible sound emerged. Bishop Arnaud's face revealed that his patience was already being tested.

'Does anyone here know who this man is?'

'His name is Philippe,' one of the guards restraining him answered. 'No-one knows what his family name is, or what happened to his family.'

'Well, I will take that to be the case unless anyone informs me to the contrary,' the Bishop said. 'Now, Philippe, you have nothing to be afraid of as long as you tell the truth. Do you understand?'

Philippe, assuming that to be his true name, nodded. Bishop Arnaud looked down, apparently at a prepared set of questions in front of him.

'What do you know of the leper conspiracy to poison wells and water-courses?'

Philippe replied whilst shaking his head vigorously. 'Nothing, m-my lord. Nothing at all.'

'Come, come. I've already told you that you have nothing to be afraid of. All we are trying to find out here is the truth. No-one is accusing you of anything.'

It was difficult to tell whether Philippe was reassured by this or not. His expression, and his level of fear, seemed unchanged.

'I know n-nothing, my lord,' he replied.

Bishop Arnaud turned to the captain of the guard. 'Who is this man's accuser?'

The captain seemed nonplussed by this question. 'Well, it's obvious he's a leper, my lord. From his skin.'

'Philippe,' the Bishop said, 'are you a leper?'

'No, my lord.'

'What about the marks on your skin?'

'I've had them since I was born, my lord. I've no marks of leprosy. Look, I'll show you.'

Philippe began to remove his shirt.

'That won't be necessary. This is a tribunal, not a physician's examination room.'

Bishop Arnaud's attention reverted to the captain of the guard.

'Captain, has this man been tortured?'

A broad smile spread across the captain's face. 'Oh yes, my lord. All night, my lord.'

'And yet still he has nothing to tell us. How do you explain that?'

'Well, um, it's obviously a very deep conspiracy. They've sworn some kind of oath, or something. Anyway, let us have him back, in time we'll tor—we'll extract the truth out of him.'

The Bishop buried his face in his hands. When it reappeared, it was not smiling.

'If this man had anything to tell us, don't you think a whole night of torture would have revealed it? Either he's innocent, or you're an incompetent fool. Which is it?'

For a moment the captain seemed to be treating this as a serious question, but the ribaldry which broke out among the crowd brought him to his senses. He scowled, and remained silent. Bishop Arnaud shook his head.

'Let him go. Bring us the next witness.'

Next up was a young woman with lank black hair. Her already ragged clothing was dishevelled, and she flicked her head from side to side, as if struggling to take in her surroundings. If she too had spent the last night being interrogated by the guards, then God alone knows what punishments were inflicted on her to induce her to speak. As she was led forward, her eyes were wide and staring.

'And what is your name?'

'Catherine.' Her voice was barely audible.

'Speak up please.'

'Catherine de Valès.'

'And are you a leper?'

'No. No, I am not.'

'Then what do you have to tell us about the conspiracy in which the lepers are alleged to be involved?'

She looked around at the captain of the guard. He nodded.

'I heard a conversation between two lepers,' she said.

'I see. And what did they say?'

'They were placing things in a cloth bag. And I heard them describe each of the ingredients as they inserted them.'

'Ingredients of what?'

The woman looked back at the captain of the guard once more, and mouthed the word 'poison', her eyebrows raised to indicate that the word was an interrogative. He nodded vigorously.

'Ingredients of poison, my lord,' she said.

The Bishop took a deep breath and raised his eyes. 'Go on.'

'I can remember the ingredients they were putting in as if it were yesterday. There was the head of a snake, the feet of a toad, and hairs from a woman's—I'm sorry my lord, modesty forbids me to say more—anyway, they were mixing these things with a black liquid, foul to look at and even more foul to smell.'

'So, you were close enough to smell the liquid. Close enough, then, to identify the conspirators as well. Are they here? Can you point them out?'

'Well . . .' She looked around at the captain again. He shook his head.

'No my lord, it was dark.'

'I see. You couldn't recognise the conspirators, and yet you could see a black liquid in the dark. And did they say what they intended to do with this fetid concoction?'

'They said they were going to seal the bag and then drop it into our well. They said this would serve the healthy Christians right for treating them as outcasts, just as the Jews had treated the Samaritans.'

'And when did this happen?'

'Recently, my lord. Not long ago.'

'Think, woman. Yesterday? Last week? Last month? Last year?'

She looked around once more, this time panic-stricken. The captain of the guard mouthed something to her, but she could not make it out. She looked at the Bishop, then lowered her eyes.

'I—I can't remember, my lord.'

'So, let me get this straight. You don't know who these people were, you don't even remember when this conversation took place, but you can remember the exact ingredients of the potion they were preparing.'

'Well, yes, my lord.'

'And if it was too dark to see, how do you know they were lepers?'

This was a question too far for poor Catherine de Valès, and she dissolved into tears.

'Because the captain of the guard told me,' she sobbed.

The rest of the day was occupied by interviews with similarly, or even more, unconvincing witnesses. Father Tomas sat through the proceedings in silence, his face becoming progressively more agitated as the day wore on. By mid-afternoon he was fidgeting in his seat with frustration, folding and unfolding his arms every few minutes, crossing and uncrossing his legs. Bishop Arnaud, to his credit, remained dogged in his cross-examination. Indeed, he seemed determined to have done with the whole matter by exposing the absurdity of the claims which had been put forward. From time to time, Father Tomas glanced at him with an expression bordering on outright hatred.

When the light began to fail and, more to the point, everyone present was stiff with cold, the Bishop wearily called proceedings to an end for the day. Roger and I walked home with our cloaks wrapped tightly around us against the bitter wind.

'Why is Tomas so anxious to pursue this nonsense?' I asked. 'Even the ordinary people can't take seriously the idea that lepers want to take over the country.'

'Tomas is a very bitter man, that's why he's dangerous. At his age, he'll never be any more than an ordinary priest—not that I'm saying all priests are ordinary, but you know what I mean. Doubtless he thinks he should have at least reached the exalted height of bishop, but he comes from a humble background and

225

doesn't have any high-born relatives in positions of influence to arrange it for him.'

'So because he can't get back at the people he really resents, the people in power, he takes his bitterness out on the rest of humanity.'

'That's how it seems to me. Then again, I loathe the man anyway, so perhaps you shouldn't take too much notice of what I say.'

XXXVII

Next day, Roger and I made our way back to the church. Unusually for that region it had snowed overnight, causing the low sun to reflect brightly off roofs and tree branches, making them gleam like silver. I could not help smiling at this unexpected natural beauty.

'This must remind you of home,' Roger said.

'For a long time I've hardly given England a thought but, yes, it can be beautiful there in winter.'

This time we managed to position ourselves near the front of the nave. The morning proceeded in very much the same way as the previous day. I wondered that the so-called witnesses were so ill-prepared, given the clear determination in certain quarters to produce some kind of foundation for the accusation against the lepers. In some cases, their testimonies were mutually contradictory. By early afternoon, Bishop Arnaud had had enough.

'I do not intend to waste any more time on this nonsense. Let all those who have perjured themselves so blatantly in this house of God look to their own souls. Unless anyone can provide some testimony which is even moderately coherent and credible, I intend to put an end to this charade.'

For a few moments there was a deathly hush, then a voice rang out from the back of the church.

'I advise you not to act precipitately, my lord. You have not yet heard the most important piece of evidence.'

The congregation turned as one in time to see Aymery de Clos himself beginning the long march down the centre of the nave, carrying a sheaf of documents. The crowd parted just enough to allow him through, and he brushed against them with obvious distaste. When he reached the table at which Bishop Arnaud was seated, he placed the documents upon it, though out of his reach.

'I have received this communication from Bishop Fournier of Pamiers. It sheds a whole new light on the accusations which have been made against the lepers.'

Bishop Arnaud made no effort to hide his irritation at this development.

'And why should the Bishop of Pamiers write to you? If he had something to pass on which was germane to this examination, he would have sent it to me.'

'You will have to ask Bishop Fournier yourself,' the Seneschal replied with barely-concealed contempt. 'See for yourself. Is that not his seal?'

Bishop Arnaud held it up to confirm for himself that indeed it was, but nevertheless remained unyielding.

'This is a matter for an ecclesiastical court. You have no jurisdiction here.'

'On the contrary,' de Clos replied. 'You will see, if you take the trouble to read what I have just presented to you, that King Philip has confirmed that the crimes involved here constitute *lèse majesté*, so that the investigation is now a matter for secular authority. I thank you for your efforts so far, but I am afraid you will now have to stand aside and allow me to continue. Indeed, I believe the contents of Bishop Fournier's letter will demonstrate that your interrogations to this point have been irrelevant.'

The Bishop stared at the Seneschal and made no effort to conceal his anger.

'How convenient,' Roger said under his breath. 'Those found guilty of treason against the King forfeit their property to him. I'm sure that can have had nothing to do with his decision.'

The crowd had by now become highly restive, most of them having witnessed the Seneschal's previous attempt to stir up public feeling against the lepers. They were not about to provide him with a compliant audience. At length he drew his sword, flourished it and then struck the table as hard as he could with the pommel. The force caused it to leap from his hand, and it clattered onto the stone floor. The sound succeeded in bringing about an uneasy silence. Aymery de Clos picked up his sword, replaced it in its sheath and positioned himself with some care immediately in front of the Bishop, so that the latter could see nothing but his back.

'Bishop Fournier,' he announced, 'has sent me the details of the sworn deposition of a leper interrogated at Pamiers recently. It will shock and astonish all those who hear it. Indeed, it appears that this conspiracy goes even farther than any of us had previously suspected.'

'Well get on and read it then,' the Bishop said in a voice audible to anyone within a reasonable distance of him. The Seneschal shuffled in annoyance and drew himself up to his full height, such as it was.

'The deposition contains the confession of one Guillaume Agasse, commander, as he chose to call himself, of the leper colony at a place called Estang in the diocese of Pamiers. He was interrogated several times by the Bishop and his officials, and slowly unveiled the depth of the conspiracy in which he was involved. Some of the less salubrious details I will gloss over for fear of shocking those of a sensitive disposition.

'The major part of his story relates to a visit which he made to Toulouse on a certain Sunday at the invitation of the preceptor of a leper colony there. When he arrived, he found himself in the company of some fifty to sixty heads of leper houses who had all received similar invitations. They gathered in the main room of the house, and were addressed by a leader of the Toulouse lepers. This man outlined the grounds of their grievance, that the healthy Christians treated them as outcasts and denied them their rightful place in society. He went on to say that it was time for the lepers to fight back by poisoning the Christians to turn them all into lepers too. When this had been accomplished, they would seize all the Christians' lands and goods and make themselves rulers of France, and eventually of the world.'

The Seneschal paused to allow the implications of this revelation to sink in, but the crowd's silent response suggested, once again, that they were more puzzled than outraged. He hurried on.

'Guillaume Agasse wondered how all this was to be achieved, but the leader of the Toulouse lepers explained further. He said that certain rich Jews shared their contempt for Christian society, but knew that they were powerless themselves because they were viewed with such deep suspicion by the Christian majority. They therefore wished the lepers to carry out their strategy for them, and were prepared to fund whatever steps were necessary to bring these things about.'

The mention of a Jewish element in the conspiracy brought predictable murmurings from the crowd. Here they were on more familiar ground.

'Not only this, but other enemies of Christ were only too willing to add their names to the conspiracy. Two prominent infidels, the King of Granada and the Sultan of Babylon, had sent their support and promised that all lepers who involved themselves in carrying out the conspiracy would be richly rewarded, provided they deny Christ and defile the holy cross. The Toulouse commander stressed that by attending the meeting they had made themselves co-conspirators, and would be expected to play their part. He directed their attention to a man standing by the door, whom Guillaume had not previously noticed. This man was tall and black, wore a helmet and a sword and carried a halberd. It was made clear that this man would behead anyone who dissented.

'They were then asked to swear an oath on a certain book which, Guillaume said, had a strange symbol on the cover which he did not recognise, and to abjure Christ, which they all did enthusiastically. He then produced a cross, which the representatives filed past in order to spit or urinate on it. The Toulouse commander told them that they would be summoned in the near future to a meeting where they would meet the King of Granada and the Sultan of Babylon in person, and concluded by reminding them that, when they had dealt with the Christians, they would themselves be masters of their own towns and villages and would be able to appropriate the lands and titles of the Christians.

'Before departing, each attendee was given a large leather bag full of poisons with which to pollute the water in his own community. The poison consisted of the defiled remnants of a consecrated host, mixed with a substance containing fragments of snake, toad, lizard, bat and human excrement. Guillaume Agasse reports that over the next few weeks he joyfully carried out the duty to which he had sworn himself, poisoning wells, cisterns and springs around Pamiers and, finally, the River Ariège itself.'

Aymery de Clos tossed the letters carelessly on the table behind him, as if daring Bishop Arnaud to pick them up and read them for himself. The Bishop did not even glance at them. By now the crowd were shouting, calling for action but seemingly in no agreement against whom it should be directed. In fact, they seemed unsure who they had just been told was their real enemy. Roger went to move forward. I grabbed his sleeve and warned him not to do or say anything rash. He pulled his arm away, made his way to a spot in front of the table where Bishop Arnaud sat, and turned to face de Clos.

'My lord Seneschal,' he shouted at the top of his voice. 'My lord Seneschal, I have a question.'

The hubbub amongst the crowd slowly died away until all eyes were straining to catch sight of the man who had dared this interruption. The Seneschal himself seemed unperturbed and stared back. Roger took hold of the edges of his cloak, performing in the manner of his profession.

'Has the King decreed what punishment is to be exacted on anyone found guilty of taking part in this conspiracy?'

'Of course. He is to be burned alive.'

'And if the conspirator is a woman?'

'The same, except that if she be pregnant or nursing, the sentence be delayed until her child is independent of her.'

'So there are to be no exceptions to the King's decree?'

'Indeed not. And why are you so interested in this point, my friend?'

I had never heard anyone say the word 'friend' with such malevolent intent. Roger took this in his stride.

'Then has Guillaume Agasse been burned?'

The crowd murmured. The Seneschal frowned. After a few moments, he seemed to realise the direction in which Roger's questions were about to lead.

'Not yet. He remains in prison.'

'Then sentence has been passed, but deferred.'

'I'm not sure. That is possible. Why are you so interested?'

'But Guillaume Agasse is a man. You told us that only pregnant and nursing women would have their sentences deferred.'

Aymery de Clos' expression revealed his increasing annoyance. The crowd, however, were hanging on his every word, clearly enjoying this unexpected exchange. Bishop Arnaud was smiling broadly, unlike Father Tomas.

'I have already told you that I am not in possession of the full facts.'

'And yet you claim to be well-informed about all other aspects of this matter. Pardon me, my lord, if I find that strange. Is it not possible, indeed likely, that this Guillaume Agasse was promised that by condemning others to the stake he would keep his own life if he put his name to this most far-fetched concoction of fantasies?'

'I am forming the impression, young man, that you are inclined to side with the lepers and Jews, with those who wish to poison us by magic and take away all that we hold dear. I advise you to be careful, very careful, what you say from now on.'

There were some hostile comments from the crowd directed at Roger, but he remained undeterred.

'And how many Christians are known to have died or contracted leprosy as a result of this alleged conspiracy?'

'Who knows? It could be thousands.'

'So you have no idea. The answer could just as easily be none, then. I will ask one more question, my lord Seneschal. You have stated, in front of all these good people assembled here, and before God, that King Philip has insisted that all accused of this conspiracy be tried by the secular arm, not by an ecclesiastical court. Yet the deposition you have just read out was made, by your own admission, in the episcopal court at Pamiers. Can you explain this contradiction?'

The Seneschal had had enough. After a few moments trying to think of an answer, his anger exploded.

'Why do we waste time listening to the ranting of this sympathiser, this man who, for all we know, is secretly a leper himself? What more evidence do we need than what the Bishop of Pamiers has already obtained? We must immediately root out those who threaten to destroy us. They are in our community carrying out their evil conspiracy as we speak. What are we waiting for?'

The crowd roared its acclaim, a man at the back of the church called for everyone to follow him out into the city to punish the conspirators, and this set off a general stampede towards the west door. Anyone who stumbled was trampled by rushing feet. Roger and I held our places, as did de Clos, his angry expression now replaced by a smug smile.

'Never learn, do you, Roger?'

He swept up his papers from the table as Bishop Arnaud looked away, then, accompanied by the captain of the guard, made his way out through the south transept door. Father Tomas was nowhere to be seen. At length, Bishop Arnaud, Roger and I were left alone.

'You should have known it would do no good,' the Bishop said. 'If it suits their purposes better, people prefer to believe an obvious lie rather than the truth.'

'The Bishop of Pamiers knows better, though,' Roger said. 'What will he gain from the massacres which are bound to follow?'

Bishop Arnaud's voice sounded weary. 'That's a presumptuous question, young man. I advise you not to ask it again.'

'My lord,' I said, 'will you be pressed to falsify your report of the depositions you've heard here, to make it sound as if the conspiracy is real?'

The Bishop seemed too melancholic to berate me for my lack of respect.

'I will do my duty before God. And his Holiness.'

He rose slowly to his feet. We bowed, he made his way into the chapel of our Lady and sank to his knees in front of her statue.

I advised Roger that we should stay in the church until after nightfall, but he insisted that he wanted to return home as soon as possible. We kept away from the busiest streets, and had nearly completed the journey when a cry came from behind us.

'It's him, the Jew-lover. Let's get him.'

We turned around to see a group of about a dozen men, some armed with staves and cudgels, running towards us. I was rooted to the spot until Roger grabbed my arm.

'This way. Run.'

We made for a narrow alley a short way ahead. I prayed that it would not turn out to be a dead-end. In fact it led out onto a chaos of tenements at oblique angles to one another. The path was strewn with rubbish and excrement, and the stench would have been unbearable had we been moving any slower. I did not dare look back, but I sensed that the sound of the mob's feet was growing closer. We turned a corner and Roger immediately pulled me through an open gateway into a tiny courtyard, closing the gate behind him. I looked up to see an old man staring at us in disbelief.

Roger put his finger to his lips. The old man shrugged and went indoors.

For some time, we listened to the sound of the mob searching the area, opening and slamming doors, interrogating people with threats. I was so afraid that I thought I would lose control of my bodily functions. At last, these sounds began to die away as the men presumably decided to vent their fury elsewhere. We waited until it was fully dark then retraced our steps, keeping away from any source of light, ducking into the pools of deepest darkness when we heard anyone approaching. By the time we completed our slow and circuitous journey back to Roger's house, I was shaking from both exhaustion and fear.

When we felt sufficiently recovered, we sat in silence for a while drinking wine. I have no idea if it was good. Roger had risked lighting a fire, against my advice. His face had taken on a fixed expression, which I read as a determination not to be cowed by the madness unleashed that day.

'Can you believe,' he said, 'that our Seneschal, Aymery de Cros, last year mobilised all the forces at his disposal to drive away the Pastoureaux because he said they brought danger to the Jews of this city, and it was his duty to protect them. The man's a flagrant hypocrite.'

'Yes, but don't forget that King Philip had it in for the Pastoureaux. Anyway, I expect he would say that his position requires him to be flexible enough to bend with the wind. More to the point, however, it seems we're both fugitives now.'

Roger smiled, briefly. 'You know how it is with mobs. Someone stirs them up, they wreak havoc, they get drunk, not necessarily in that order, they sleep it off and then they can barely remember what they've done or why.'

'Nevertheless—'

'Nevertheless, we just have to sit it out until they come to their senses, or what pass for senses in their case. Things will die down. They always do.'

I drew back a curtain as far as I dared. The overcast sky hinted that more snow might be on the way. Above the city, the nocturnal clouds reflected a deep red glow from burning buildings below. The air was heavy with smoke. From time to time we heard shouting and screaming. Several groups of armed men ran past and, from what I could see, as the night went on the violence became more and more indiscriminate.

'I would say that God's given you a strong signal not to prolong your stay in Carcassonne,' Roger said. 'Much as I'd be happy for you to remain longer. But the Cardinal's men will be snooping around after this, you can be sure.'

'I can't leave now. Not while you're in danger.'

'I've told you, for me the danger will soon pass. For you, it may not.'

We watched through the night. I have no idea how much wine we consumed, but this time it did not have the effect of lightening our mood. After some hours, the sounds of murder and destruction began to grow more faint as the mob's fury exhausted itself. God alone would know how many innocents perished that night.

I closed my eyes and fell asleep in my chair.

XXXVIII

When I awoke the next morning, stiff and aching, Roger was nowhere to be found. If he had been taken by force, the commotion would surely have roused me. I washed and breakfasted on what I could find in his sparsely-furnished food-store, then sank back into my chair, absorbed in my thoughts.

A hammering on the door made me leap from my seat. My hands balled themselves into fists.

'Who's there?'

There was no response, but the hammering resumed, if anything more insistent. With my foot behind it, I opened the door just wide enough to see an elderly woman, probably at least sixty years of age. She was pacing up and down in agitation. I could see no-one else in the vicinity, so I opened the door wider. She had no time for introductions.

'Are you the priest who's staying with Roger the lawyer?'

'Why do you want to know?'

'If you are, my father's asking for you. He's dying.'

I calculated the likely age of this woman's father.

'I'm the one you're looking for. You'd better take me to him.'

It was no surprise that she led me, albeit by a more direct route than I had previously travelled, back to the house of Guilabert. The old man lay on a rough mattress on the floor, covered by a blanket, his face ashen, his eyes closed. We knelt at his side. I confirmed that he was still breathing, but it was evident that his life was ebbing away. Above the staleness I had noticed before, there was another scent in the air.

'Can you hear me, Guilabert?' I caught his daughter's surprise that I knew his name, but she said nothing. 'I'm Nicholas. You told me your tale a few days ago, about Montségur. Do you remember?'

His eyes flickered. He tried to raise his hand, and I took hold of it. It was icy cold.

'There's nothing to fear. I'll stay with you until—for as long as you need me. Your daughter's also here. I'd like to say some words of comfort, Guilabert, although I know they're not the words you would really like to hear. Are you happy for me to do that?'

I felt his hand give mine the slightest of squeezes. I recited the words of Extreme Unction, knowing that if by some miracle a Cathar perfectus had walked through the door at that moment, I would gladly have given way. Whether Guilabert could understand the Latin words I was speaking, there was no way of knowing, but I hoped that he was at least receiving some measure of comfort. His daughter remained silent, but tears flowed freely down her cheeks.

I sensed that his soul was about to pass from this life, and recalled being told once that hearing is usually the last of our faculties to go before death. I leaned forward and spoke into his ear.

'I will make sure that your tale is known to future generations, Guilabert. I'll write it down and take it to a place where chroniclers will read and study it. I give you my word on this.'

I thought that the merest hint of a smile passed across his lips, but could not be sure. A few moments later, he gasped, his body became rigid, and then subsided. His hand fell lifeless from mine. His daughter began to sob, and I was forced to hang my head to conceal my own grief. At length our eyes met, we rose to our feet, and she stared at me.

'Did you mean what you said to him?' she asked.

'Every word.'

'You realise that—'

'He was an unrepentant Cathar. Of course. Judgement is, thankfully, God's responsibility, not mine.'

When I returned to Roger's house, there was still no sign of him. I delved in the bottom of my bag and retrieved an old scrap of vellum, sat at his desk and wrote down in the fullest detail, in his own Occitan tongue, what Guilabert had told me of the siege of Montségur, using his own words as far as I could recall them. When the task was complete, I still had no idea how to fulfil my promise to make it available to posterity. Would any chronicler wish to record the testimony of an avowed heretic? If the sum of my experiences since setting foot in France were any guide, a way of keeping my word to Guilabert would present itself sooner or later.

I turned over the piece of vellum and allowed my thoughts free rein, roaming across all the events which had occurred since my departure from England, and what I had learned from the remarkable people I had met. In many ways, I was not the same Nicholas who set off from Croyland in bad grace so long ago that—well, it did seem as if a whole lifetime had intervened. Some time later, I found that I had written the following, in English:

The words of Nicholas of Croyland, written on the occasion of his visit to the city of Carcassonne in the year of our Lord thirteen hundred and twenty-one, recording the following propositions:

One. Men and women of independent thought have come to differing but equally valid conclusions, based on their own often brutal experience, regarding the reason for God's having placed us upon this earth, or indeed the absence of any such reason.

Two. I have watched others die many more times in the last half-year than in the whole of my previous life, and have concluded that death is invariably, on one level or another, a release from life.

Three. I am shaped, directed and limited by my own past. The single event which dominates my childhood memories, and which continues to haunt me through adulthood, I have only ever felt able to reveal to a child. In order to achieve any degree of absolution from my guilt, I must become like a child again myself.

Four. Power and wealth are corrupting influences on all men. Jesus Christ during his ministry possessed nothing. He told the rich young ruler who wanted to enter the Kingdom of Heaven that it would be necessary first to dispose of all that he owned. The apostles possessed nothing when they set out to preach the Gospel to all humanity. My head rings with the words of Jesus Christ and his apostles, not those of archbishops and cardinals.

Five. Hope and despair are, in equal measure, essential components of the human condition.

Six. When I wish to inspire myself with hope for the future, I think of Madeleine and everything she taught me. When I am in the depths of despair, the face which appears in my thoughts to reassure me and give me courage is that of Esclarmonde. They were little more than children, but experience had made them wise beyond their years, and far wiser than I.

Seven. I will never return to the stifling security of a closed spiritual community.

I folded the sheet of vellum and placed it in the back of my copy of St Augustine's *Confessions*.

Roger returned later in the day, apparently in good spirits. He said nothing of how he had spent the day until I asked him directly.

'I've been pursuing my profession,' he said. 'Even a man of the people needs to eat, drink and pay his bills. You were sleeping peacefully, so I didn't like to disturb you.'

'I don't know about peacefully. Weren't you worried, going out after last night?'

'Why? As I expected, our pursuers were all sleeping off their exertions, most of them in a drunken heap in the street. I just stepped over them.'

'And the victims?'

Roger's eyes moved towards the window. 'I was due to see a certain Jew, Isaac, this morning. When I got there, his house had been ransacked and set on fire. There was no sign of Isaac.'

'Perhaps he had enough warning to make his escape.'

'Hmm. Perhaps.'

Given the recent murderous attentions of the Pastoureaux towards the Jews, and the evidence I had seen in both Narbonne and Carcassonne of the ease with which feeling against them could be whipped up, I wondered how long it would be before there were no Jews left in southern France to persecute. Events of the last few days indicated that those with a will to do so could find other ready victims if necessary.

'How are lepers treated in England?' Roger asked.

'Most large towns have a leper hospice. People fear the disease, of course, but by and large they also see it as a duty to show charity towards the victims.'

'It used to be like that here,' he said. 'But a certain royal physician, no less, has pronounced that one of the causes of leprosy is having sexual intercourse with a woman while she's menstruating. He also declared that the physical deterioration of lepers is the outward sign of a simultaneous inner moral deterioration. When you wash the blood of a leper through a cloth, black stains are left behind as a sign of the evil which is inside him. Did you know that?'

'Strangely enough, I'm sure that wasn't covered in my education. But from what you say, it's no wonder that lepers form a ready target. Still, don't we always have to ask, who's getting what out of stirring up this ill-feeling against them?'

'Indeed we do, and the answer is, it's not yet clear. We'll have to wait and see who's considerably richer in a year or so.'

'From what we've heard, it'll be King Philip.'

'Well, if our kings are able to destroy the once-mighty Templars to get their hands on their wealth, I suppose a few miserable leper houses won't present much of an obstacle.'

'Changing the subject, Roger, did you mean what you said last night?'

'I said lots of things last night.'

'About God giving me a sign to leave Carcassonne.'

'You're His servant, I'm not. Signs from God aren't my speciality.'

'But you must have said it for a reason.'

'Must I? Perhaps God inspired me, then.' He grinned. 'Of course I'd be happy for you to stay, Nicholas, I enjoy your company, but what is there to stay for? Whatever you're searching for, you're not likely to find it here.'

'What makes you think I'm searching for something?'

'Your hungry expression. You have a restless mind. I get the feeling that you've embarked on some kind of pilgrimage. Not to Rome or Jerusalem, perhaps a journey into your self, if that makes any sense.'

'And my destination?'

'I could say Truth, or Knowledge, or Wisdom. Perhaps all of those. But you're in a better position to know than I am.'

Roger poured us some wine and we sat in front of the fire.

'When I arrived in Narbonne,' I said, 'just as the plague broke out, Pierre begged me to leave before it was too late. I spent the night praying to God to speak to me in some way, to show me whether I should stay or not. I heard only silence. The next morning, I arrived at the main gate intending to take Pierre's advice, but something I saw by chance made me change my mind. Wasn't that God speaking to me through events?'

Roger shrugged. 'As I say, you're closer to Him than I am. But can I say something heretical in confidence that you won't inform on me to the Inquisitors?'

I smiled and sipped my wine, and that seemed to provide him with the reassurance he sought.

'I've often heard people say that God spoke to them through some apparently remarkable coincidence, as you've just done. I always feel tempted to ask them: what about all the coincidences you've seen which didn't lead to any major change in your life, which didn't help you to make a decision, which just happened and then you went on with your life? Surely you can't just pick and choose like that, decide that God's directing you on one occasion and not another simply because of the eventual outcome?'

'An interesting thought,' I said, 'though hardly heretical.'

'But suppose you take the same line of reasoning and apply it more widely. Think of all the reasons which have been given over the centuries for believing in God. Let's keep it simple and just say the Christian God. What if you start from the other end and ask yourself: how would the world be different if God didn't exist, at least the kind of God we've been taught to believe in?'

I drank slowly to give me time to consider how far Roger might be intending to take this line of argument.

'If God didn't exist, neither would the world, since He created it.'

'Ah, you say that because we've been conditioned to think that's the only way the world could have come into existence. But suppose our world and the moon and the planets and the stars weren't created, they came to be through some perfectly natural process we don't as yet understand? Suppose even that they never were created, they've simply always existed. Imagine a universe where one of these hypotheses were true. How would it look different from the universe we see around us today? How would the world be different? How would our lives have changed?'

'But you're only postponing the problem,' I said. 'In your universe, who created the animals and plants which populate the world? Who created humanity?'

'As a lawyer, I refer you to my previous answer. Listen. Sometimes when men are digging in quarries around here, they discover animal bones, the remains of creatures like none alive today, limb bones from animals which must have been five times the size of a horse, some so old that they've turned to stone. What were they? The cattle of giants or titans?'

'Perhaps the remains of creatures which perished in the great Flood.'

'But doesn't the Book of Genesis tell us that God commanded Noah to take into the ark two of every kind of animal then living on the earth? Did Noah disobey that command? Or maybe there were some he just couldn't catch in time.'

My mind went back to my discussions with Zacharias, and the ways in which he challenged my admittedly conservative way of interpreting Scripture. I also recalled the first of the propositions I had written down just a short time before, and which was coming under immediate challenge.

'God never promises us that we'll understand everything however much we study and exercise our reason, at least this side of death. Perhaps accepting that is the first step towards real faith.'

Roger watched me for a few moments in silence. I cradled my empty cup, but for once he did not offer to refill it.

XXXIX

Next day, I found Roger pacing the room in a state of agitation. He did not wait for me to ask the reason.

'I've had two pieces of news. You may or may not be pleased to know that Narbonne has a new Archbishop.'

'Is his name Raymond de Savigny, by any chance?'

'I see you're ahead of me,' he said. 'Anyway, perhaps he'll be an improvement on the last incumbent.'

'He can hardly be worse. You said there were two pieces of news.'

'Pierre is under arrest.'

'What?'

'You heard me. What did you expect? The Cardinal will know he must have helped you to escape.'

'I told Pierre he'd be in danger,' I said, 'but he was the one who insisted I go. He said he could talk his way out of any situation, and didn't seem to think the Cardinal would care that much about me anyway.'

'Well, it seems he was wrong on both counts. Cardinal de Savigny doesn't take no for an answer, and he doesn't forgive people who cross him. But Pierre will have known that.'

'I must go back to Narbonne. If it's me the Cardinal wants—'

'Don't be ridiculous. If you go back, the whole story will come out. As long as you stay out of sight, Pierre can continue saying he doesn't know how you got away or where you've gone, and eventually they'll have to let him go.'

I sank into a chair. Roger sat opposite me and leaned forward.

'Pierre knew what he was doing. I thought having Madeleine with him would give him everything to live for, a reason to just keep his head down, but obviously I was wrong.'

I took a deep breath. 'Madeleine died. Of the plague.'

Roger spent a long time digesting this information, then stood up with his back to me and put his hands on his head.

'You must leave. Leave now.'

'So soon?'

He turned around, lowering his hands. His voice was hostile.

'Trouble seems to follow you around, Nicholas, doesn't it? If de Savigny really wants to hunt you down, he'll find you in Carcassonne. For your sake, for my sake, for Pierre's sake, just go. Get as far away from here as you can, as quickly as you can, and for God's sake don't tell me where you're going.'

Despite my distress at the way in which Roger and I had parted, for a while I was animated by an unexpected energy. This stemmed partly from a desire, born out of fear, I readily acknowledged, to put as much distance between myself and Carcassonne in as short a space of time as possible. But the knowledge that now I was totally dependent on my own resources was strangely exciting.

When the light began to fade, and I to tire, I hailed a passing farmer to ask for a ride on his bullock-cart. He proved to be as charitable as those who work on the land generally are. When he asked me how far I was going, I said without premeditation, and yet without hesitation, that I was heading northwards to Rocamadour. He nodded and smiled. A little further on, he observed that I would not reach a village before nightfall, and insisted that I spend the night with him and his wife, to which I readily agreed.

Their farmhouse was simple but clean and well-appointed, and his wife young and energetic. When I watched them together, they smiled and touched one another readily, being evidently very much in love. We sat around an open hearth to consume a meal of bread and broth, and afterwards drank a fiery concoction which the farmer said he distilled in an outhouse from grapes left over from, or not suitable for, the wine harvest. I sipped it gingerly, while my hosts scoffed at me and emptied their cups in one go. I recounted some of my more appropriate adventures, and they told me of the difficulties they had faced in the last few years because of the poor harvests, including the loss of their first child. When I offered to pay them for the food and lodging they provided for me, however, they took the deepest offence. It seemed I was becoming adept at upsetting those whose hospitality I enjoyed.

By the next morning, my offence had been forgotten, or at least politely consigned to history. My hosts provided me with bread and water for my journey, but warned me that the way north lay through the Black Mountains, and that the only road along the main valley had been closed since the beginning of winter by a landslide. The shepherds knew other routes through the mountains, but without their help I should not even attempt to cross. When I set off, however, the sun was shining, and I felt sufficiently refreshed to be confident of my ability to navigate my way unaided.

It was not long before the mountains began to loom in the distance, and when the sun disappeared behind a bank of cloud the reason for the name of this range became apparent. For long periods I saw no other human being, let alone the shepherds the farmer had advised me to look out for. I also had no idea what the extent of the Black Mountains was; would it take me hours, days or even weeks to see my first glimpse of fields and rivers on the other side? I had not the slightest idea. There were, by my reckoning, four or five hours of daylight remaining, and I still had some of the bread and water the farmer and his wife had given me. I began to climb.

At first the ascent was gentle and I made good progress, now feeling more confident that I had made the right decision. I even encountered a shepherd with his flock on the lower pastures, and asked him the best way to get across the mountains. He stared at me with what I can only describe as suspicion, then replied in a strange accent, if indeed I interpreted correctly what he told me, that he was accustomed to drive his sheep straight over the top, but travelling alone I could take a shorter route along a narrow path skirting a gorge. He pointed into the distance, but I could see neither gorge nor path. I asked how far away, and he replied that it was not too far.

Continuing upwards in the direction he had indicated, I did eventually see a sharp-sided valley in the distance. As I stood at the top and looked down, I decided that, if path there were, it must be an exceedingly narrow one, too narrow for the human eye to pick out. After staring for a while, however, I noticed a descending ledge, strewn with rocks, which led around a crag and presumably farther. My feet slid on the loose shale, and my progress was painfully slow. To compound my anxiety, a distant storm rumbled and growled

245

somewhere further down the valley, but I did not dare quicken my pace. It grew darker, and the wind picked up.

I hugged the cliff face, terrified that the force of the wind might cause me to lose my footing at any moment. Pressing myself against the bare rock, I prayed to God for deliverance, barely daring to close my eyes for a moment. I plucked up the courage to look down; the drop below was precipitous and my head began to spin. It was then that I noticed what appeared to be a series of caves a short way ahead. If I could reach them, they would provide some measure of shelter until the storm abated.

Rain now began to fall, or more aptly to be hurled downwards, lashing my face and hands. In great trepidation I edged forward over pebbles which continually slid away from under my feet, and lacerated my hands and knees when I tried to make progress on all fours. After what seemed an eternity, I reached the first cave and saw to my surprise that the path between the various cave-mouths appeared to have been swept clear of debris. The first was empty but exposed to the force of the wind, and with great caution I moved on to the next. Inside, to my astonishment, was a pile of clothing, together with some water containers. In truth, it seemed that God in His grace had provided me with a ready-made shelter for the duration of the storm, and I sat on the cold, hard stone floor, feeling myself to be the luckiest man alive.

I took out the last of my bread and sated the worst of my hunger, grateful to be out of the storm. After a while, my spirits were restored to the point where I decided to check the remaining caves, and in the next I received the surprise of my life. At first I could see little, but as my eyes adjusted to the dim light they picked out at the back of the cave a human figure, a very old man wrapped in blankets, his back against the cave wall. Whether he was alive or dead I could not at first tell. When the shock of this discovery had abated, I entered further and crouched next to him. He was breathing but was completely motionless. His eyes were open and blinked occasionally, but there was not the slightest flicker when I placed my hand in front of them.

'Friend,' I said, 'my name is Nicholas. Nicholas of Croyland. Will you do me the honour of telling me yours?'

There was no response. His eyes continued to stare blankly out of his skeletal face, framed by his long, fine white hair. He appeared to be in some kind of trance. I sat down and waited, and eventually his breathing quickened and his eyes flickered, as if he were slowly emerging from his former state. He began to rock slowly backwards and forwards. Finally, with a deep sigh, he stared directly at me, his eyes no longer unseeing. I shivered.

'Nicholas,' he said, in a voice like the breeze whispering through a wheat field. Clearly his senses had still been functioning. For some time we stared at one another, and the old man did not seem to be the slightest discomfited by this. I asked him again: 'What is your name?'

'I no longer have a name.'

'Then what was your name previously?'

'What does it matter? It was someone else's name.'

I began to wonder whether I should have suppressed my curiosity and remained in the adjoining cave after all, but an instinctive curiosity drove me to want to know more about this strange hermit.

'How long have you been here?' I asked.

'All my life.'

'But how can that be?'

'My life began when I came to this cave. Before that my existence was a dream.'

'What made you come here?'

The old man closed his eyes, then said, 'God revealed to me that I was living in a world of shadows. I came here to find reality.'

'And do you find reality when you close your eyes?'

He opened them and looked deep into mine before replying. 'The only true reality is God residing in us. We cannot find Him by looking outwards.'

'But surely,' I said, 'we find Him in some way when we partake of the Eucharist, when we eat the body and drink the blood of His divine Son?'

I think the hermit snorted, but I cannot be certain. In any case, he made no reply to my proposition.

'If the only true reality is inside us,' I continued, 'does it not follow that the external world, these mountains, this cave, perhaps even our own bodies, are nothing but a figment of our imagination?'

'Hmm. Perhaps,' he replied, 'they are a figment of God's imagination.'

This made the old man chuckle. Was he playing a game with me? Or had his life of solitude left him unhinged?

'Where did you study, Brother Nicholas?'

'Why do you call me Brother?' I said.

'Please answer my question.'

I was beginning to feel more than a little confused.

'As you've somehow already surmised, I was raised and educated at an abbey, of the Benedictine Order.'

'Ah. That tells me much. May I give you a word of advice? If you are truly seeking knowledge, as you try to deceive yourself you are—no, please don't interrupt—then you will have to put behind you everything you have learned about logic, rhetoric and, yes, theology. Only then will your mind be clear to see what is important and what is real.'

'But I can no more unlearn what I've learned than I can throw off my own body and exchange it for another.'

'Then there is no hope for you, Brother Nicholas. What did Jesus reply to the man who said he would follow him so long as he could bury his father first?'

'Jesus told him, "Leave the dead to bury the dead."'

'Exactly.'

'I still don't understand.'

'Jesus also said that it's necessary to die and be re-born in order to see the Kingdom of Heaven. Have you ever really thought what those words mean, Brother Nicholas?'

'I assume you're telling me that I must die to my old self, treat my past as having been consigned to the grave.'

He gave a slight nod. I still found it difficult to judge whether he was raving. Christian mystics had often been considered insane by their contemporaries. The old man had not finished with me.

'You believe that you are an educated man, clinging to your learning like a drowning man to a spar of timber, but you are a fool, Brother Nicholas. The bishops and cardinals, yes, and popes, will never see the Kingdom of Heaven because they surround themselves with worldly wealth and become attached to it. But you are no better. In your case, it is what you have been taught about the world and about God that you cannot bring yourself to give up.

You are arrogant because you think you are learned, but you have been taught nothing.'

What kind of learning was there which did not depend on drawing on the wisdom of the great teachers of bygone ages? He suddenly looked weary, as if the no doubt unaccustomed use of his voice had drained him of strength. He looked back at me, and through the gloom it seemed that his eyes had grown moist.

'It is so hard for you,' he said. 'You are young, you think that you are immortal, and you believe what you are told by people you look up to. I was once like you. As a young man I travelled to preach the Gospel in India, and that was where I learned that wisdom cannot be taught in the classroom. Indians believe that souls migrate to a new body at death, either upwards or downwards in the hierarchy of existence. The goal of earthly life is thus to secure rebirth at a higher spiritual level in the next lifetime. Yes, I know that the Cathars hold to a garbled version of this belief, but banish that from your mind. When a soul has been through many rebirths, and is not far from the ultimate state of Nirvana, it is characterised by its quiet wisdom and its instinctive spirituality. In everyday speech, the Indians refer to someone who has attained that level as an "old soul". I sense in you, Nicholas, that despite your arrogance and your slavish devotion to your learning, you have the potential to become an old soul. Does that shock you? Then so be it. Nothing I have said to you today seems important or meaningful to you now, but perhaps I have planted a seed. We shall see if it flourishes.'

The hermit leaned back once more against the cave wall. Before long his breathing resumed its slow, regular rate and his eyes lost any focus on this world. He reminded me of an animal in its winter hibernation. I watched him for a while, then rose, left the cave and settled myself to spend the night in the adjacent one. Outside, the storm was beginning to abate.

XL

The following morning the storm had fully blown itself out. When I looked into his cave, there was no sign of the nameless old hermit. My first thought was that my ordeal the previous day had so disordered my mind that I had imagined his very existence, that our strange discussion was nothing but a figment of my imagination. However, my nose alerted me to a roasted hare on the floor of the cave, presumably left for him by one of the shepherds. Its aroma was so enticing, and my stomach so empty, that I ripped off the two back legs and devoured the flesh greedily, looking over my shoulder in the hope that the hermit would not return. Of course he would know full well who the thief was, but hopefully he would sympathise with my overwhelming need. In any case, his ascetic life probably enabled him to survive on little food.

Rather than risk following the precipitous path further, I decided to retrace my steps, and scrambled back up to the top of the gorge. All I knew was that my direction of travel had to be generally northwards, so I set off briskly in the hope that the mountains could be crossed in the course of a day. Among the mountains it proved difficult to navigate, and the regular need to detour around obstacles left me disoriented and frequently lost. In early afternoon, however, I looked down into the valley and saw the site of the avalanche which had blocked the way along its floor. I spent some considerable time descending the side of the valley, but managed to emerge beyond the obstruction and proceeded from there onwards along the well-marked path with renewed enthusiasm, remembering to give thanks to God for what I saw as my deliverance from peril.

Even so, the path was rocky and did not make for easy walking, and several times I twisted an ankle as fatigue set in. But the mountains now began to taper downwards, and just as the light was fading I rounded a crag and saw in the distance ahead of me open fields and vineyards. I knelt on the spot to pray, but found my eyes misty with tears, whether from relief or exhaustion or some mixture of the two I had no idea. There was nowhere to shelter so I pressed on. Fortunately the night was clear and moonlit, and just when I felt it impossible to walk another step, I stumbled upon a small isolated cottage. The elderly occupants, seeing my condition, gave me what food and drink they could spare, then led me to a bed recessed into the wall of their one living room and covered me with blankets. For a few minutes I was conscious of their muted voices in the background, then knew no more.

Within another couple of days, I reached the town of Castres. This turned out to be a bustling, thriving community whose prosperity, to judge by the size of the local sheep market and the number of emporia selling its products, was based heavily on the wool trade. Along the river were rows of colourful houses, many built out over the water, which I was told were the homes of weavers and dyers. In places there were surviving remnants of the Roman fortifications from which the town clearly took its name. I visited the Benedictine monastery at its heart, and in the church made obeisance before the earthly remains of the blessed martyr St Vincent.

In a local inn I made the acquaintance of a group of merchants who were heading northwards, and who invited me to ride with them on one of their pack mules. The relief to my sore and blistered feet was more than welcome, even if their conversation often bordered on the vulgar. I accompanied them as far as the strikingly beautiful hilltop town of Albi. At one time it had been considered to be the place of origin of the Cathar heresy, hence the alternative name by which Cathars are sometimes known, Albigensians. Seeing no evidence that the place any longer formed a hotbed of heresy, I decided to rest there for a day or two to allow my body to restore itself to strength, not to mention healing the blisters which had seemingly transferred themselves from my feet to my nether parts.

It transpired that a number of pilgrims visited Albi, most following the route to the great shrine of Santiago, but I met a group who were making the detour to Rocamadour before once again heading westwards towards the Pyrenean Mountains. I continued my journey with them and found them a very mixed bunch, but on the whole most congenial company. Several were Italian, so my ability to converse with them was strictly limited, but the majority were from southern France. Their number included a friar named Ricardo, a jovial character with an enormous love for all humanity, it seemed, and a humble devotion to his calling, quite in contrast to the charlatan who had turned up in Narbonne soon after the outbreak of the plague. Ricardo, by contrast, appeared able only to see the better qualities of those he met. Any coin or surplus food which came into his possession would almost immediately find its way into the hands of the nearest pauper.

We stayed one night at a wayside monastery, and several more at hostels which had been set up along the route especially for pilgrims. No-one had enquired up to this point about my background, although one or two commented on the curious hybrid accent I had acquired. One night, however, while we were relaxing over some wine, Ricardo asked me how I came to be heading for Rocamadour. Such was my affection for him that it seemed quite natural to tell the whole tale of my travels from England to Avignon, then to Narbonne and Carcassonne. He listened in silence, then thought for some time, never taking his eyes from me.

'I understand,' he said at length, 'that you didn't choose the life you've experienced since you left England. Doubtless God has a purpose in leading you through all this remarkable sequence of events. But the fact remains that you're leading an undisciplined life, my friend, one which breaches all the commitments you made when you entered holy orders. That will remain the case until, or unless, you either return to the Benedictine fold, or ask to be released from your vows.'

'I'm well aware of that. But I think that, in my position, you'd feel this was a question that could be resolved in the fullness of time. The Benedictine Order hasn't exactly been principled in its dealings with me.'

'People do what they feel they have to do. Compared with the treatment handed out to many of the saints over the centuries, I don't see that your grievances are anything remarkable.' He lowered his voice. 'Consider how many good Christians among the Knights Templar were condemned to burn on the basis of the most outrageous charges. Think about them, then tell me that you're the victim of a gross injustice.'

I knew, of course, that on one level he was right. Such sufferings as I had endured were of no account by comparison with those of the Church's many martyrs and, yes, in recent times the Templars. Nevertheless, his unsympathetic response angered me. After long reflection, I had concluded some way back that I entered the Benedictine Order through something bordering on compulsion, rather than by vocation. What choice did I have as a child? In consequence, my initially uncomfortable situation had long since ceased to appear a matter requiring urgent resolution. I had discovered a world outside the cloister, sometimes exciting, occasionally frightening, but always more enticing than the numbing certainties of monastic life. I smiled.

'You're right, Ricardo. After I've paid homage to our Lady at Rocamadour, I'm heading back to England. Despite the circumstances under which I left, since I don't seem to belong anywhere else, I shall return to Croyland Abbey. I'll discuss the situation with Father Simon, the Abbot, and decide what's best to be done. Whatever the Order decrees, I'll accept the outcome as God's will.'

The friar kept his eyes fixed on me. No hint of a smile crossed his lips. He clearly did not believe a word I had said.

From then on I avoided Ricardo's company, although on the road I often sensed his eyes watching me. The onward journey to Rocamadour took us about another week, so sparsely settled is this vast land. I kept myself to myself, finding that I was content on the whole to be alone with my thoughts. The undulating terrain as we approached our destination was a visual delight, even if a relentless strain on our legs. It could in no sense be described as a region of high mountains, but from time to time we found ourselves without warning at the summit of a deep gorge, at the bottom of which a small, meandering river would glint in the intense sunlight. It seemed a landscape sculpted by a divine artist. I was enchanted, and found that amidst all my uncertainties one fact now presented itself as incontrovertible. After all I had been through, the vicissitudes of the last year, the wonder of a new land, all the pain and the joy and the fascinating people I had met, I had no desire under any circumstances to return to England.

XLI

WHEN WE FINALLY ARRIVED AT Rocamadour, I was surprised to find it little more than a village, a busy and attractive place, totally dominated by its Abbey and church containing the shrine of St Amadour after whom the place took its name, a saint about whom, to my shame, I knew precisely nothing. It clung in spectacular fashion to the top of a cliff at the side of a colossal gorge, a deep crack in the earth which appeared to have been chiselled out by an errant titanic stone-mason. Having secured a bed at one of the hostelries, I joined a large crowd in shuffling on my knees up a flight of more than two hundred stone steps—I counted them all as a distraction from my discomfort—a feat of endurance which turned out to be a considerably more damaging ordeal than I had imagined. By the time I reached the top my shins were raw and bleeding, and I could barely stand for the pain in my back, neck and calves.

Forcing all this to the back of my mind, I joined the other pilgrims in walking barefoot into the church. This entailed passing a selection of the most wretched of God's children, who waited outside pleading for alms: the halt and the lame, the deaf, the blind and the dumb, lepers, the possessed and the cruelly disfigured. By this stage I had little money left and could not afford to give to all of them, so I gave to none. Doubtless their most urgent physical needs are met by the brothers of the Abbey.

The church was not large but pleasantly cool, and despite the great press of pilgrims gave off an air of sombre tranquillity. On shelves inside the door stood row after row of wax images, many deliberately damaged or pierced with sharp objects, presumably to reflect the nature and location of the affliction suffered by the man or woman who had placed it there in the hope of relief. I joined the back of a throng, all of us waiting patiently to see the object of our visit, the renowned miracle-working image of the Black Virgin (black from candle-soot, I heard one doubting Thomas suggest). In front of us penitents pleaded for forgiveness, the sick and deformed begged to be cured, the lonely and desperate prayed for solace. After some time, I reached a point where I could see clearly the image of our Lady. Her soft features and outstretched hands seemed to me to reflect a serenity born of suffering, the suffering of someone who had lost a son in the most cruel way imaginable. Her face did not suggest that she had been a passive vessel for the divine will, but had actively participated and paid a heavy price. For how is it possible to show true compassion without having suffered?

When my time came to fall at the feet of the Virgin, I had nothing I wished to pray for. Instead, I allowed my sense of the Virgin's compassion to envelop me, and smiled as a feeling of peace and contentment surged through my soul. For a brief moment I felt at one with the whole of creation, as if God, His world and I were indivisible. It was the most intensely joyful moment I could ever remember, and only the brusque and vocal promptings of those waiting behind forced me to tear myself away.

I retired to the back of the church to gaze for one last time on the face of the Virgin, and was taken aback when a soft female voice spoke to me over my shoulder in English.

'The Virgin of Rocamadour is of special importance to us, you know.'

The owner of the voice proved to be a young woman with undeniably attractive features. Wisps of black hair straggled from beneath the wimple, of a design which I had not seen since leaving England, which otherwise covered her head.

'Women come to pray to her,' she continued, 'to ease the pain of impending childbirth. Or for help in conceiving.'

I stared at her, unable to think of any appropriate response. It did not even occur to me to ask how she knew that I was English. She smiled, I responded in kind, then she turned and made her way out of the church.

I moved on to the Abbey where the prior, having satisfied himself as to my credentials, kindly allowed me to browse in the library. There I found myself diverted by several volumes of miracle stories collected over the years by the monks to demonstrate the power and grace of our Lady and her shrine at Rocamadour. Many were variants of tales told far and wide to extol the virtues of a particular church and the saint whose relics it held, some involving the healing of patients whom physicians had long since given up, others positively relishing the gruesome punishment of a miscreant who had offended our Lady.

One such involved a thief who robbed three pilgrims on their way to the shrine, making off with their purses. Strange to relate, he soon found that the hand in which he gripped the purses became so tightly shut that he could no longer unclench it. He came across a knight, to whom he unwisely related everything that had happened, and asked for his advice. The knight responded that there was only one remedy he knew, at which he removed the reins from his horse and hanged the thief from the nearest tree, giving praise to the Virgin and declaring it an act of vengeance on the enemies of Christ. I must confess to being a little taken aback by the gleeful tone in which the climax to the story was related, particularly when I recalled watching at first hand the mortal fate of the two thieves who attempted to rob me on the way from Avignon to Narbonne. It seemed doubtful to me that our Lady could take positive delight from watching a man, whatever his crime, struggling for life at the end of a rope as his eyes bulged, his tongue lolled from his mouth and he defecated uncontrollably.

Another tale took place in the year eleven hundred and sixty-six from the birth of Christ. A community was beset by attacks from a particularly vicious pack of wolves, who had carried off children and caused widespread panic. One day, two of the wolves savaged a woman named Stephana and dragged her mangled body, barely clinging to life, away to the forest. With what little breath remained she prayed to the Virgin of Rocamadour for help, and immediately the wolves desisted from their attack, and indeed became her protectors. The next day the villagers found her, but by now her wounds were pus-ridden and worm-infested, and although they took her home her appearance was so appalling, and the stench of decaying flesh so overpowering, that none could bear to remain with her.

Her neighbours resolved to place her in a cart and take her by night to a distant village, where they abandoned her to her fate. The residents of this village were no more sympathetic, and tied her to a mule and drove it away. The mule dipped its head to drink in a river, thus precipitating her into the water. Just as it seemed that her misfortunes could become no greater, she prayed to our Lady of Rocamadour, whereon she was carried along by the river and cast ashore to be found and taken to the property of a nobleman. He took pity on her and ordered that she should be cared for. In the fullness of time, she regained enough strength to indicate that her only chance of full recovery was to make a pilgrimage to Rocamadour to pray directly at the Virgin's shrine. Needless to say, when she eventually arrived, her prayers were answered. Whether those who previously treated her cruelly were subjected to concomitant punishment, like the thief, the account did not say.

Reading these words made me think of the plight of those sick and crippled souls outside the church who had clearly not benefited from any miracle of healing. Had their prayers not been fervent enough? Or was the age of miracles over? Wiser and more devout scholars than I had grappled for centuries to explain why some prayers appear to be answered but not others, and why God seemingly allows some to continue to suffer irrespective of whether they are pure in heart or mired in sin. The families of many plague victims in Narbonne had prayed and pleaded with God night and day to spare their loved ones, had made generous offerings to the Church and pledged themselves to make pilgrimages, but still the disease swept all before it, saint and sinner alike.

That night I lay in the hostelry's dormitory, with six or seven other pilgrims. My thoughts ranged so widely that I felt very far from sleep. The door opened slowly, and a figure, clad from head to toe in a dark cloak and hood, entered hesitantly. It crept from bed to bed investigating the occupants, peering closely in the near-darkness. Curious and slightly alarmed, I propped myself up on my elbow. The figure turned and tiptoed towards me. When it leaned over me, I saw to my astonishment the face of the young English woman who had spoken to me in the church earlier in the day. Turning round to check once more that the other residents were sleeping, she placed her finger over her lips and slipped off the cloak. Underneath, she was naked.

I welcomed her into my arms. I had no idea what to do next, and was embarrassed to admit as much, so I lay back and allowed her to take control, which she willingly did. After what seemed all too brief a period, I experienced an ecstasy surely as great as that of any mystic discovering the presence of God. Afterwards, she lay for a while with her head on my shoulder while I stroked her hair.

Before long I drifted into the most contented sleep I had known. When I awoke at first light, she was gone. During our two brief encounters, I did not speak a word to her. Although I had shared a deeper intimacy with her than with anyone I had ever met, I did not even know her name.

In the morning I decided to climb to the top of a tower which, I had been told, offered a panoramic view of a large part of the surrounding region. As I was crossing the street in front of the Abbey, however, I saw walking towards me a man wearing a uniform which marked him unmistakably as in the service of his Holiness. As he drew closer, I recognised him as one belonging to the circle of those in Avignon whose primary allegiance appeared to be towards Cardinal Bertrand de Savigny rather than to Pope John. To my alarm, it was clear that he also recognised me and was heading in my direction. He drew uncomfortably close before stopping.

'You're Nicholas the Englishman, are you not?' he said.

I looked back at him, sweating and frantically considering whether to respond in the positive or the negative, or simply to turn and run. He raised his hand to withdraw something from his cloak. It turned out to be a rolled-up piece of parchment. He thrust it into my chest, crumpling the edge.

'This'll be for you then.'

He fixed me with a hard stare, then turned on his heel and strode away without looking back.

I glanced down at the parchment, tucked it into a pocket in my tunic and proceeded to the tower. After a long ascent, the view along the gorge from its summit made the effort worthwhile. The morning sun was glinting on the sheer sides of the canyon, creating an illusion that it held its own light source, a deep yellow glow radiating upwards from its depths. I took out the document which the papal servant had given me, considered throwing it over the side of the tower, then decided at the last moment to open it. It turned out to be a letter. I looked straight down to the signature and felt a smile form on my lips.

My dearest Nicholas

If this letter reaches you it will be little short of a miracle, given the sloth and incompetence of the administrators in the Palace, and yet I must fulfil, if belatedly, the promise I made to write to you from Bologna. Believe it or not, I have engrossed myself in my legal studies to such an extent that I have become a very dull scholar, of the kind which in the past I so despised. I find in the law a refuge of certainty in the midst of this world's turbulence. Perhaps, in a way, it is the same certainty which others find in the cyclical rituals of the monastic life. I will leave it to you to make that judgement.

Do you remain enclosed within the folds of the cloak of St Augustine? I continue to study his works with alacrity, and yet a nagging uncertainty afflicts me. If I understand his teaching correctly, he believed that we are all irredeemably mired in sin and can only be saved through the grace we receive via the Church's sacraments. This means, for instance, that infants who die before baptism are damned to the tortures of hell. Can our God really be such a cruel Master? Augustine also teaches that the medium through which our essential sinfulness is transmitted is sexual intercourse, which according to him is inherently sinful if not reserved exclusively for the process of procreation. I must apologise in advance if my words shock you, dear Nicholas, but I struggle with the idea that a natural act between two human beings, which is capable of inducing ecstasy and deepening the bond between them in such a magical (dare I use that word?) manner, can be the ultimate source of all the ills of this world. I have begun a piece of writing, provisionally entitled Secretum, *in which I imagine myself in dialogue with the blessed Augustine, and in which I will try to work through my doubts about his teaching. When it is completed, I will send you a copy in case it should prove of any interest.*

Still, enough of such weighty matters. I continue to collect old manuscripts with a fanatical zeal. I now have a large collection of the works of Plato in the original Greek, which some day I must learn how to read. For how can a man call himself a true scholar if he cannot read Greek? I feel a deep anxiety that some unenlightened age in the future will cease to admire and respect these works, and

259

*consign the books containing them to oblivion. Were that to be the
case, I believe our civilisation would enter a new age of darkness
from which the light of wisdom and knowledge might for ever be
excluded.*

*But I have saved my most important news until last. A short while
ago whilst in church I found my attention dragged, as helplessly as
a condemned thief in chains, from the holy office being celebrated
before the altar. A little way in front of me was the most exquisite
creature ever created by God, a young woman of such astounding
beauty that, while I gazed at her, the world around me fell into
silence, became without form and void. I have seen her several
times since, and have smiled at her with, I think, the merest hint
of a decorous yet positive response. She walks outside with her head
uncovered, so I am sure that she is unmarried, though even if that
were not the case it would do nothing to undermine my devotion
to her. I do not yet know her birth name, but in my mind I have
christened her Laura since her eyes speak this name to me whenever
they meet mine. She fills my waking and sleeping thoughts. I have
discovered the true meaning of the word adoration.*

*My father still toils away at Avignon, so perhaps at some point I will
find a pretext to visit him so that we may spend more time in one
another's company and resume our friendship from the point where
it was so abruptly truncated. All I beg of you is that you do not allow
yourself to become narrow in mind like my father and those who
work alongside him. Travel whenever the opportunity arises, meet
people from every walk of life, both good and bad, do not allow your
God-given intelligence to be shackled and constrained. Never cease
to question. Do not fear mysteries. Follow the path which leads to
the sun-kissed uplands.*

Your dearest friend, Francesco Petrarca

A feeling of warmth flowed through me as I rolled up the letter
and looked out from the top of the tower. Above the gorge, an
eagle glided lazily on the breeze, and I longed for the power to soar
above the world, to see into the distance with the piercing clarity
of this bird's eyes. It was humbling that Francesco, a young man

surely destined for renown, perhaps even greatness, had taken the trouble to fulfil a promise made to someone of no consequence he had known for a single day. I retrieved from my bag the parchment on which I had written down Guilabert's account of the tragic events of the siege at Montségur, and re-read it with tears poised at the corners of my eyes. It was still unclear how I could fulfil my vow to him to ensure that his story would be recorded for future generations, but I would move heaven and earth to do so, preferably far from the reach of the tentacles of the Inquisition.

Father Simon said when he told me of my impending departure from Croyland that one day I would look back and see that as the day on which God changed my life for the better. Perhaps he was more prescient than I appreciated at the time. I still recalled word for word the challenge he had thrown down to me:

'From time to time we need to subject our faith to the crucible of action. To expose ourselves to all the evil and the temptation which the world can throw in our way, and to show courage and resolution in standing opposed to it. Only in this way can we be sure that our faith is as robust as we believe it to be. At least once in our life, we have to test ourselves to the limit.'

The Brother Nicholas who left Croyland so long before had ceased to be. And although I had arrived at a destination, I felt no sense that anything had been completed although something important, a transformation, a metamorphosis, had begun. I resisted the temptation to review once more the places I had visited, the people who had changed me and the challenges which had tested me since leaving Croyland, though I knew the memories would always remain vivid if I chose to draw on them. A chain of events had led me from a secluded monastic life in the fens of eastern England to the top of a tower at Rocamadour, yet whether the guiding hand behind this process be named God, Providence or Coincidence no longer seemed important. What did matter was that I had never in my life felt more alive.

If the past was a country I had travelled through and left behind, the future was a misty upward path along which I would have to find my way step by step. England was closed to me, and there were many reasons for not retracing my steps through southern France. I ran my fingers through my hair, stroking the crown where I had long since allowed it to grow across my tonsure.

I remained in principle a member of the Benedictine Order, yet cast adrift and rootless. Of one thing I was certain, however: I had not undertaken the journey up to this point in order to sink back into the secluded ritual of monastic life. Father Simon had surely foreseen this also, that my destiny lay elsewhere, even though he could have had no more idea than I precisely where.

I still had the copy of St Augustine's *Confessions* which the Abbot gave me, although sadly I would not have been able to fulfil my offer to return it in its original state even if he had wanted me to. In any case, he clearly knew that he would never see me again. I found myself wondering what had become of Brother Peter, so rigid and set in his ways that he had lost the ability to open his heart to others? Or Brother Stephen, happier among the creatures of the farmyard than among his fellow men and women? A tear came to my eye as I recalled poor Brother John; had Father Simon contrived to find a way of laying his body to rest in hallowed ground, or would he be forever damned as a suicide? I offered up a fervent prayer for his soul, whatever the fate of his mortal remains.

St Augustine wrote of God that:

> *You fill everything, but do You fill it with Your whole being? Or can it be that the universe itself is not big enough to hold You, and so contains only a part? If so, is this part of You present in all things at the same time? Or are You present in different measure, greater in larger things and lesser in smaller things?*

Augustine was an infinitely wiser man than I could ever be, yet even he struggled to understand the true nature of God, and was often reduced to expressing his sense of wonder through unanswerable questions.

As I watched the figures below me setting out on the road which heads west from Rocamadour, I wondered whether to join them and head for the shrine of the blessed St James at Compostela, since by all accounts barely a day passed without a party of pilgrims setting off in that direction. Some had begun their pilgrimage in England. Immersed in a noisy throng, however, would I hear God if He called to me? St Augustine detected God's voice decisively, not in a spectacular vision but in the overheard words of a child: 'Take up and read, take up and read.' He opened his Bible by chance to St Paul's Epistle to the Romans, and his eyes lighted upon the passage which changed his life: *Let Christ Jesus himself be the armour that you wear; give no more thought to satisfying the bodily appetites.*

I sensed that, if God spoke to me, it would be through one of His creatures whom I met along the way, through experiencing the glories of His creation, or perhaps from within my own soul. From there onwards, whenever I heard the moaning of the wind, the crashing of waves, the chatter of crowds in the market-place or the cry of a new-born child, I would listen for a still, small voice.

I looked down from the tower and saw walking far below the English woman who had come to me during the night. By chance, she looked up at the same moment. She beckoned me to come down to her.

Author's Postscript

Although The English Pilgrim is a work of fiction, some of the characters appearing within its pages are historical, including Simon, Abbot of Croyland, Aymery de Cros, Seneschal of Carcassonne and, of course, Francesco Petrarch. Those referred to indirectly in the accounts of the burning of Béziers, the siege of Montségur and the events surrounding the supposed leper conspiracy are also historical.

There is no reason to suppose that the inhabitants of Narbonne and Carcassonne, cities of which I am very fond, were any more or less virtuous, self-seeking or anti-Semitic than those of other medieval cities. It is a matter of historical record, however, that the years around 1320 were particularly turbulent in France, especially in the south, and that social stress was rife. Poor harvests had caused hardship for several years, outbreaks of violent anti-Jewish feeling occurred on a regular basis, the nefarious activities of the Pastoureaux are well-documented, and even the bizarre belief in a Jewish-incited leper conspiracy to poison wells and water-courses is rooted in historical fact. On the other hand, I am not aware that Narbonne suffered a devastating plague in 1320, although outbreaks were frequent throughout western Europe in the fourteenth century, both before and after the Black Death.

The Catholic crusade to eradicate the Cathars in the first half of the thirteenth century was ruthless and brutal, and the story of the siege of Montségur has passed into legend. Even the Nazis searched the site for evidence of the Holy Grail. Catharism did survive into the fourteenth century in isolated communities; the last Cathar perfectus, Guillaume Bélibaste, was tried by the Inquisition at Pamiers under Jacques Fournier, and burned at the stake in 1321.

Sadly, little of Croyland Abbey, in the Lincolnshire community which now goes by the name of Crowland, remains above ground. The north aisle of the once-splendid Abbey church still serves as the parish church. Claremont Abbey is fictional.

All Biblical quotations are taken from the New English Bible (second edition, 1970). Quotations from St Augustine's *Confessions* are my own translations from the online Latin text at http://www.stoa.org/hippo/index.html (accessed June 2013).

Lightning Source UK Ltd.
Milton Keynes UK
UKOW05f1402060913

216654UK00001B/7/P